SCANDINAVIA AND THE UNITED STATES

An Insecure Friendship

Twayne's International History Series

Akira Iriye, Editor
Harvard University

SCANDINAVIA AND THE UNITED STATES

An Insecure Friendship

Jussi M. Hanhimäki

London School of Economics

TWAYNE PUBLISHERS • NEW YORK
AN IMPRINT OF SIMON & SCHUSTER MACMILLAN

PRENTICE HALL INTERNATIONAL • LONDON • MEXICO CITY • NEW DELHI
•SINGAPORE • SYDNEY • TORONTO

Twayne Publishers
An Imprint of Simon & Schuster Macmillan
1633 Broadway
New York, NY 10019

Library of Congress Cataloging-in-Publication Data

Hanhimäki, Jussi M., 1965–
    Scandinavia and the United States : an insecure friendship / Jussi M. Hanhimäki.
        p.   cm. — (Twayne's international history series)
    Includes bibliographical references and index.
    ISBN 0–8057–7935–3 (alk. paper)
    1. Scandinavia—Foreign relations—United States.   2. United
States—Foreign relations—Scandinavia.   3. Cold War.   4. United
States—Foreign relations—1945–   5. Sweden—Foreign
relations—1950–   I. Title   II. Series.
DL59.U6H36   1997
327.48073—dc21   96–44455
                                                                                      CIP

10 9 8 7 6 5 4 3 2 1

Printed in the United States of America

To Holli
for everything

Lyndon Johnson at Stockholm's Arlanda Airport with Swedish Prime Minister Tage Erlander during Johnson's Scandinavian tour in September 1963.
Courtesy of the Lyndon B. Johnson Library.

CONTENTS

FOREWORD

Twayne's International History Series seeks to publish reliable accounts of post–World War II international affairs. Today, more than 50 years after the end of the war, the time seems opportune for a critical assessment of world affairs in the second half of the twentieth century. What themes and trends have characterized international relations since 1945? How have conceptions of warfare and visions of peace changed? These questions must be addressed if one is to arrive at an understanding of the contemporary world that is international—with an awareness of the linkages among different parts of the world—and historical—with a keen sense of what the immediate past has brought to human civilization. Hence Twayne's International History Series. It is hoped that the volumes in this series will help the reader to explore important events and decisions since 1945 and to develop the global awareness and historical sensitivity required for confronting today's problems.

The first volumes in the series examine the United States' relations with other countries, groups of countries, or regions. The focus on the United States is justified in part because of the nation's predominant position in postwar international relations, and also because far more extensive documentation is available on American foreign affairs than is the case with other countries. The series addresses not only those interested in international relations, but also those studying America's and other countries' histories, who will find here useful guides and fresh insights into the recent past. Now more than ever, it is imperative to understand the linkages between national and international history.

This volume outlines the fascinating story of U.S. relations with the five Scandinavian countries since the Second World War. The story is fascinating for a number of reasons, geopolitical, economic, and cultural. The Scandinavian countries, as the author shows, were united in their perception of the Soviet Union, but not always in their view of the United States. They had different histories and often conflicting approaches to the problem of national security. Because they were not among "the great powers," moreover, during the Cold War they developed a sense of mission: they sought to contribute to the easing of international tensions and to solve local conflicts through and outside the United Nations. In the economic sphere, they were often adamant in insisting on the protection of their economic (for instance, fishing) interests. Furthermore, the Scandinavian countries, particularly Sweden, came to exemplify the modern welfare state, characterized by an extensive state role in ensuring the health and well-being of the citizens. In this, Scandinavia represented the opposite of the largely privatized, free-enterprise system of social welfare to which the United States adhered. Thus, as the book demonstrates, U.S.-Scandinavian relations often took on intellectual and social coloration.

Dr. Jussi Hanhimäki is well positioned to document and analyze this story. Born in Finland, receiving a doctorate in the United States, and teaching at the London School of Economics, he is a superb embodiment of the internationalized scholarship that is a precondition of any study of international relations. It is hoped that the book will be read widely, not just in the United States and Scandinavia but elsewhere, for the insights it contains have much relevance to the ways in which we come to an understanding of the contemporary world.

PREFACE

It is hard to imagine a less equal postwar relationship than the one between the United States and the five Scandinavian, or Nordic, nations (Denmark, Finland, Iceland, Norway, and Sweden).* On the one side is a continental superpower, rich in both natural and human resources and blessed with unequaled wealth and apparent military omnipotence, which have allowed the United States to exert its power, for better or worse, on other nations around the globe. On the other side is a group of sparsely inhabited countries whose populations together have comprised less than 10 percent of the U.S. population at any given time, tucked away between northwestern Russia and Greenland, dependent on foreign trade, and relatively speaking, almost defenseless against foreign invaders. Moreover, while the onset of the Cold War magnified the United States' position as the undisputed leader of Western democracies confronting the, perhaps exaggerated but nonetheless real, Soviet threat, logic dictated that such small democracies as the Scandinavian countries—located at the USSR's doorstep—should have become steadfast supporters of American containment policy. On the surface at least, it seems that they could have ill afforded otherwise.

Yet the Scandinavians shied away from unequivocal support for the United States and persistently searched for a third way. While Finland (restrained though it was by its treaty commitments to the Soviets) and Sweden practiced neutrality, Denmark, Iceland, and Norway set limits and conditions to their NATO memberships. They became, in effect, "semi-allies." Whether allied or

*I am using the terms _Scandinavia_ and _Norden_ (or _Scandinavian_ and _Nordic_) interchangeably in this study, although, strictly speaking, _Scandinavia_ as a geographical term would not include Denmark, Finland, or Iceland.

not, all Nordic countries acted as bridge builders between the blocs and could claim at least some of the credit for the eventual unfolding of détente in the late 1960s. They would claim a self-appointed role as the moral voice of the international community, championing such causes as nuclear nonprolifera-tion and lavishly criticizing such misguided interventions as the American involvement in the Vietnam War. At the same time, the Danes, Finns, Ice-landers, Norwegians, and in particular, the Swedes perfected their welfare societies. With Social Democrats at the helm throughout most of the postwar era, the Scandinavians presented the Middle Way—a social system that, ide-ally, lay somewhere in between the capitalist (read the United States) and socialist (read the USSR) extremes—as an avant-garde solution to be imi-tated by others. More important for this study, the Middle Way (or the Nordic Model) represented a departure from the polarized vision of the socioeco-nomic competition between socialism and capitalism that was one of the cen-tral characteristics of the Cold War. With their very success, at least until the 1970s, the Scandinavians appeared to provide a challenge to both sides. They had, it seemed, found a way to put convergence theory into practice.

The study that follows differs from most other works in the field of U.S. for-eign and international relations. It is not a story of confrontation or alliance. Nor is it a chronicle of an intense diplomatic and political relationship, or an analysis of a clash of cultures. Rather, what follows is a discussion of a complex web of relationships, both bilateral and multilateral, formal and informal, eco-nomic and cultural, military and political, that linked the destinies of Den-mark, Finland, Iceland, Norway, and Sweden together with that of the United States during the Cold War and beyond.

In the first chapter, I explore the period up to 1945, beginning with Leif Erikson's discovery of North America at the end of the first millennium, but focusing particularly on World War II. The following chapter is devoted to a discussion of the early Cold War years. The focus is on the birth of the Nordic Balance, a security structure that remained largely in place throughout the Cold War. Its main features were "semi-neutral" Finland, tied to the Soviet security system via these countries' 1948 treaty of Friendship, Cooperation and Mutual Assistance (FCMA); neutral Sweden; and "semi-allied" Denmark and Norway, both of which joined NATO in 1949 while they continued to reassure the Soviets that their soil would not be used for offensive purposes. These arrangements provided the basic strategic setting for Scandinavia throughout the remainder of the Cold War.

Chapters 3 and 4 explore the years 1950 through 1961 and place more emphasis on domestic and cultural developments, as well as the images that Scandinavians and Americans held of each other during the height of the Cold War. In contrast, chapter 5, focusing on the 1960s and the first half of the 1970s, emphasizes the Nordic countries' role as bridge builders, a function highlighted as first Europe and later the United States and the Soviet Union embraced an era of détente. The chapter ends with the signing of the Helsinki Accords in August 1975 and is followed by an analysis of the years 1976 through 1989, when Soviet-American détente first evaporated (although the European element still lingered on) but then returned with the ascendancy of Mikhail Gorbachev. The last chapter provides a brief discussion about the implications of the end of the Cold War and the new search for security and identity that provides the main future challenge to both the Americans and Scandinavians alike.

One added dimension of this study warrants a mention: the inter-Scandinavian relationship. At no other time in history has Nordic integration been at the same time more successful and more disappointing than during the years following World War II. Although they formed the Nordic Council (NC), eased restrictions on the freedom of movement among the five countries, and established thriving cultural cooperation and exchanges, the Scandinavians, despite their evident commonality of interests, could not agree on more substantial forms of integration. Plans for an economic union and effective cooperation on foreign and security policy were thwarted by outside pressures and by internally imposed limits. And yet there was enough common ground, an adequate measure of "cobweb integration," and cooperation in various international organizations (including in the United Nations, the CSCE, and for some, NATO), to justify the study of a relatively unified Nordic bloc. While they never created a formal union, the Danes, Finns, Icelanders, Norwegians, and Swedes certainly believed they shared a common identity and a vision of a good society that was best preserved by keeping international tensions outside of Northern Europe. Their success—and the United States' role in it—forms a major part of the story that follows.

During the preparation of this work, I have incurred a number of professional and personal debts. For financial and institutional support I would like to thank the Finnish Academy (*Suomen Akatemia*), Harvard University's Charles Warren Center for Studies in American History, and Ohio University's Contemporary History Institute. I am grateful to the many librarians who assisted me at Harvard University, the London School of Economics and Political Science, Ohio University, Princeton University, the University of Cincinnati, and the University of Helsinki. The staffs at the Truman, Eisenhower, Kennedy, Johnson, Ford, Carter, and Reagan Presidential Libraries and at the National Archives were extremely helpful.
 I would like to express my gratitude to Akira Iriye for encouraging me to undertake this project and for setting an example for many diplomatic historians with his groundbreaking work on intercultural relations. Keith W. Olson took the time to read through the manuscript and saved me from many potential embarrassments, for which, as well as for his friendship in good times and bad, I remain deeply grateful. For supporting, as well as criticizing, this work in

various direct or indirect ways, I would also like to thank Frank Costigliola, Seikko Eskola, John L. Gaddis, Ernest R. May, Arnold A. Offner, Keith W. Olson, Olli Vehviläinen, and the many colleagues and friends at Boston University, Harvard University, and the International History Department of the London School of Economics. At Twayne Publishers, the help of Margaret Dornfeld, Patricia Mulrane, and others has been invaluable. For a superb job of copyediting, I am grateful to Karen Dorman and to the people at Impressions Book and Journal Services. Needless to say, while all of the above should share some of the credit for the completion of this work, they are not to be criticized for anything included in or excluded from this book.

Last, I wish to thank my wife, Holli Schauber, who has never failed to support me during yet another exotic writing project. There are no words that adequately express my love and gratitude, but perhaps dedicating this book to her will go part of the way.

ABBREVIATIONS

ACC	Allied Control Commission
AFNORTH	Allied Forces Northern Europe
AP	Agrarian Party (Finland)
CDE	(Conference on) Confidence and Security Building Measures and Disarmament in Europe
CIS	Commonwealth of Independent States
COMBALTAP	United Baltic Command (NATO)
CSCE	Conference on Security and Cooperation in Europe
ECA	Economic Cooperation Administration
ECSC	European Coal and Steel Community
EDC	European Defense Community
EEA	European Economic Area
EEC	European Economic Community
EFTA	European Free Trade Association
ERP	European Recovery Program
EU	European Union
FCMA	Treaty of Friendship, Cooperation, and Mutual Assistance (Finno-Soviet)
FCP	Finnish Communist Party
FINEFTA	Finland-EFTA Free Trade Agreement
FPDL	Finnish People's Democratic League
FRUS	*Foreign Relations of the United States*
GNP	Gross National Product
HUAAC	House Un-American Activities Committee
IDF	Icelandic Defense Force
INF	Intermediate Nuclear Forces

MDAP	Mutual Defense Assistance Program
MLF	Multilateral Force
NATO	North Atlantic Treaty Organization
NC	Nordic Council
NFSG	(U.S.-Norwegian) Northern Flank Study Group
NIU	Northern Interparliamentary Union
NNAs	Nonaligned Nations
NNWFZ	Nordic-Nuclear-Weapons-Free-Zone Proposal
NORDEK	Nordic Economic Union
NSC	National Security Council
OEEC	Organization for European Economic Cooperation
PfP	Partnership for Peace
PRC	People's Republic of China
RNAF	Royal Norwegian Air Force
SACEUR	Supreme Allied Commander Europe
SDI	Strategic Defense Initiative
SDU	Scandinavian Defense Union
SFO	Swedish Foreign Office
SG	Standing Group (NATO)
SLBM	Submarine-launched Ballistic Missile
UN	United Nations
UPP-SP	United People's Party–Socialist Party (Iceland)
USIA	United States Information Agency
USIS	United States Information Service

LIST OF ILLUSTRATIONS

chapter 1

ATLANTIC CROSSINGS

Before Christopher Columbus there was Leif Erikson. The legendary voyages of this Viking warrior and his adventurous troops bridged the European and North American continents five centuries prior to the time the Italian explorer planned to travel to India by sailing westward around the globe. The difference, of course, was that after the Vikings landed in Vinland (what is known today as Newfoundland), they were not followed by a flood of fortune hunters and conquistadors as were the explorers who sailed under the Spanish flag and accidentally ended up in the Caribbean. Both returned to tell their tales, but unlike Columbus, who charmed Queen Isabella with the fabulous spoils of his journey, Erikson, who earned the nickname "Lucky" for surviving his voyages, went home almost empty-handed. Although a few other fearless Norse explorers set out from Greenland and Iceland to follow Leif Erikson's route, the Vikings did not leave a permanent mark on North America. Their brief flirtation with the new continent was forgotten (or dismissed) until the discovery of a Viking settlement in L'Anse aux Meadows, Newfoundland, in the 1960s confirmed that the saga had more than a grain of truth in it. By stepping from one island to the next, from Iceland to Greenland to Newfoundland, the Vikings had stumbled on the continent that, almost a millennium later, would host the most powerful nation on earth and play a major role in the affairs of the Vikings' descendants.

Although the Norsemen disappeared as quickly as they had arrived, Scandinavians did form a part of the European settlement of North America. In 1638 a group of Finns and Swedes (Finland was at the time part of Sweden) settled on the banks of the Delaware River, establishing a colony proudly named New Sweden. A formidable regional power in Northern Europe at the time, Sweden thus joined, albeit unsuccessfully, the race to colonize the new continent. With these early settlers came one of the most important Scandinavian contributions to the Europeanization of the New World: the log cabin, which was to become one of the staples of the American frontier experience and a symbol in the popular mythology of U.S. presidents in the nineteenth century. The colony of New Sweden itself, however, was soon overrun by Dutch and English settlements, and the first permanent Scandinavian inhabitants of North America soon blended with the rapidly growing mass of white immigrants and settlers. By the time of the Declaration of Independence, they had lost their ties to the old homeland and had become British subjects.

The second and much larger wave of Scandinavian immigration occurred in the nineteenth century. Initially, a group of 53 Norwegians arrived in 1825, settling first in Orleans County, New York, and then moving in the 1830s to the Fox River Valley in Illinois. Most Scandinavian immigrants eventually gravitated toward the Midwest. The land there resembled what these people, almost exclusively farmers, had left behind in Scandinavia. They were lured further by the stories of the early settlers, by the promise of inexpensive land made by the Homestead Act of 1862, and by the lack of fertile soil and opportunity at home. The flow of Scandinavian immigration grew steadily during the mid-nineteenth century and reached its peak in the 1880s, when more than 650,000 Scandinavians arrived in the United States. Although the flow of immigration later slowed down—in the 1930s more Scandinavians migrated out of rather than into the United States—by the 1920s there were approximately 2.5 million American citizens of Scandinavian ancestry, mostly in the Midwest (Wisconsin, Illinois, and Minnesota being the states with the largest Scandinavian populations).

Their success in America was undeniable. In large part, it was due to most Scandinavian immigrants being fortunate enough to be born white, blond, and blue-eyed. On the other hand, a large portion of the Scandinavians were relatively highly skilled; they brought with them new skills and techniques in such fields as architecture and engineering. Many of them became successful farmers in the Midwest, and while not all became distinguished members of their new communities in the United States, the Northern Europeans blended easily into the mainstream of white America. For them, it was the land of opportunity, or as the distinguished American scholar of Scandinavia Franklin D. Scott puts it:

> By the mid-twentieth century most of them were so wholly a part of America itself, so completely integrated in the new environment, that their origin was forgotten. They assimilated with ease, partly because they willed it so, partly because their inherited ideals and patterns of life were basically the same as the ideals and patterns earlier established in American life and appropriate to the American environment.[1]

At the same time, however, the mass movement across the Atlantic had its impact on Scandinavian societies as well. Concern over large-scale migration, as well as the influences brought back by those who returned to Northern Europe after a stint in the United States, propelled the Nordic governments to improve the lot of their people. The result was progressive social legislation that in many cases went much further than in the United States. Women, for example, were extended voting rights in all Scandinavian countries during the early twentieth century. (Finland, although at the time part of the Russian empire, was the first to do so in 1906, 14 years before the United States.) Beginning with Denmark in 1899, Scandinavian labor unions were given the right to conduct collective bargaining at the turn of the century. In many other fields as well, the Scandinavian countries were, by the early twentieth century, as progressive as the United States or more so. Public education, child welfare, and government-sponsored social security were gradually embedded into Scandinavia, long before the term *Middle Way* was coined by Marquis Childs in the 1930s as a general description of the socioeconomic structure in Northern Europe (and particularly in Sweden).

The cross-Atlantic interchanges were not, however, the only, or even the main, catalyst behind the change of Scandinavians from feared Viking warriors in the Middle Ages to peaceful and progressive social legislators in the twentieth century. Indeed, between Leif Erikson's adventures and the dawn of the atomic age, the five countries that by the end of World War II would be considered the quiet corner of Europe had been involved in numerous wars against each other and suffered from several outside interventions. Some of the countries, particularly Denmark and Sweden, had been formidable regional powers whose military forces had terrorized modern-day Germany and stood up to the growing power of imperial Russia. Eventually their meager natural resources and small population bases, as well as the rise of other European powers (first Russia in the seventeenth and eighteenth centuries and then Prussia/Germany in the nineteenth), relegated the Scandinavian countries to a minor role in international politics. After the Napoleonic wars—when Sweden, for example, lost Finland to Russia—the Scandinavians were but minor pawns in the continental power struggles that concerned, in particular, Russia, Prussia, Austria, and France. By the early twentieth century, Norden had clearly become a periphery.

During the Great War, their relative insignificance to the strategic calculations of the great powers enabled the three independent Scandinavian countries—Denmark, Norway, and Sweden—to practice neutrality. It was not, however, strict neutrality. Denmark, for example, was pressured into placing mines in the narrow straits that separated the Baltic Sea from the North Sea, thus restricting the British and Russian fleet movements. While protesting the British imposition of a blockade on Germany, the three countries acted as reexport centers and made a considerable profit by circumventing London's restrictions. The Danes, who were in the most precarious position as direct neighbors of Germany, went the furthest. For instance, they imported 12 times as much lard as they had prior to the war. The lard was then sold to Germany, where it was turned into glycerine and used to produce explosives.

Such duplicity aside, it was the Russian Revolutions of 1917 that significantly changed Scandinavian, as well as American, attitudes toward the belligerents. For the United States, the March 1917 overthrow of Czar Nicholas II made it much easier to justify entrance in the war; it could now be seen as a crusade "to make the world safe for democracy." For Sweden and Denmark, the turmoil in Russia might have allowed for a decisive German victory with severe implications for the future of the power balance on the Baltic Sea; thus their sympathies shifted toward the Allied powers. Yet it was the Bolshevik Revolution eight months later that had the most profound impact on Scandinavia.

Because of it, Finland declared its independence on 6 December 1917 and secured recognition from Lenin in early 1918. Scandinavian countries followed suit, while the Western allies, including the United States, stalled, hoping that the Bolshevik regime in Russia would collapse. In the end it did not, but Washington waited until 1919 before it recognized Finnish independence. The hesitation was a result of the turmoil within Finland that allowed the Germans to play a major role in the early phases of what eventually became the first Nordic republic (at one point it had appeared that the Finns would have a German-born king). In January 1918, a civil war between the Reds and the Whites erupted in Finland when a radical faction of the Finnish Social Democratic Party led by Otto W. Kuusinen seized power in Helsinki. Headed by C. G. E. Mannerheim, a former general of the Russian Imperial Army, and helped by German troops who landed in southern Finland in April, the Whites eventually triumphed over the Reds in May 1918. The prospect that the Baltic Sea was becoming a *Mare Germanicum* appeared strong, especially since the Germans had negotiated an advantageous peace agreement at Brest-Litovsk with the Bolsheviks in March.

It was not to be. Despite Germany's success at the Eastern front, the country surrendered in November 1918 and appeared weak and humiliated. At the same time, the ongoing civil war in Russia made the "eastern problem" appear, for the moment, less threatening. Scandinavians had not only succeeded in remaining outside the war, but Finland had gained its independence and the two great powers that represented potential security risks to Northern Europe had been defeated, had lost territory, and appeared unable to rebound quickly. In addition, at the Paris Peace Conference in 1919, an American president put forward a proposal that had the potential of guaranteeing future security for even the smallest countries.

Much like Woodrow Wilson, the Scandinavians were enthusiastic about the League of Nations and the promise of collective security. Finally there appeared to be a solution to the problem of small state vulnerability, the ever-pervasive danger of falling prey to the aggressive designs of great powers. Had Wilson—although his own citizens eventually rejected U.S. participation in the League—come up with a formula that answered the needs of the small Scandinavian countries?

He had not. Although the League offered many successful resolutions (including its effective decision in 1920 to grant the Åland Islands to Finland, despite Sweden's demand that it should have control over this Swedish-speaking island group between the two countries), the League of Nations could not live up to its founding father's rhetoric, in part because the United States failed to join in. The League had no ability to use force and was rendered impotent when crises broke out in Manchuria, Ethiopia, and elsewhere. By the early 1930s, with the Soviet Union and Germany rebounding from their losses in World War I, the Scandinavians were searching for other types of security guarantees. Neutral cooperation was one option, and the Oslo agreement of 1930—signed by Sweden, Denmark, Norway, the Benelux (Belgium, The Netherlands, and Luxembourg), and later by Finland—appeared to provide a possible solution. However, the Nazi takeover in Germany in January 1933 and Hitler's subsequent decision to leave the League of Nations in October (the Soviets joined the next year) shook the security calculations in a fundamental way. In the end, the Scandinavians turned increasingly toward Nordic cooperation, hoping that closer links and a united front might guarantee their neutrality in the future.

It was an unattainable goal. In the 1930s, cooperation among the Scandinavian countries did become more intense, but it was mostly limited to increased inter-Scandinavian trade. In annual meetings that started in 1932, the foreign ministers agreed to appoint specific officials to handle mutual relations and, in 1934, established committees—the so-called Neighbor Country Boards—to study possible ways of further increasing regional economic cooperation, mostly as a way of limiting the harmful effects of the worldwide economic downturn. Although the Scandinavians were reasonably successful in this endeavor, they could not agree on preventive defense measures. The persistent, but illusory, hope that Scandinavia could stay neutral in the increasingly likely event that another continental war might break out, meant that the Nordic countries, much like the United States, were relatively unprepared for the rapid succession of events that led to the outbreak of World War II in 1939.

In the interwar years, the diplomatic and political relations between the United States and the Scandinavian countries were limited, a reflection of a general American retreat from direct involvement in European affairs in the 1920s.

Nevertheless, with the onset of the Great Depression in the late 1920s, Scandinavia, and particularly Sweden, played a role in the development of American thinking about their domestic difficulties. As President Franklin D. Roosevelt acknowledged when he launched the New Deal, the traditional "American way"—relatively unrestricted competition—had clearly failed to provide any kind of social safety net for millions of people hit hard by the economic turmoil.

Not only were the United States and the West in general suffering the hardships of the Great Depression, but the Soviets were, to the disbelief and consternation of many observers, making apparent headway with Stalin's five-year plans. Nothing approaching outright socialism would ever be tried in the United States, of course, but many people began thinking there may be something in between.

There was. The Swedes had apparently perfected a social democracy that had enabled them to prevent, even in hard times, the great escalation of poverty and homelessness that so marred American society in the 1930s. With the publication of Marquis Childs's *Sweden, The Middle Way* in 1936 and spin-offs such as Arthur Montgomery's *How Sweden Overcame the Depression* in 1938, Americans were exposed to a paradise of sorts: a society that provided for its citizens in hard times. Indeed, Scandinavians seemed to have put Keynesian models in practice with great success: they had increased public spending in order to boost the economy and reduce the effect of the worldwide slumps. To be sure, critics rightly asked whether the Scandinavian experience held much relevance for the United States, given the wide differences in the populations, the structure of the economy, and the sheer size of the countries. During the 1930s, moreover, the New Deal programs instituted a measure of social security to the United States. By the end of the decade, when the public began discussing the promise and applicability of the Middle Way, the United States was about to be drawn out of the doldrums of depression, not because of Keynesian models, but because of the carnage in Europe. As the most devastating war in human history unfolded, few had time to think about the Middle Way. It would have to wait, perhaps indefinitely.

Hitler's rise to power in 1933 and the subsequent militarization and expansion of Germany (e.g., Austria and Czechoslovakia) naturally concerned the Scandinavians. The Danes, who shared a border with Germany, were particularly worried. Much like the Norwegians and Swedes, however, the Danes hoped that by remaining neutral, as they did during World War I, they could stay outside the war that began with the German invasion of Poland in September 1939. At the outbreak of war, the Scandinavians jointly declared their neutrality after a meeting between the four countries' foreign and prime ministers in early September. For a brief moment that action appeared to provide a solution. Then, in late November of 1939, Finland was attacked.

Given its status as a former part of the Russian empire and the long Finno-Soviet border (more than 600 miles), Finland was the most vulnerable of the Nordic countries. As he worried about Hitler's increasingly aggressive stand, Stalin was searching for additional security guarantees on his western borders. Finland, along with Poland, Estonia, Latvia, and Lithuania, eventually fell prey to the Kremlin's design. In 1938 the Soviets initiated talks in Helsinki about potential border changes and Soviet occupation of a number of key islands off the Finnish coast. The Finns, unlike the Balts, never gave in, despite the shock delivered by the Nazi-Soviet Pact in August 1939 and the division of Poland following the German assault in September. Frustrated with Finnish intransigence and assured by the secret protocol of his agreement with Hitler that placed Finland in the Soviet sphere, Stalin decided to stop the fruitless haggling over slices of territory. Instead, he went for the whole pie. On 30 November 1939, Soviet troops attacked Finland, refused to recognize the Helsinki government, and established the "Government of the Democratic Republic of Finland" under the leadership of Otto W. Kuusinen. He was joined by other Finnish communists who had lived in the USSR since 1918 when the Finnish Civil War ended. Four hundred fifty thousand Soviet troops crossed the border into Finland, supported by 2,000 tanks and 1,000 planes. They faced an apparently inferior opponent: the Finnish Army totaled approximately 300,000 men, but at the start of the Winter War they could not all even be provided with rifles. Finland appeared doomed.

The Winter War of 1939–1940 proved not only that hopes of neutrality were futile, but that the Scandinavians could not count on any meaningful support from the Western powers. Starting in late November 1939, the Finns, although they found a sympathetic audience in the United States and even among their Scandinavian neighbors, had to endure a life-and-death struggle without significant outside help. Under pressure from the Germans—still de facto allies of the Soviet Union—the Swedes even refused to allow troop transits through their territory. Potential, although unlikely, Western aid was blocked. In the end, the Finns survived in part because of their own heroism—tales of skiing Finnish soldiers fighting a numerically superior enemy in sub-zero temperatures became commonplace in American newspapers during the winter of 1939–1940—but mostly because of the weakness of the Soviet armed forces. Among other things, Stalin's purges of the officer corps in the late 1930s had relieved the Red Army of its most talented leadership. Notwithstanding their ability to prevail, however, the clear lesson for the Finns was that security could not be guaranteed by trusting in support from other Scandinavian nations, regardless of their sympathies.

The Winter War that ended with the Moscow Peace Treaty of March 1940 was only the beginning of Nordic troubles. The Germans needed Swedish iron ore for their war efforts and were concerned that a possible British occupation of Norway would severely hamper such deliveries. The Danes had the misfortune of being directly on Germany's path to Norway. On 9 April 1940, the Germans occupied Copenhagen, and the Danish government capitulated without resistance within a few hours. The Norwegians, attacked simultaneously, put up a fight and although most of the country was under German occupation by early May, the Germans did not obtain full control of Norway until a month later. On 7 June 1940, the Norwegian government decided to end hostilities and continue its struggle from exile in Great Britain.

The German occupation of Norway and Denmark had significant effects on the positions of Sweden and Finland. In Stockholm, Prime Minister Per

Albin Hansson's cabinet had little choice but to practice qualified neutrality and allow German troops to travel through Sweden to Norway. The iron ore trade provided little consolation for such violations of sovereignty. In 1940–1941, however, German power was too awesome to be challenged. As Hansson noted in his diaries: "Our cherished and strictly maintained policy of neutrality was broken because of the realization that it was unreasonable to risk war in the present circumstances."[2] Finland, on the other hand, began to gradually gravitate toward increased cooperation with Germany. With the memories of the Winter War fresh in their minds, the Finns naturally searched for a counterweight against future Soviet aggression. It soon became obvious, however, that the Germans were after much bigger game than simply securing their backs in Scandinavia. With some hesitation, Finland's President Risto Ryti and his cabinet committed their country to an eventually ill-fated mission against the USSR. In early June 1941, in preparation for "Operation Barbarossa," 75,000 German troops moved into northern Finland via Sweden.

So it was that in the same year that the United States joined the Allies, Finland began to participate as cobelligerent in Hitler's invasion of the Soviet Union, and Sweden clung to its neutrality by making concessions to the Germans, who had, effectively, surrounded the largest Scandinavian country by occupying Denmark and Norway and sending troops to northern Finland. Only Iceland—occupied by the British after the German takeover of Denmark but turned over to American forces in 1941—was free from German influence. Later on it acted as a way station for the eventual attack by the Allies on Germany.

Scandinavia, of course, was not among Franklin Roosevelt's foremost concerns after December 1941. With the exception of Iceland, the Nordic countries were too far from the traditional U.S. sphere of influence to generate much interest in Washington. This did not mean that Americans had no policy in Northern Europe. To ensure the control of Iceland as a base for European operations and a stopover point for troop transits, for example, Washington ended a defensive alliance with the exiled government of Denmark. The United States continuously, albeit unsuccessfully, pressured Sweden to join the war on the Allied side, and despite Soviet pressure to declare war on Finland, tried to broker an agreement between Finland and the Soviet Union from 1941 to 1944. In the end, the Moscow Armistice in September 1944 that ended the Finno-Soviet Continuation War (a Finnish term, adopted to distinguish the 1941–1944 conflict from the Winter War) did not come as a result of American mediation efforts. Rather, the Finns sued for peace after the invasion of Normandy proved that Germany's demise had progressed far enough to prevent it from orchestrating a successful revenge. According to the terms of the Moscow Armistice, however, the Finns had to fight yet another war, to expel the remaining German troops from Finnish Lapland. It was only in April 1945, a month before Germany's final surrender, that the guns fell silent in Finland.

Washington's relatively low-key approach to Scandinavia during World War II reflected Roosevelt's Grand Design for the postwar world. After the defeat of Germany and Japan, the American president assumed that security would be guaranteed by a great power consortium of "Four Policemen"—the United States, the USSR, Great Britain, and China—and that each would be responsible for security in its respective area, or sphere, of influence. Their geographic location and past histories placed the Scandinavians, with the possible exception of Iceland, in either the Soviet or the British sphere. Because the Nordic countries had not loomed large in Franklin Roosevelt's mind, only Finland received any attention at the February 1945 summit in Yalta.

World War II reaffirmed an earlier pattern in American-Scandinavian relations. Ideologically, economically, culturally, and politically, the United States and the five Nordic countries shared a great deal. A belief in democracy was as firm in Finland, Denmark, Iceland, Norway, and Sweden as it was in the United States. And yet, to preserve national security, the paths that the individual Scandinavian countries chose during World War II were very different from what their shared ideological legacy might have suggested. Sweden had clung to its neutrality, despite having to pay a high price in terms of concessions to Nazi Germany. Its traditional national security policy thus proved—alone among the five countries—successful in the turmoil of World War II. In the postwar era, Sweden experienced little internal pressure to move from neutrality to some other form of foreign policy. Norway and Denmark, however, could no longer regard neutrality as an acceptable security policy in view of the German occupation. While acting as a major military base for the North Atlantic theater, Iceland gained its independence in 1944. It was intricately linked to the Western Allies' military operations at its very birth and would retain its strategic significance in the postwar era. Finland had fought three separate wars—two against the USSR, one against Germany—during its search for security. Because of Finland's proximity to the USSR, which emerged from the war as the foremost Eurasian power, Finland's future seemed the bleakest of the Nordic countries. Yet, the Finns not only had survived, but had been able to avoid foreign occupation.

From such legacies grew distinct security policies during the immediate postwar years. The common feature was that in framing their policies, each of the Nordic countries not only consulted their neighbors about the potential Soviet threat, but also regarded the United States as a potential guarantor against the insecurities so evident to small countries in the postwar world. For the first time, the United States had a significant role to play in security considerations for all Scandinavian countries. Simultaneously, a part of the Americans' search for security involved a reversal of the trail traveled by Leif Erikson a millennium earlier. This time there would be no turning back.

chapter 2

QUEST FOR SECURITY, 1945–1949

"It is a time for peace, a time when those who have suffered will begin rebuilding the terrible damage and destruction inflicted upon us by a senseless war," Finland's Prime Minister Juho K. Paasikivi commented in a speech on Finnish radio on 7 May 1945. He added: "The eyes of all people are turning particularly upon those statesmen whom destiny has placed to lead the three great victorious powers. [Like all other people] We Finns hope that the end of the war and the beginning of the peace will ease our economic troubles."[1]

Indeed, Paasikivi was reflecting the feelings of many leaders and ordinary citizens of small European countries in the aftermath of Nazi Germany's defeat. He could have been speaking for Danes, Icelanders, Norwegians, and Swedes, all of whom, in one way or another, had to begin a search for security and a struggle to regain their prosperity in the aftermath of the most destructive war in human history. Most Scandinavians agreed with his reference to the leaders of the three great powers—although it soon became apparent, as Great Britain's power began to fade, that there really were only two. It was time for a new search for security after a war that had left few of the traditional economic, strategic, and power relationships in Europe untouched.

In Scandinavia, this search for security would mean a process replete with half-hearted alignments with the West, constant reassuring of the East, and an attempt to define a middle ground between the two extremes. Some Scandinavians hoped that the United Nations could provide enhanced security, but the history of the League of Nations in the interwar period advised otherwise. Gradually most Scandinavians—except for the Finns, who lived under the constant shadow of the Soviet Union—leaned increasingly toward the West. Even the Swedes, although not participants in the war, would respond positively to the offer of Marshall Plan aid and viewed the Soviets as the only significant threat to their independence. Inevitably, if not uniformly, the American and Scandinavian perceptions of threat and security converged in the late 1940s.

TRIUMPH AND UNCERTAINTY

Victory for the Allies in Europe meant something very different to Americans and Scandinavians. V-E Day was the symbolic beginning of America's unprecedented influence over postwar developments in Europe and the world at large. With its military and industrial might, the United States had certainly provided the edge necessary for the Allied triumph over Germany. Dwight D. Eisenhower's leadership of the Allied Expeditionary Force was in many ways a symbol of the role of the United States as the first among equals in what was initially a hot war against Germany, but within a few years developed into a Western alliance directed against the USSR. The war had left the United States and its infrastructure untouched, while Europeans had experienced destruction throughout the war, thus adding to the economic inequalities between the United States and its European allies (and, of course, its former enemy soon turned ally, Germany). With the dropping of the atomic bomb a few months later, American superiority had yet another dimension. The nation seemed virtually indestructible, omnipotent. Indeed, as the "good war" ended, much better times seemed to be in store for the United States. No wonder huge parades and celebrations erupted in American cities from coast to coast, first with the surrender of Germany and later with the capitulation of Japan.

In the streets of Helsinki, however, there was no parade. For the Finns, Allied victory came at the heels of the final end of Finland's six years of continuous military conflict, twice against the Soviets, once against the Germans. The German defeat was received with mixed emotions, because that nation—whether ruled by Hitler or someone else—had always been a counterweight of sorts against the growth of Soviet power at the expense of Finnish independence. Now a new era was beginning, an era in which the Finns were, seemingly at least, at the mercy of their old archenemy (a loose translation of the Finnish term *perivihollinen*). Although the Finns had avoided occupation, they were faced with the following situations: the Soviets dominated the Allied Control Commission in Finland (with Andrei Zhdanov as the titular head of this mission); the Soviets occupied a naval base in southern Finland (Porkkala); the Finns were committed to paying reparations to the Soviets; and Finland's March 1945 elections had given the Finnish Communist Party and its umbrella organization, the Finnish People's Democratic League, 23.5 percent of the popular vote and several important cabinet posts. Prime Minister, and later president, Paasikivi launched a new foreign policy—the Paasikivi Line—that was built on the premise that the Soviets indeed had certain legitimate security interests in Finland. Under Paasikivi's leadership, the successive Finnish gov-ernments embarked on a foreign and security policy that was meant to satisfy those interests by convincing the Soviets that Finland would never again be used as a base for an attack against the USSR. And, surprisingly enough, they were to receive support from Washington.

In Stockholm, the final defeat of Germany signaled the end to years of uncertainty and continued balancing between German demands, Soviet com-plaints, and Western pressures. V-E Day in Sweden was greeted with enor-mous relief and jubilation. Unlike Finland, which had lost 11 percent of its territory and 2 percent (approximately 85,000) of its population, the Swedes had emerged from the war physically untouched. It had been, to an extent, a good war. The Swedish economy, although affected by sanctions and other measures of economic warfare, was intact and ready to serve the needs of an otherwise destroyed continent. In fact, Swedish GNP had risen by 20 percent between 1939 and 1945. The Social Democratic Hansson government could herald its successful policy of neutrality as one that had kept the country out-side the destructive war without compromising internal democracy. Yet, even in Sweden, the Soviet Union's role in defeating Nazi Germany seemed to have an early spillover effect into Swedish domestic politics: the communists received 10.3 percent of the votes in the September 1944 *Riksdag* election. The prospects for foreign trade with such traditional trading partners as Poland also appeared dim given the Soviet hold over that country. And while the Finns had received rounds of sympathetic commentary in the United States during World War II—particularly during the Winter War of 1939–1940—the Swedes had fewer admirers in the country that was about to play such a significant role in postwar Europe.

The Norwegians and the Danes had suffered outright occupation for five years. The German domination and the cooperation of some politicians in both these countries—most notoriously the Norwegian Nazi leader Vidkun Quisling—left an imprint on the nations' foreign and domestic policies. In Norway, 25 collaborators were executed and 20,000 were sentenced to prison terms; in Denmark, 46 were executed and 10,000 were sentenced to prison terms. The first postwar Norwegian prime minister, the moderate socialist leader of the Labor party, Einar Gerhardsen, had spent part of the war in a German concentration camp. Moreover, at the end of the war, Soviet troops established their presence in northern Norway and in the Danish island Born-holm on the Baltic. Economically the two countries were no better off than other Western European countries and desperately needed foreign aid. In foreign policy both had traditionally been pro-British, but that country's ability to guarantee their security had been compromised during the war and was to be seriously questioned as the island empire's strength dwindled in the aftermath of war. Both Danes and Norwegians—as well as other Scandi-navians—were distrustful of continental European powers, whom they viewed as responsible for the troubles of the previous decade. Although much less so than Finland, Norway and Denmark also shifted left after the war: the Norwegian communist party gained 11.9 percent and the Danish communist party gained 12.5 percent of the popular vote in October 1945, and the social democratic (or labor) parties emerged as the leading political force in both countries. Indeed, the general mood had swung so far to the left that one conservative Danish parliament member lamented in June 1945: "We have all become socialists."[2]

The Icelanders, far removed from the center stage of World War II in Europe, had experienced an occupation of a different sort. In the midst of mild protests, the British had landed on the island in 1940 but a year later the Americans took over. Concurrently the two countries signed a defensive alliance with the exile government of Denmark, which was in charge of Iceland's foreign policy. Although Iceland had seen little of the war, and its economy had indeed benefited from the American troops that had occupied the island throughout the war, the local communists were in a strong position, holding several seats in the first independent cabinet (1944–1947). Yet it was obvious that the Icelandic communists had few ties to Moscow and that their electoral success was largely based on the anti-American attitude that had surged in the population as a result of a long period of occupation and of the social problems caused by the existence of 45,000 American service personnel among a population of merely 125,000. Newly independent and eager to establish themselves as a sovereign nation, the Icelanders found the message of the extreme left, a harsh criticism of the presence of foreign troops, appealing.

Scandinavians, when comparing the two emergent rivals, the United States and the Soviet Union, found little affinity with the giant of the East, but many reservations about the United States as well. In the interwar period, many Scandinavians, particularly such Swedish intellectuals as Gunnar Myrdal, had vehemently criticized the United States' record on race relations. At the same time, the American economic system appeared to be far too laissez-faire and too excessively uncaring about the unemployed, the elderly, and the otherwise downtrodden to appeal to the Nordics. The Great Depression had, naturally, given ample evidence to these critics of American society and, indeed, even encouraged some Americans, such as the journalist Marquis Childs, to herald the social democratic Scandinavian countries as models of economic tranquility.[3] All in all, in 1945 the United States was at best a stranger, at worst a socioeconomic monster, to most Scandinavians.

The Scandinavians also had little desire to be bogged down into continental European power politics, something that many Scandinavians saw as the breeding ground for war and destruction. In the first few postwar years, Denmark, Norway, and Sweden retreated to the confines of neutrality and even proclaimed themselves as bridge builders between East and West. Yet, as the Cold War sharpened, as the Soviet-American rivalry began to overshadow everything else, and as the expansion of Soviet power bore uncomfortable resemblance to the expansion of Nazi Germany, second thoughts appeared.

Security for a small country appeared again in jeopardy. In such a context of past, present, and future dangers, the Scandinavians eventually chose different paths to security, paths that, in one way or another, all involved the interests of the United States and the Soviet Union.

THE FRIENDLY DEMOCRACY

Finland was a very special case. In 1944–1947, the country increasingly became a symbol of what "might-have-been." Finland was used as an example during the Yalta Conference in February 1945 of how successful interallied cooperation could be. Everything seemed to be running smoothly in Finland: the Soviet-dominated ACC had been relatively easy on Finland, allowing the Paasikivi government to function according to Finnish law and the Finnish press to operate with considerable freedom. Finland was not a trouble spot like Germany or Poland, but a symbol of interallied cooperation at a time when that cooperation was beginning to crack. Although this situation was largely because the Americans had not been at war against Finland and thus could not claim a seat in the ACC, the events in Finland in late 1944 and early 1945 seemed to encourage the possibility that those neighbors of the USSR that had fought for Germany might in the future have governments that were both friendly toward the Soviet Union (as Stalin insisted at Yalta) and democratically governed (one Western concern regarding these nations). As it turned out, however, Finland was the only country where the Yalta agreements worked.

Despite increased East-West tensions, the American foreign policy establishment treated Finland in a way that seemed to contradict the Manichaean world view that evolved during the onset of the Cold War. In the diplomatic scene, Washington distinguished Finland's position early on from that of other former German allies. For example, at the July–August Potsdam Conference, American leaders (Secretary of State James F. Byrnes and President Harry S. Truman) insisted that of the small European "losers" (Finland, Bulgaria, Hungary, and Rumania), only Finland's political establishment was stable enough to warrant formal recognition by the great powers. Symbolic of the coming of the Cold War, the Big Three failed to reach an agreement on this issue. On 17 August 1945, Truman and Byrnes instead decided to recognize Finland's postwar government unilaterally. As a result, Finnish-American diplomatic relations were formally restored on 1 September 1945 when Benjamin Hulley became the American *chargé ad interim* in Helsinki.

Aside from restoring diplomatic relations with Finland without formal Soviet consent, however, there is little evidence of any American attempt to intervene in the development of Finno-Soviet relations after World War II. During the "war responsible" trials in early 1946, for example, the United States abstained from making any official policy statements. At the London Council of Foreign Ministers meeting in September 1946, the Americans also accepted the Soviets' argument that because the United States had not declared war on Finland it would not have the right to vote on matters concerning the drafting of the Finnish peace treaty at the Paris Peace Conference. When the American delegates later suggested a reduction in Finland's war reparations during a meeting of the Economic Council of the Peace Conference on 4 October 1946, an angry Soviet response quickly convinced the U.S. representatives to remain silent on Finland.

Even if the Americans did not publicly make Finland an issue in the brewing confrontation with the Soviets, they took some economic steps. Economic aid to Finland began in December 1945 when the Export-Import Bank approved its first credit to Finland, for $35 million. This credit was extended by another $32 million in January 1947. The credits were an example of "the Finnish argument" in practice, a view prevalent at the Northern European division of the State Department and shared by most of the American legation in Helsinki. The Finnish argument called for refraining from any acts or public expressions that might be seen as a challenge to the predominance of the USSR in Finland. Although supporters of the Finnish argument were willing to provide economic aid to Finland, they would do so only if it produced no complications for Finno-Soviet relations. In dealing with Finland, the Americans were not out to tease the bear.

It was, indeed, a rather sophisticated view that recognized both the special circumstances of Finland's delicate position and the limits of American power in an area so close to the Soviet heartland. At the same time Finland, along with Czechoslovakia until February 1948, was a symbol of the type of relationship that the United States hoped could be established between the Soviet Union and all its Western neighbors. In the long run Finland would, however, remain the only "friendly democracy" of this kind.

BRIDGE BUILDERS

Bridge building was the official name for the foreign policy practiced by the Gerhardsen Labor government of Norway, the Knud Kristensen *Venstre* (left) government of Denmark, and the Hansson (from October 1946, Erlander) Social Democratic cabinet of Sweden in the immediate years following World War II. In part an expression of the moderate leftist views of the parties in power, bridge building was also based on the desire to go back to the interwar neutral policies and a belief that this could only be achieved through "reassurance" vis-à-vis the Soviet Union.

In as early as June 1945, the Norwegian foreign minister and future secretary general of the United Nations, Trygve Lie, had emphasized that in the postwar world, Norway had to safeguard its security "in co-operation with the Atlantic Great Powers and the Soviet Union."[4] Similarly, on 18 September 1945, Foreign Minister Christmas Møller had declared that Denmark would maintain good relations with both the East and the West. Although preoccupied with questions related to postwar reconstruction and, particularly in Norway's case, with the removal of foreign troops from their territory, the Danes and the Norwegians also placed some hope in the United Nations as a mechanism for preserving their security. Yet, they were well aware that much depended on how well the victors would get along with each other.

The Swedish notion of a Middle Way between capitalism and extreme socialism that had been preserved with some pains throughout the war also led the Hansson Social Democratic government to pursue policies regarding the East-West confrontation similar to those of the Danes and the Norwegians. The wasteful butchering of millions of young lives, the plight of the hundreds of thousands of refugees that came to Sweden during World War II, and the fates of their neighboring countries convinced the Swedes that they had chosen the right path. *The Middle Way*, a title of an admiring 1936 book on Sweden by the American journalist Marquis Childs, was to be continued, not only in domestic politics, but in Sweden's relations with the outside world as well.

The eagerness to make statements stressing cooperation early on in the postwar years were also partly motivated by the presence of Soviet troops in Denmark and Norway. In a sense, then, the idea was somewhat akin to the premises of the Paasikivi Line practiced by the Finns: the Soviets had security concerns in Northern Europe that needed to be satisfied by reassuring the Kremlin that they had nothing to fear from Northern Europe. In this regard the Oslo and Copenhagen governments seem to have been successful: the Soviets left northern Norway by September 1945 (some British troops stayed in Norway until November of the same year) and Bornholm in April 1946. But verbal reassurance was also a result of domestic factors, the search for a kind of Middle Way in what, to most intelligent observers, was likely to be a political, strategic, economic, and ideological, if not necessarily outright military, confrontation between the Western Allies and the Soviet Union.

In the 1940s bridge building did not arouse much interest from the outside world, largely because the policy itself was never clearly defined but represented a rather vague transitional stage between traditional neutrality on the one hand and eventual participation in NATO on the other. From the U.S. perspective, bridge building was of no immediate negative consequence in 1945–1947, because the Scandinavians who practiced it were understood, quite correctly, to be leaning toward the West and only practicing cordial relations with the Soviets as a way of avoiding any unwelcome intrusions in their domestic affairs. As a way of showing its support to the Scandinavians, the United States sold them some military equipment, including naval vessels to Norway, torpedo boats to Denmark, and aircraft to Sweden.

No significant American criticism surfaced during the two immediate postwar years regarding the power of the Social Democrats, hardly the ideal choice from the U.S. perspective. Indeed, they could be seen as an important counterweight to the abhorred prospect of communist rule. At times the containment of communist influence by the Social Democrats and American sales of military equipment could even be tied together. For example, in March 1946, when the Swedes made another request for the purchase of Mustang aircraft from the United States (they had bought 50 in 1945), the acting director of the Office of European Affairs and later ambassador to Finland in the 1950s, John D. Hickerson, supported the deal by referring to the American "interest in the continuance of the Social Democratic government now existent [in Sweden]."[5]

As the Soviet-American confrontation gradually intensified and the doctrine of containment began to take shape in 1946—due in no small part to George Kennan's famous Long Telegram—bridge building came under increased scrutiny and criticism. As Moscow and Washington were unable to reach any meaningful accommodation on Germany and as the disturbing rebellions in Azerbaijan, Greece, and Turkey strained Soviet-American relations even further, bridge building became far too "pro-Soviet" for the Americans. U.S. dissatisfaction became evident in 1946.

Viewed from Washington, the Kremlin seemed to have an easy time intimidating the Swedes. In 1946, for example, the Swedish government felt compelled to return to the USSR Baltic refugees who had fled from Estonia, Latvia, and Lithuania after joining German service in 1941. Also in 1946, the Swedes granted the Soviets a one-billion-kronor credit (approximately $300 million). Although Washington was critical of these Swedish policies, the East-West tensions that were to become so prevalent in the next two years had not yet reached the point at which such actions would incite more than mild protest from the United States.

At approximately the same time, questions about Norway's bridge-building policies and the general character of the Gerhardsen Labor government surfaced in connection with the election of the first secretary general of the United Nations. Indeed, Gerhardsen himself had been a one-time admirer of the Russian revolution, having visited the Soviet Union for the first time in 1920. However, he soon became disillusioned by Stalinism and the Nazi-Soviet Pact of 1939. The same applied to Foreign Minister Trygve Halvdan Lie, who was sworn in as the first U.N. secretary general in February 1946. Indeed, the State Department had a file on Lie that extended as far back as September 1919, when he, along with 400 other Norwegians, had been identified as "a bolshevist." If Lie had been one, his ideas had changed with those of Gerhardsen and the Labor Party in general. Nor did Lie have much admiration for the Soviets. As the foreign minister of the Norwegian exile government in London during the war, he had visited Moscow in November 1944 and been bullied by Molotov into granting rights to the Soviets in the northern Svalbard islands, a question he had been carefully evading. Nevertheless, as the foreign minister in 1946, Trygve Lie was very much the symbolic torchbearer of Norwegian bridge building. He would carry this role to his new post by insisting on building a genuinely international organization, one that would be able to function as a true mediator in conflicts between the great powers in a way that a small country like Norway never could. The task was doomed to fail in the international climate of the late 1940s and early 1950s.

Even Lie's election in early 1946 reflected the difficulties ahead. His election was the result of a hard-fought battle that exposed East-West divisions that would severely hamper, if not outright paralyze, Lie's ability to handle the job. Lie's name surfaced for the first time in the fall of 1945 as the last option on a tentative list drawn up by the American representative on the United Nations' Exploratory Commission, Edward R. Stettinius. However, Stettinius, who had served as Franklin D. Roosevelt's secretary of state in 1944–1945, was not eager to have the post held by a socialist from a country that was potentially under strong Soviet influence. Accordingly, a number of names were thrown around in the election process—including the future Canadian Prime Minister Lester Pearson and the Belgian Foreign Minister Henry Spaak (future secretary general of NATO)—that became a hotly politicized contest between the Soviets, the Americans, and the British. On 17 December 1945, the Soviet representative to the Exploratory Commission, Andrei Gromyko, proposed Yugoslavia's ambassador to the United States, Stanoje Simic. It was only fair, the future Soviet foreign minister argued, that since the headquarters would be in New York, the secretary general should be from Europe. He offered no alternative candidate. By this time it had become clear that a trade-off would be necessary. The kind of person acceptable to the Big Five (China, France, Great Britain, the United States, and the USSR) was, in the end, one from a small unoccupied European country. Two names were left: Lie and Spaak. After serious maneuvering of votes, the two men ended up splitting the top posts of the world organization, with Spaak as the first president of the General Assembly and Lie as the secretary general.

Suspicions of the Norwegian's abilities continued throughout his tenure. In June 1946 Truman agreed with Stettinius's argument that the United States "had made a mistake in picking a dud as secretary-general." A socialist, a consensus candidate, and from a country that shared a border with the USSR, Lie was suspect from the very beginning. Although the U.S. embassy in Oslo assured the State Department that Lie would not be "pro-Russian," it seemed clear that the Russians had wanted Lie over Spaak and thus scored a victory of sorts. From Lie's perspective, however, his election was a symbol of "Norway's balancing act between east and west." Although future Secretary of State Dean Acheson described him as an "unimpressive candidate," the new secretary general symbolized not only the difficulties emerging in East-West relations that led to his election, but also the efforts of Norway—and Scandinavia at large—to play the role of bridge builders in the immediate aftermath of World War II. Although he gained U.S. support during the Korean War because of his support for sending U.N. troops to restore the 38th parallel, Lie himself eventually became exasperated by the impotence of the new organization to act independently. No wonder he would describe it to his Swedish successor, Dag Hammarskjöld, as the "most difficult job in the world."[6] Lie would, nevertheless, pursue peace and try to act as a credible mediator in the international crises that faced him during his seven-year tenure. In a sense, then, although acting under the auspices of the United Nations, Lie was setting a precedent for the notion that small countries with little to gain except international acknowledgment could be effective mediators or facilitators during times of crisis; something that was dramatically illustrated by his fellow citizens almost a half-century later when the Palestinians and Israelis reached their initial peace settlement in a country house located 200 miles north of Oslo in August 1993 (see chapter 7).

Despite doubts about Lie's political leanings and ability to handle his new job, American criticism of the Scandinavian notion of bridge building remained mild until 1947. The basic, and largely correct, assumption that the three core countries of Scandinavia were Western-oriented and only accommodated the Soviets as a way of deterrence remained firm. The Danes', Norwegians', and Swedes' economic ties to the West remained strong and were not to be shaken by credits granted to the USSR. To be sure, at that time the Americans themselves were confused about the exact nature of the Soviet threat and how best to counter it. Thus, the first two years following V-E Day were hardly a reliable barometer of the rapid changes that took place in American-Scandinavian relations after the summer of 1947, changes due, in part, to the rise in strategic significance of the High North and the North Atlantic to American military planning, which had already begun to sour American-Icelandic relations.

THE NEW NATION

At the end of World War II, Iceland was an anomaly. Occupied by American troops since 1941, the small island had become independent in 1944, and its first independent cabinet, headed by the conservative Independence Party leader Olafur Thors, included several members from the local Communist party. Although the Icelandic communists had virtually no direct ties to Moscow, the situation was a disturbing state of affairs for the U.S. State Department, especially because the communists made demands to remove foreign troops from the newly independent nation's soil. Indeed, if there was a strong current of anti-Americanism in Scandinavia, it was to be found here, in the country closest to the United States and important for the air routes between North America and Europe. As Hans W. Weigert wrote in the October 1944 issue of *Foreign Affairs*, it was not just mildly desirable to keep an American (or possibly British) base in Iceland after the war, but "Iceland must remain forever an integral part of the mutual defence system of the two countries (U.S. and Britain) and must never be permitted to fall into the hands or under the influence of a potential enemy."[7]

The Icelanders, however, were reluctant to accept the continued presence of foreign troops. As soon as the war ended, they made demands that American troops be withdrawn and rejected a U.S. proposal to sign a 99-year lease for the Keflavík air base. Most Americans left the island by October 1946, although the Thors cabinet allowed approximately 600 civilian specialists to remain in Keflavík to run the communication links with U.S. occupation troops in Germany. The Icelandic parliament, the *Althing*, approved this deal on 5 October 1946. Because the communist members resigned in protest over the deal, the Keflavík agreement also caused a cabinet crisis that eventually led to the formation of a new government in February 1947 under the leadership of social democrat Stefan J. Stefansson. To the considerable delight of some American observers, there were no communist ministers in the new cabinet, nor would there be any until the mid-1950s.

Following the exodus of American troops, however, the country soon found itself in economic trouble. During the war the GIs themselves, the continued construction projects at the Keflavík base, and the decreased foreign competition in the fishing markets (Iceland's dominant source of employment), had created an economic boom that almost eliminated unemployment. But during the war inflation had become a problem: prices were three times as high in 1946 as they had been in the 1930s. While inflation continued its upward spiral in 1946–1947, the sudden end to construction and the decrease in the demand for different services led to unemployment, and increased competition in the newly invigorated fish markets cut the country's exports (40 percent of the economy was geared to exports) and in effect created both an unstable economy and a rather temperamental electorate.

With the combination of all these forces—economic dislocation and the growth of nationalism that often displayed itself in the form of anti-Americanism (perhaps simply because the Americans were the only foreign target available)—the emergence of the Cold War seemed a rather distant issue for most Icelanders. And yet, their island's strategic significance was rising in a dramatic fashion as the Soviet-American rivalry came to have important strategic implications in the northern Atlantic.

U.S. BASE RIGHTS AND THE EMERGING POLAR STRATEGY

Any significant great power interest in Northern Europe tended to focus on the island possessions of Norway and Denmark in the Northern Atlantic: Spitsbergen and Greenland. Already in 1944 the Soviets had expressed an interest in acquiring a base in Norway's northernmost islands and in 1946 continued to press for, at the minimum, a joint governorship of the Spitsbergen archipelago. With protests from the West and the refusal of the Norwegian parliament, *Storting*, to make concessions, however, the Soviets eventually dropped their claims in early 1947. In the meantime, the Americans continued to press the Danish government to sign a treaty continuing Washington's base rights in Greenland and looked for a way of guaranteeing access to the Keflavík airport near Reykjavík.

Why was there such a growing American interest in the northern Atlantic? The answer lies in the emergence of the so-called polar strategy.

At the end of the war, American strategic planners were already thinking about establishing a circle of bases around the world as a way of deterring and, if necessary, countering future threats to the security of North America. The major potential threat was, early on, identified as the Soviet Union, around which most U.S. bases were eventually located. In the context of Northern Europe, the base rights issue revolved around both denying the Soviets easy access to the North American continent and securing for the United States adequate communication links with Western Europe. The communications problem did not affect Spitsbergen and was eventually settled through links over Greenland and Iceland, but the proximity of the Norwegian-owned islands to North America caused much consternation, especially because the Soviets also wanted base rights there.

In 1946 and 1947 polar strategy gained a more prominent position in the minds of military strategists and national security planners in Washington. The air force experts, for example, argued quite convincingly that in the future, once a new generation of long-distance bombers was built, the most likely direction from which a Soviet attack on the United States could be launched was via the northern polar basin. Not only was that region virtually uninhabited and without any early warning systems, but, as the Joint Chiefs of Staff (JCS) pointed out in 1947, Spitsbergen was 500 miles closer to New York than any other potential Soviet base. Thus, the JCS continued, if the Soviets were to acquire an air force base on that island, they would be capable of reaching the largest U.S. city 5 to 10 years earlier than if their aircraft would have to be launched from Soviet soil. The arctic region's future military potential thus gave rise to a polar strategy, which in turn gained increased attention concurrently with the gradual increase in Soviet-American tensions. In late 1947 the newly founded National Security Council (NSC) focused much of its energies into understanding the exact nature of the Soviet threat and into searching for ways of minimizing it. Northern Europe, because of its proximity to the USSR and because of the Scandinavian countries' strategically significant possessions in the North Atlantic, was one of the first areas to be assessed.

The document that was devoted to exploring the significance of Scandinavian possessions to American national security was NSC 2/1, which assessed in detail the prospects and importance of having U.S. bases in Azores, Greenland, and Iceland. The document was released on 25 November 1947 and its message was clear: the United States needed to have bases in the northern Atlantic for offensive, defensive, and communicative purposes. The islands were "primary base areas" where U.S. installations were not only desirable, but "required." Thus, acquiring base rights from Iceland and Denmark (for Greenland) was one of the highest priorities of the NSC in late 1947, because: "It is difficult to conceive of a war in the next 15 to 20 years in which Greenland [and] Iceland . . . would not be of extreme importance to our war effort. Present

planning therefore is severely hampered by the indefinite status of our negotiations for base rights in these areas. We need such rights and feel that our government should take the strongest appropriate action to obtain them. It
appears, in any case, that in the event of war it would be necessary to occupy
these areas to prevent their use by the enemy."[8]

Indeed, a quick glance at the map easily confirms the significance vested in
base rights in the two largest islands of northern Atlantic. Iceland, for example, was relatively close to the "only conceivable enemy" (i.e., the USSR), it
offered suitable weather and terrain for air operations, it was reasonably defen-
sible, and, naturally, it was located along the most likely enemy attack route
against the United States. Having the Soviets be in a position to use Iceland
for their own purposes was unthinkable. Greenland was significant for the
same reasons. In particular, NSC 2/1 noted, the United States "would be inca-
pable in the near future of operating directly against the potential enemy from
bases anywhere other than in Iceland and Greenland." The two islands were,
in short, both the potential first line of defense as well as the prime launching
path for offensive operations.[9]

In the first two postwar years the North Atlantic had thus emerged as one
of the most significant areas for U.S. national security. And although the
Greenland-Iceland-Spitsbergen triad would gain even more attention in the
1950s, it was already clear from the growing strategic interest in Scandinavian
possessions by both superpowers that the Scandinavians would have a hard
time continuing their quasi-neutral policies. At the same time bridge building
was, clearly, a less than well defined foreign policy for both the Norwegians
and the Danes. It can best be characterized as a "holding pattern," employed
by two small countries that were searching for their place in the postwar international system. As the base rights issue clearly indicated, moreover, the two
countries, not unlike Iceland and Finland, were prisoners of the geography
that determined their strategic significance in the East-West confrontation. In
this regard, they had far less room to maneuver than did the Swedes.

In the spring of 1947 the Cold War was further minimizing the chances for a
policy of bridge building. With the Truman Doctrine and the American
takeover of the British effort to counter communist gains in Turkey and Greece,
the United States took decisive steps in its policy in Europe. To the Scandinavians these actions clearly showed that Washington meant business, and that
the United States was to be a major player in Europe. On the other hand, these
actions also indicated the growing impotence of the British, and caused concern
among the Danes and the Norwegians, who traditionally had relied on England
as a security guarantor. A few months later the Americans made another move.

AMERICA TAKES CHARGE: THE MARSHALL PLAN AND NORDEN

On 5 June 1947 Secretary of State Marshall announced the United States'
offer to help European postwar recovery. In Scandinavia the Marshall Plan

received immediate popularity, but also became one of the thresholds and defining moments in the postwar positions of the five countries. It decreased the anti-American sentiments in Iceland and paved the way for that country's eventual alignment with NATO. It meant the beginning of an end to the bridge-building policies of Norway and Denmark, it resulted in the clarification of Sweden's postwar economic interests, and it provided an example of Finland's delicate balancing act with the Soviet Union. From the U.S. perspective, the European Recovery Program (ERP), the official name of the Marshall Plan, was the first time that its presence was concretely felt in postwar Northern Europe. Yet, the generally positive reception was not a resounding approval of containment; even the countries that chose to participate did so with some hesitation.

To be sure, the U.S. offer was too luring economically to be turned down. Much like the rest of Western Europe, Denmark, Norway, and Sweden were all either facing or about to face a serious dollar shortage. This concern was most acute in Denmark, which simply could not afford to pass up the prospective loans and grants. By the fall of 1947 the Norwegians were in a similar situation, while the Swedes, who received only loans from the United States, were better off. The Swedes' economic prowess also allowed them to interpret participation in the ERP as a nonpolitical act and thus it did not interfere with their traditional policy of nonalignment.

Meanwhile the Finns, facing the dual burdens of postwar reconstruction and reparations obligations, were probably the most eager for assistance but felt compelled under diplomatic pressure from the Soviets to turn down the invitation to attend the July 1947 conference in Paris. After Marshall's speech at Harvard on 5 June 1947 and particularly after Ernest Bevin delivered the British view on the American proposal, the Finnish government had seriously considered the possibility of participation. President Paasikivi himself was optimistic when the Soviets attended preliminary talks in Paris in late June 1947. The Soviets withdrew from the planning in early July, however, and the mood in Helsinki began to sour, despite the fact that Finland was among those countries receiving an invitation to participate in the ERP. In a rather threatening voice the Soviets let the Finns know that attending the Paris conference would be considered a hostile act toward the USSR. Aware that the Soviets had not yet ratified the Finnish Peace Treaty and that the ACC was still in place in Finland, President Paasikivi turned down the invitation on 11 July 1947.

The Finnish decision produced a schism within the American government, especially within the military branch. While the JCS suggested an outright termination of trade agreements with Finland in October 1947, the State-Army-Navy-Air Force Coordinating Committee (SANACC) took an opposite view. Finland should not be penalized on its refusal to join the Marshall Plan, SANACC argued, because "[it has] not been Sovietized to the same alarming degree as the Balkan satellites." Their argument carried the day.

Thus, despite their somewhat heretical behavior—the turning down of the Marshall Plan and a pronounced friendship policy toward the USSR—Finland was still considered to be part of the larger framework of a liberal world order. Or, as the SANACC's report concluded, Finland had not been "lost," but rather represented "the only penetration yet achieved in any part of the [Iron] Curtain."[10]

The question, then, was how to best sustain such a penetration. The answer had been formulated in the immediate postwar years and was perhaps best expressed by one of the more "hawkish" members of the State Department's European Division soon after the Finns had declined the Marshall Plan invitation. H. Freeman Matthews said on 15 July 1947 that in order to keep the Finns outside total Soviet control, the United States should refrain "from acts in Finland which might reasonably be regarded by the USSR as a challenge to its essential interests."[11] At least in this case the term "essential interests" seems to have meant a Soviet perception of the potential security threat that might accrue if Finland was more closely associated with the West. Perhaps paradoxically, an integral part of U.S. containment policy, as it applied to Northern Europe, was an effort to keep a certain distance to Finland in order to ensure the continuance of its Western ties. The Finns continued to receive loans and credits, although the numbers came nowhere near the figures afforded to Marshall Plan countries.

The Finnish decision may have had an impact on the attitudes of their neighbors to the west. Although Sweden, Denmark, and Norway were not eager to take a definitive stand in the brewing conflict between the United States and the Soviet Union, the fact that, with the exception of the Finns, only East European countries refused the American invitation convinced the two most important Swedish leaders—Foreign Minister Bo Östen Unden and Prime Minister Tage Erlander— that a refusal to participate meant siding with the Soviets. This was something that even the neutral Stockholm government was unable to stomach in the summer of 1947. Unden used, with apparent success, the prospect of siding with the Soviets as an argument to sway the Norwegians, who were initially reluctant to join in a scheme that would undermine the idea of bridge building. The Soviet threat that was so evident in Moscow's pressure on the Finns thus worked to push the other Scandinavians closer to the West.

The Copenhagen, Oslo, and Stockholm governments, however, were not ready to join the Marshall Plan without questioning its potential political implications. In particular, all three countries, in order to underplay the divisive political effects of the ERP, lobbied for the plan to be administered by the United Nations. Norwegian Foreign Minister Halvard Lange publicly indicated his desire for such an approach as early as 25 June 1947, the anniversary of the U.N. charter. In a meeting in Copenhagen on 9 July, Lange enlisted support for this approach from his Danish and Swedish counterparts, and it became one of the cornerstones of the Scandinavian countries' early attempts to undermine the political effects of the Marshall Plan by modifying its actual implementation mechanism. In addition, Lange suggested that the Scandinavians should begin exploring wider cooperation among themselves, apparently as a way of undermining the clear push toward broader Western European integration imbedded in the U.S. demand that countries wishing to receive aid should coordinate their efforts rather than ask for individual help.

Lange's efforts bore little fruit in 1947. At the Paris conference that opened on 12 July, the Scandinavians carried relatively little weight. The suggestion of a greater role for the United Nations was rejected outright by the two most powerful attendants, France and Great Britain, nor did the Paris conference allow for a discussion on the principles regarding the participating countries' relationship to those countries that remained outside the ERP. If anything, the Scandinavians attracted some embarrassing positive attention from the Soviet press, which commented favorably on the Scandinavians' efforts to oppose the further division of Europe, although these comments soon gave way to accusations about the spread of American economic imperialism to Northern Europe once the three countries capitulated to the majority at Paris. As their efforts proved fruitless, the combined Scandinavian front began to break down in the late summer of 1947. The Danes—who were facing the most serious economic problems—joined the Icelanders in backing the British viewpoint on most issues (such as opposing a proposal for a customs union that was supported by France, the Benelux, and Italy), while the Norwegians stayed closer to the emerging neutral "grouping" of Sweden and Switzerland.

Although the Soviet threat played a role in the decisions of Norway, Denmark, and Sweden to join the Marshall Plan, the governments of these countries were far from ready to take a definitive side in the Cold War. Indeed, this was one of the arguments presented in favor of participation in the Marshall Plan, because remaining outside would certainly have been a more decisive gesture than taking part in it. All three, and particularly Sweden and Norway, also continued to play down the political side of the Marshall Plan and insisted that the programs were purely economic.

Concurrently, the Scandinavians, including Iceland, which had been absent from the 7 July meeting, began to explore ideas of closer cooperation among each other. Resisting the idea of wider European integration and a broad customs union—both of which would entangle them in continental politics—the Nordic foreign ministers agreed in August 1947 to explore all possible Scandinavian options. In February 1948 they established the Common Nordic Committee for Economic Cooperation, a group whose mandate was to study the possibilities for establishing a customs union, the gradual removal of tariffs between the Scandinavian countries, the creation of a common labor market, and the expansion of cooperation in trade policy vis-à-vis the outside world.

These moves were not going to bear fruit until the early 1950s. Instead, by late 1947, it was becoming clear that the bridge-building policies envisioned by the Scandinavians in the first postwar years no longer sufficed. Denmark was already showing a clear interest in moving closer to the West, if largely for economic reasons. The Norwegians were more hesitant, but as their economic needs grew in the latter half of 1947, their political allegiances also shifted in the same direction as those of their southern neighbors. In contrast, the Swedes, who were in no dire straits economically, were determined to stick with their traditional neutrality. The three countries' attitudes were to a large extent preambles of their stands toward European economic cooperation in general: Denmark would be the first to join the European Economic Community (EEC) in 1972, while Norway and Sweden, for different reasons, rejected it at that time. The core countries of Northern Europe were, in short, being torn in different directions by the effects of the American initiative. The trend continued when events in Finland once again brought the Cold War home for other Scandinavians by increasing their sense of vulnerability to Soviet pressure.

FINNS IN BLUEBEARD'S CASTLE

Finland's unique postwar situation and the cautious American policy toward that country became clear as developments in Finno-Soviet relations unfolded in the spring and summer of 1948. On 23 February 1948 Stalin invited the Finnish president, Juho Kusti Paasikivi, to Moscow to negotiate a treaty with the USSR similar to those signed by Hungary and Rumania in 1947. The invitation was hardly a surprise to the Finnish leadership. As early as 1944–1945 the Soviets had suggested a defensive pact with the Finns, but Paasikivi had averted a treaty by referring to the Moscow Armistice of September 1944, which prevented Finland from joining any military alliances before the official final peace treaty was signed. In 1947 the Paris Peace Treaty removed that block. The Soviets signed a series of defensive military pacts with Hungary, Bulgaria, and Romania in 1947, and it seemed highly probable that the Finns would soon be asked to do the same. Stalin's invitation was therefore a culmination of a long series of Soviet approaches and Finnish rebuffs. President Paasikivi realized that this time he could not take a rain check.

Not unexpectedly, Stalin's invitation triggered negative Western speculation. Given the Czechoslovakian coup d'etat in late February, it seemed only logical that Finland would be the next target of Soviet-directed communist aggression. George Kennan, chief of the U.S. Policy Planning Staff, captured the general attitude in Washington by arguing that the Soviet Union would not tolerate an independent neighboring state that had not modeled itself as a people's democracy. Indeed, even before Stalin's invitation, Kennan, author of the famous "Origins of Soviet Conduct" article that appeared in the July 1947 issue of *Foreign Affairs,* had predicted a Kremlin-directed tactical maneuver by the Finnish communists. Nor was he alone in his pessimism. The French, for example, were ready to declare Finland the latest addition to the

Soviet empire, and the British agreed that Finland was becoming a test case of Western resolve. Lord Pakenham made the strongest public statement to this effect when he told the House of Lords on 3 March 1948: "Now the unhappy government of Finland [is] being embraced with the kiss of death and being invited to visit Bluebeard's [Stalin's] mansion."[12]

Pessimism and calls for action were also evident in the American press and on the floors of the House and the Senate. In its first report on Stalin's letter on 28 February 1948, the *New York Times*, for example, speculated that it was the "first step of a long plan for the seizure of power by Finnish Communists." Groups of Finnish-Americans approached President Truman expressing concern about Finland's potential fall under Soviet hegemony and pleading for the U.S. government to do something "to help Finland in what appears to be a final stand for that country." Representative Charles Vursell described Finland as "teetering on the brink of communism." Similarly, Senator Kenneth Wherry of Nebraska expressed his concern in a speech at Congress: "Now, without any aid from us, Finland is going to be taken over by the Russian sphere of influence. I wonder if there is anything in the world we could do unless we were to have an outright break with Russia." He then asked: "What is our responsibility?"[13]

Good question. The answer? To keep quiet.

Indeed, the United States was prepared to, or could, do very little. Secretary of State Marshall could not advise the U.S. Minister to Helsinki, Avra M. Warren, to give the Finns any hopes of American help aside from offering to support the Finns if they took their case to the United Nations. By 1948, however, the United Nations, to which Finland did not even belong, had proved to be a rather impotent tool for solving conflicts or helping small countries under pressure from a more formidable power. The Finns were not encouraged by memories of prior Western promises to support them against the Soviets, such as those made in 1940 during the closing stages of the Winter War. President Paasikivi, after weeks of stalling, eventually accepted Stalin's invitation on 9 March. Negotiations in Moscow began on 23 March 1948.

In the end, the Finno-Soviet Treaty of Friendship, Cooperation, and Mutual Assistance (FCMA), signed on 6 April 1948 in Moscow, differed significantly from the treaties that had been completed between the USSR and its East European satellites the previous year. While those treaties had been virtual preambles of growing Soviet hegemony in Eastern Europe, the Finno-Soviet FCMA Treaty recognized the limits of Soviet influence in Finland. It was directed specifically at avoiding the possibility of a renewed use of Finland as a springboard for an attack against the USSR. The most significant part of the treaty reflected Soviet fears of a revitalized Germany that might ally itself with anti-Soviet Western powers. Article One committed Finland to preventing any attack via its territory against the Soviet Union, specifying the attacker as "Germany or any country allied with Germany." The Finns were not required to send troops to fight with the Soviets but merely to protect their own territory. Thus, while the FCMA Treaty may not have represented Soviet expansionist hopes in Finland, it certainly demonstrated that the Kremlin was attempting to build a security zone on its Western border to counter any repetition of Operation Barbarossa. Never again, the treaty spelled out, would Germany—or its Western allies—be able to use Finland as a springboard for aggression against the USSR.

From the Finnish viewpoint, the most troubling clause of the FCMA treaty dealt with potential Finno-Soviet consultations about joint defensive precautions if a threat from Germany seemed imminent. Although the treaty did not obligate Finland to accept Soviet military assistance if such a threat were on the horizon, the fear was that the Soviets might manufacture a threat and demand consultations, perhaps even military bases, in Finland. For example, if West Germany rearmed, the Soviets might use such an occurrence as a basis for suggesting military talks between themselves and Finland. Indeed, 13 years later, in the fall of 1961, such fears seemed to come true (see chapter 5). In the end, according to political scientist George Maude, the FCMA Treaty did not make Finland a "full member" of the Soviet security system in Eastern Europe because the pact fell short of being a military alliance. In fact, the treaty paradoxically served to strengthen Finland's neutral aspirations. Article Four of the FCMA Treaty prohibited either party "from participating in alliances directed against the other party." In the long run, this clause served to enhance Finland's efforts to remain outside the East-West conflict. Thus, the FCMA Treaty became the cornerstone of much of Finnish postwar foreign policy, a fact that Paasikivi and his successor as Finland's president, Urho K. Kekkonen, would often mention.[14]

Why were the Soviets so soft on Finland? The Soviet Union's need for security had apparently overcome any expansionist dreams about Finland that the Kremlin may have had. Given the memories of World War II, Soviet security concerns naturally focused on doing everything to prevent a renewed attack from the West, especially from Germany. In this context, Finland was not the strategic hot spot that many Central European states, like Czechoslovakia, were because it did not lie directly between Germany and the Soviet Union. Thus, the FCMA Treaty satisfied Soviet security concerns in Finland in a way that a similar treaty with Poland or Czechoslovakia could not. Nor did Finland lie directly between the USSR and its other Cold War adversaries. Neutral Sweden, which was much more likely to stay neutral if Finland was not forced into a military alliance, was an added bulwark between the USSR and the West. In short, the FCMA Treaty seems to indicate that, dictated by their larger security interests in Europe, the Soviets had limited aims in Finland.

The aftershocks of the FCMA Treaty were, moreover, viewed positively in the United States. Throughout the spring of 1948, a communist coup d'etat had appeared to be a serious possibility in Finland. The FCP leadership—with the exception of a key member, the Minister of Interior Yrjö Leino—were ready and willing to attempt such a coup. There was, however, no green light from the Kremlin, which kept a tight leash on the FCP's policies. As the Finnish historian Kimmo Rentola writes: "Military security and state-to-state relations were foremost in Stalin's mind, and when he got a satisfactory arrangement on those accounts, the Finnish communists had fulfilled their task."[15] Thus, not only did a coup d'etat never occur but the *Eduskunta* elections in July 1948 resulted in defeat for the FCP/FDPL (down to approximately 20 percent from 23.5 percent in 1945), and their removal from the Finnish government. They were not to hold ministerial posts again until the mid-1960s. The Finns, in their own way, seemed to have "contained" the expansion of communism.

The Finns themselves were quick to capitalize on the Soviet-American confrontation and the evident eagerness in Washington to give aid to those allegedly threatened by communism. In the summer of 1948, the Finnish minister to the United States, K. T. Jutila, went to great lengths in Washington to press for a "little Marshall Plan for Finland."[16] Apparently he was successful after the electoral defeat of the FCP, because when American foreign economic policy, particularly the number of export licenses and the type of products allowed to be exported to given countries, was designed, Finland was not put in the same category as the USSR's East European satellites. Also, in the wake of the elections, the United States took a favorable view on Finnish loan and credit requests (which had been put on hold during the spring of 1948) and the Finns were granted, for example, a $5 million cotton credit on 1 September 1948 and a $10 million loan to the Finnish woodworking industry two months later.

The Finnish drama—Stalin's letter, the negotiations in Moscow, the signing of the FCMA Treaty, and the prospects of a communist coup d'etat—was followed by growing concern in other Northern European countries. Here, finally, seemed to be disturbing proof of the USSR's real intentions in Scandinavia. But each of Finland's western neighbors interpreted the evidence quite differently.

NATO OR SDU?

The Soviet pressure on Finland and the rumors that the Soviets would soon invite the Norwegians to sign a similar pact, led the Oslo government to study previous Soviet-Norwegian treaties, particularly the nonaggression pacts of 1928 and 1930. In combination with the Czechoslovakian events (the Norwegian and Czech foreign ministers, Halvard M. Lange and Jan Masaryk, were personal friends), Stalin's letter to Paasikivi and the Finno-Soviet negotiations increased the pressure toward strengthening the Norwegian defense forces. The Norwegian Foreign Ministry even drafted an appeal to the United States and Great Britain in the event that an invitation to sign a Soviet-Norwegian treaty actually arrived from Moscow. Similarly, the Danes reacted to the combination of the Czechoslovakian coup d'etat and the Finnish crisis with increased suspicion toward the internal communists, and the Danish army was on alert during the Easter holidays. In April 1948 the Danish Foreign Minister Gustav Rasmussen also guaranteed the United States that the Danes had no intention of demanding an abrupt end to the 1941 Greenland defense agreement. Meanwhile, the Swedes, although expressing some concern over the potential for a political shift, particularly in Norway, also increased their military preparedness. There was, however, a long road to be traveled before the Danes, Icelanders, and Norwegians joined NATO as founding members in April 1949.

Although leaning toward some kind of a collective security pact that could deter the Soviet Union's expansive designs, the Scandinavians were still conscious of alleviating Moscow's threat perceptions. They tried hard during 1948 to come up with a solution that would not tie them too closely to the USSR's adversaries. Concern over the impact that membership in a general Western military alliance might have on Finno-Soviet relations, and by extension to the position of the rest of Scandinavia, was particularly significant to Sweden. The Social Democratic Erlander government and particularly the long-time Swedish Foreign Minister Bo Östen Unden were determined to stick with the country's traditional policy of neutrality. Viewing the Americans and the Soviets as simply playing power politics, a type of zero-sum game, Unden thought that only the continuance of neutrality provided the Swedes with ongoing security. As he maintained in April 1948:

> The most severe disadvantage [of joining a Western military pact] is that Swedish involvement on the side of the Western powers would, in peacetime, seriously damage relations with the Soviet Union. The Soviets would, not unreasonably, regard the matter as proof of Swedish readiness to establish bases within their territory for the use of future enemies of Russia. Russia would have a strong interest in counteracting such a Swedish policy. Sweden would become the object of a struggle between the USA and the Soviet Union for political influence. Sweden would become a centre of unrest.[17]

A few weeks later, on 3 May 1948, Unden arrived in Oslo with a proposal of a neutral Scandinavian Defense Union (SDU) that he presented to the Danes and the Norwegians. He did this in part out of Sweden's own sense of insecurity, but also to try and prevent the Norwegians from joining a Western pact and from dragging the Danes with them. Although realizing the unlikelihood that Norway, with a small defense force and a joint border with the USSR, would opt for the security guarantees of the less-than-formidable Swedish armed forces when the North Atlantic option offered so much more in terms of potential military aid, Unden hoped that the Oslo government still believed strongly about continuing their bridge-building policies. In the end, although the Danes were willing to seriously consider this type of pact, the Norwegians were already convinced that only a formal tie to the Western powers could guarantee that the Soviets would not approach them as they had the Finns. The SDU proposal was a last-ditch effort by the Swedes to both continue their neutrality and keep Sweden from being increasingly sandwiched between East and West. They would find that only the first of these goals could be attained.

The Norwegians and Danes were just as willing as the Swedes to consider options other than joining a Western military pact to safeguard their security concerns. Well aware of their preference to continue as bridge builders, Sweden's Prime Minister Tage Erlander maintained that one of the goals of his government was "to do what was possible to reduce the areas of contention between the blocs."[18] But even such statements could not draw the Norwegians and Danes to opt for a neutral SDU. The memories of World War II and the swift Nazi occupation that had been all but condoned by the Swedes left little trust in a purely Scandinavian option. The Norwegians—concerned over the impact that association with the United States might have—had also explored the possibility of a separate British-Scandinavian security agreement, but such hopes had quickly evaporated when Foreign Secretary Ernest Bevin informed Lange in March that British resources were too limited to guarantee Norwegian security without American help. From that point on, the Norwegians and Danes gradually drifted toward NATO membership despite the Unden proposal.

That is not to say that the SDU could not have materialized. But the main issue that divided the Scandinavians was that while the Swedes wanted the alliance to be an independent and a neutral one, the Norwegians and the Danes wanted a Scandinavian treaty that included defensive arrangements with the West. The pressure exercised by Great Britain and the United States also pulled the Norwegians and the Danes further away from the Swedish viewpoint. The Brits were traditionally interested in the defense of the North Atlantic and keeping the long Norwegian coastline from being open to potential Soviet influence, while the Americans' primary strategic interest was to secure their base rights in the Danish-governed Greenland. Because the Danes were expected to follow the Norwegians' lead, however, the United States also approached the Oslo government. Indeed, during the summer of 1948, Washington was pushing for the same arrangement that the Norwegians were: a Scandinavian pact with strong ties to the West. The problem was that the Swedes would not compromise their neutrality.

By early fall of 1948, as the SDU negotiations continued concurrently with the planning of NATO, the NSC issued its first major policy paper on Scandinavia. It reflected the dilemmas the United States was facing in Northern Europe. NSC 28/1, "The Position of the United States With Respect to Scandinavia," first noted that the April 1948 Finno-Soviet FCMA treaty had "greatly increased the apprehension in Norway and Denmark that Soviet expansionist pressure may be applied against them." Therefore, the paper concluded, these two countries were quite willing to join a Western defensive alliance. In contrast, Sweden's strong traditional adherence to neutrality was chastised, and the NSC called for influencing "Sweden to abandon [its] attitude of subjective neutrality and look toward eventual alignment with other western powers." According to NSC 28/1, the problem was the Swedes' fear of provoking the Soviets coupled with their belief that they were "not directly threatened at the present." In other words, while the Swedes thought neutrality was the best guarantee for security, the Americans believed that only a strong defense alliance could guarantee anyone's security in the face of an aggressive USSR. The British, who at times pressed for a defensive alliance harder than the Americans did, were even more hostile toward Swedish neutrality.

As American pressure increased, the Swedes found yet another way of arguing against abandoning the doctrine of neutrality. In October 1948 Unden argued during his visit to Washington that Sweden's joining a Western military pact would have an "adverse effect on Finland." During the meeting Unden further added that Finland occupied a unique position among the states directly bordering Russia, because while it "was not being Russianized," any "Western step" (such as joining a military alliance) by Sweden would lead to "a direct change in the position of Finland."[19]

Although this argument did not convince many officials in Washington, most Finns, including President Paasikivi, preferred the continuation of Swedish neutrality. In an interview with a Swedish journalist on 28 November 1948, Paasikivi said that although it was impossible to predict how the Soviets would react to it, he did not wish to see Sweden joining NATO, because it might prompt the Soviets into reconstructing *their* security arrangements in Northern Europe. Paasikivi, for whom Finland's postwar foreign policy is named, could see the basis for Finland's coexistence with the USSR being shaken by Sweden's possible move away from neutral ranks. By placing Finland directly between the two blocs, such a move could irreversibly change the geopolitical realities that the Finnish president viewed as the foundation of his country's foreign policy. Moreover, when the Swedish parliament, *Riksdagen*, held hearings about military alliances in February 1949, most members preferred continued neutrality, but only if Finland's situation vis-à-vis the Soviet Union remained the same. In the wake of the NATO talks, therefore, most Swedes and Finns considered Swedish neutrality as a necessary precondition to Finland's continued independence.

By that time, the failure of the SDU was already clear. Although a meeting of the three countries' foreign ministers in Karlstad, Sweden, in January 1949 did produce a vague compromise formula of sorts, the conditions attached to it by the Swedes—one of which was that Scandinavians could receive Western military aid without formal ties—were objectionable to the United States. Indeed, the United States had already made it clear to the Danes and the Norwegians that participation in a larger security arrangement was a precondition to military aid from Washington. Because of the World War II experiences of both countries—relying on their self-declared neutrality only to be overrun by Germany—the Norwegian and Danish leaders were, more than their Swedish counterparts, looking for protection against potential aggressors. To them, the Soviet Union had emerged as a threatening geopolitical reality and ideological nemesis that only a protective American umbrella could keep in check. In that context, Stockholm's attempts to convince their neighbors that the Swedish defense forces alone would provide a significant military deterrent were unconvincing.

The Danish and Norwegian governments' decisions, which were supported by all political parties in these countries except the communists, probably also provided the final push for the Icelanders. As a result, all three became founding members of NATO in April 1949. However, although they joined the alliance, the Danes and Norwegians took into account the possible anxiety that their decisions might cause in Moscow. Indeed, the Soviets had bombarded the Scandinavians with diplomatic notes and articles in prominent newspapers that condemned even the idea of joining a military alliance as a hostile act. As a way of reassuring the Kremlin, the Norwegian government guaranteed in a diplomatic note sent to the Soviets on 1 February 1949 that it would not allow foreign bases or troops in its territory "as long as Norway is not attacked or subjected to threats of attack."[20] When they joined NATO the Danes, along with the Norwegians, also insisted that no military installations would be stationed in their territory in peacetime. As a result, the two countries did not become "full" members of the Atlantic Alliance. Rather, they were—and remained throughout the Cold War—"semi-allies" and continued to reassure Moscow by emphasizing the defensive nature of their actions. In 1949, even Iceland refused to allow foreign troops to enter its territory (although it would agree to give the United States base rights two years later). The Norwegians and Danes, although opting for NATO membership, still wished to maintain a certain distance from the United States, if only to appease the Soviet Union. Nevertheless, after April 1949, the Cold War ushered its way into Scandinavia, and the five Nordic countries had to make decisions that shaped their fortunes for the next forty years.

SOCIAL DEMOCRATS' GAINS

The intensification of the Cold War in 1947–1949 and the long period of vacillating that ended with the creation of NATO coincided with a clear swing to the right among the electorates of the five Nordic countries. The communist losses in Finland in 1948 had led to the creation of a Social Democratic minority government by the former speaker of the *Eduskunta*, K.-A. Fagerholm. A similar shift occurred in other countries. In Iceland the communists, represented by the United People's Party-Socialist Party (UPP-SP), had lost their government seats already in 1947, although the UPP-SP, partly because of its status as an opposition party, lost only one out of its ten seats in the *Alth-ing*. (It retained the 19.5 percent of the popular vote it had received in 1946, however.) Also in 1947, the Danish elections showed a decline in popular support to the local communists by almost half from what it had been two years earlier (from 12.5 percent to 6.8 percent of the popular vote). In Swe-den, the *Riksdag* elections in 1948 meant a decline from 10.3 percent (in 1944) to 6.3 percent for the Swedish communists. Finally, in 1949, the Nor-wegian communists lost all their seats in the *Storting*. A shift to the right, or at least toward the more moderate left, was clear.

The communists' losses in 1947–1949 can largely be explained by the effects of the Cold War and, perhaps with the exception of Iceland, by the per-ception among the general public that communists were Moscow's agents, undermining the independence of their respective countries. In part this per-ception was because the social democratic parties refused to join into political alliances with the communists. In Finland, for example, the social democrats campaigned actively against the FCP, one of their most famous slogans being, "It's enough!" (*Jo riittää!*)—an unmistakable and politically successful refer-ence to the power vested in the communist members of government.

The social democratic (or moderate labor) parties thus dominated the political scene in Northern Europe in the late 1940s. Ideologically they were distant from either major political party in the United States. Nevertheless, the Scandinavian social democrats represented a bulwark of sorts against the spread of Soviet power and communism in the region, particularly among the working class and within the national labor unions. Often the Scandinavian social democrats themselves—as in the slogan mentioned earlier—con-sciously took on the role of such a bulwark. For example, when two labor advi-sors of the Economic Cooperation Administration (ECA) came to Oslo to meet with the Norwegian labor leaders, they were told that "the Communists were in process of being weeded out" from the Norwegian Federation of Labor.

The social democratic parties were beginning to lean toward, or complete adopt, a more bipolar worldview as a result of the Cold War. Indeed, in the late 1940s, internal discussions about international relations within, for exam-ple, the Danish, Norwegian, and Swedish social democratic parties stressed a division in the world between two camps (democratic and dictatorial) rather than three (capitalist, communist, and socialist) as had been the case during the first two postwar years. In short, if the United States viewed them as a tool of containment, the Scandinavian social democrats—largely independently, it seems—began to view themselves in the same role.

Of course, this role was not clear-cut. From the U.S. perspective, the social democrats did not represent an optimal political ideology but rather a murky Middle Way. The United States had very little sympathy for the type of wel-fare state ideas that the Scandinavians championed during the postwar era. But Washington also had no real alternative. Because of the limited interest that the United States had in Northern Europe and the de facto attainment of most of their security goals by 1949, the political ideology of the Scandinavian governments had to be considered secondary. Put another way, the expansion of American power to the region had clear limits and did not extend into the arena of domestic politics.

American expansion had clear limits, that is, with the possible exception of Iceland. After the first official NSC Policy Statement on Iceland, which noted the relatively strong position of the Icelandic communists, was approved in August 1949, the State Department was charged in November 1949 with the implementation of a program titled "Design to Decrease the Vulnerability of the Icelandic Government to Communist Seizure of Power." Yet even this program focused on "Icelandic self-help" rather than on overt U.S. measures. During informal talks with Iceland's foreign minister, Bjarni Benediktsson, and other government members, the U.S. minister to Reykjavík, Edward B. Lawson, attempted to convince the Icelanders of the need to create a home guard or other internal defense force, to develop a counterintelligence organization as a watchdog of communist activities, and to take other measures to strengthen internal Icelandic security. In addition, the State Department planned to increase contacts between U.S. and Icelandic labor groups as well as to "encourage Scandinavian labor groups to send representatives to Iceland to suggest ways of combating communism in Icelandic labor groups."[21] Keeping the Keflavík air base in American hands was not to be jeopardized by the possibility of a communist coup d'etat.

The concern over the Icelandic communists, however, leaned in a slightly wrong direction. To be sure, continued economic problems could play into the communists' hands. Yet they made no headway in the October 1949 elections to the Althing (they lost one of their ten seats), and they remained outside the cabinet. Any problem in obtaining permanent base rights on the small island republic was due mostly to the continued strength of Icelandic nationalism, which did not die with the country's participation in the Marshall Plan or its membership in NATO. As a May 1950 State Department Policy Statement said: "Icelandic parochialism and nationalism continue to be a significant factor in Icelandic behavior and remain as an obstacle to closer relations between Iceland and the [United States]." Such nationalism was preventing a successful completion of a bilateral American-Icelandic agreement for U.S. base rights, a concern that was becoming an increasingly significant issue for the U.S. security planners. Soon, they would turn to NATO for help in solving this dilemma.[22]

THE UNITED STATES AND COLD WAR NORDEN

In the 5 April 1945 issue of Current History, Julius Moritzen, a Scandinavian specialist with the New York Herald Tribune, had speculated about the possibility—in his mind almost a certainty—that Scandinavian countries would create a regional federation in the aftermath of the war. This, he argued, "would lift Scandinavia to a position of eminence in Northern Europe once more, and enable the constituent parts [he included Finland in this analysis] to fulfill their broader responsibilities."[23] It became clear soon after the capitulation of Germany, however, that Moritzen's prediction was a pipe dream.

The four years after V-E Day had seen a remarkable change in the role of the United States in Northern Europe. The coming of the Cold War and the failure of the United Nations to become a guarantor of a peaceful world order led to Scandinavians' concern over their security, and the very survival of their democracies seemed to come under a serious threat from the East. In such a situation the hope, entertained by observers like Moritzen, that Northern Europeans could stick together and remove themselves from the turbulence of the continent also quickly diminished. By 1949 three of the Northern European countries had joined a military alliance led by the United States, one stuck with its traditional neutrality, while the fifth continued an uneasy coexistence with the Soviet Union. Nordic integration seemed like a distant dream as Scandinavians were drawn in radically different directions by the harsh realities of the Cold War.

But even though cooperation among all Scandinavians had proven impossible in the military sphere, it was possible in the economic arena. The traditionally large amount of intra-Scandinavian trade kept the countries drawn together both formally and informally, no matter what their respective security arrangements were. Concurrently with the planning of the ERP, talks regarding inter-Scandinavian economic cooperation commenced. During a late August 1947 meeting of the foreign ministers of Denmark, Iceland, Norway, and Sweden, the countries had already agreed to take steps in this direction. In a similar meeting in Oslo the following February, plans for common tariffs, the reduction of inter-Scandinavian trade barriers, and a joint approach to trade with other countries began to take shape. This type of Scandinavian economic cooperation was bound to increase in the 1950s.

Indeed, with the alliances and security concessions of the late 1940s, the military-strategic situation of Scandinavia was stabilized for most of the remainder of the Cold War, as the "full" NATO membership of Iceland, the restricted memberships of Denmark and Norway, the neutrality of Sweden, and the security pact between the USSR and Finland seemed to create what a Norwegian political scientist later dubbed the Nordic Balance.[24] The area was to be "the quiet corner" and remain virtually immune to serious international conflict throughout the remainder of the Cold War. As a result, the social democrats, who emerged as the most potent political force in Scandinavia, were able to direct the northern European countries toward becoming the most advanced welfare states in the world.

Although the American perspective on social democracy as an ideology was far from favorable, the United States considered the situation in Northern Europe in 1949 largely positive. The three Scandinavian countries' decisions to join NATO had been welcomed. These decisions guaranteed that, in the event of hostilities, the Soviets would not have access to the strategically important islands of Greenland and Iceland, nor would the Americans have to worry about securing North Atlantic communication links between the United States and Europe. The Soviets had also been denied base rights in the High North, which had been an important goal in the emerging polar strategy. In addition, Sweden was soon to be linked to the Western security structure in an informal way through the sale of military equipment that helped strengthen the Swedish military's deterrence factor. Contacts between the military planners in Norway, Denmark, and Sweden were also under way. Nor did the Finnish situation cause too many headaches in Washington. After all, as long as the "friendly democracy" formula worked and Finland did not become an outright satellite, it was, in its own way, containing the expansion of communism.

If there was a concern, it was linked to the idea of neutrality. Charles Ulrich Bay, the U.S. ambassador to Norway, captured the essence of this problem in a cable from Oslo in January 1949. He noted that "Russian aggression [in Scandinavia] may not necessarily be [in the form of] direct military attacks, but with Scandinavian neutrality could take the form of slow aggression as in Finland."[25] Bay, one of the leading American diplomats in northern Europe, thus suggested a theme that would become increasingly prevalent in U.S. thinking vis-à-vis Scandinavia by suggesting that neutrality, if it gained popularity, opened the door to the gradual growth of Soviet-communist influence through nonmilitary—assumably cultural and economic—means. This approach seemed to characterize Soviet policy toward Finland after the security pact of 1948. Such a Soviet policy might be successful in neutral Sweden, and neutralism might, indeed, find fertile ground among the reluctant cold warriors in other parts of Scandinavia as well. Despite being excluded from the cabinet, the Icelandic communists still received close to one-fifth (19.5 percent) of the vote in 1949. The Scandinavians' strong reluctance to involve themselves in continental European affairs and alliances could also play into the Russians' hands and hinder the consolidation of a unified anti-Soviet Western front.

Despite their evident acknowledgment of the Soviet threat, even the NATO countries of Scandinavia were not considered to be firmly committed to the cause led by the United States. Although willing to extract money and security guarantees as ways of avoiding economic chaos and deterring the Soviets, they were not eager to just follow the American lead. Their close contacts to neutral Sweden and their continued wish to reassure the Soviets made them keep the United States at arm's length. As the Cold War entered a new and dangerous phase in the early 1950s, some of these attitudes began to change.

chapter 3

FROM WAR TO THAW, 1950–1955

On the morning of 25 June 1950, the phone rang at Tage Erlander's mother's house in Ransäter, Sweden, where the Swedish prime minister was relaxing for a few days with his wife, Aina, and his two sons. Sven Dahlman from the foreign ministry in Stockholm was calling to inform the prime minister that North Korean troops had crossed the 38th parallel into South Korea. Erlander, just into his fourth year (out of a record-breaking 23 successive years) as the Social Democratic Party leader and prime minister, never doubted that the Soviets, in some way, had prompted the aggression. He realized that the events in northeast Asia were bound to cause an uproar among the Swedish public similar to the one two years earlier after the Czechoslovakian coup. "At that time we had been able to hold onto a neutral foreign policy. Would we be as successful this time?" he wondered.[1] It was not going to be easy.

The outbreak of the Korean War stands out as one of the seminal events shaping the Scandinavians' outlook about the East-West confrontation. In late June 1950, a genuine war scare was evident from Helsinki to Reykjavík. It strengthened the anti-Soviet attitudes in all five countries and led to increased defense spending in Denmark, Norway, and Sweden. It resulted in closer NATO cooperation by the three Nordic members of that organization and to the acceptance by Iceland of the return of an American-run—albeit under NATO auspices—base in Keflavík. The end result was that in Northern Europe, except for Finland, the U.S. position and influence grew stronger.

These developments went hand-in-hand with the hardening of attitudes in the United States that had been evident already in 1949 as a result of the "loss of China" and of the first successful Soviet testing of an atomic bomb. With the replacement of George Kennan by Paul Nitze as the director of the State

Department's Policy Planning Staff and with the subsequent militarization of American containment policies (so evident in NSC 68, one of the seminal documents of U.S. Cold War strategy), little room was left for compromise between the Soviets and the Americans. In addition, the early 1950s was the heyday of that fervently anticommunist (and anti-intellectual) trend in U.S. domestic politics known as McCarthyism. These factors all contributed to a hardened U.S. attitude that lacked any desire for accommodation. In large part, the question asked of the northern Europeans in no uncertain terms was whether they were "in" or "out." For the most part, albeit with characteristic qualifications, they chose to be "in."

Yet the Scandinavians never completely abandoned the idea of bridge building. Trygve Lie, in his position as the secretary general of the United Nations, seemed positioned to become the great symbol of such mediation in the early 1950s. But he was in an impossible situation. The former foreign minister of a small country that had recently joined NATO could muster little support for his various peace initiatives. To his credit, Lie never stopped trying. Throughout the fall of 1950 and all during 1951, Lie attempted to mediate a cease-fire as he shuttled back and forth between different capitals. His efforts were to no avail. Because the United Nations itself was a belligerent in the conflict, it was extremely hard for the world organization to act as an effective mediator. Thus, hostilities dragged on, intermittently, until July 1953.

Lie's inability was also due in part to his independence, which made the Norwegian a pariah for both the East and the West. The Americans could not forgive or forget that already in 1949 Lie had supported the seating of the People's Republic of China (PRC) in the Security Council. Such support played into the hands of the McCarthyites, who began painting a picture of the Norwegian as, at worst, a communist, at best, a "fellow-traveler." His reputation in the United States was restored briefly in June 1950 when Lie emphatically supported a U.N. resolution to brand North Korea as the aggressor. The Soviets were boycotting the Security Council because of the rejection of the PRC, so the U.S.-sponsored resolution passed, and under U.N. auspices, the North Korean attack was, in due course, countered. But such action also meant that Lie lost his admittedly tentative Soviet support as well. Lie gradually began viewing the Soviets as a complete menace to world peace. This stance probably spoiled his efforts to mediate an end to hostilities in 1950 and 1951; his anti-Soviet comments, for example, soured a secret channel with the Communist Chinese that he had been able to establish after their entrance to the war in late October 1950. Lie was undone by the same force that had made his election possible in 1946: the Soviet-American confrontation. On 10 November 1952, the stout Norwegian announced his resignation, although his term was not due to expire until 1954. When he passed the torch to the slightly eccentric Swede Dag Hammarskjöld on 7 April 1953—a man Lie himself described, unfairly and incorrectly, as one with "no administrative experience and [the] record of a dilettante" or, at his bitterest moments after he realized that his secret bid for reelection would not succeed, as a "fairy"—Lie solemnly welcomed his fellow Scandinavian to "the most difficult job on earth."[2] In a sense, however, Lie was also passing the mantle of bridge building from Norway (and to some extent Denmark) to neutral Sweden (and in the long run, Finland).

By the time Hammarskjöld replaced Lie, the world situation had changed significantly. Stalin had died and the war scare that was so evident in the aftermath of the North Korean invasion had faded away. In some quarters, including northern Europe, the scare was replaced by a gradual rise in neutralist sentiments in the mid-1950s. In Scandinavia, America's "moment"—which in reality was more of an anti-Soviet moment—lasted only a short period, and disappeared concurrently with the fading of the shadows cast by a faraway war. The shadows did, nevertheless, leave a significant, permanent legacy.

KOREA'S LONG SHADOW

The outbreak of the Korean War strengthened the U.S. national security and foreign policy establishment's resolve to keep Denmark, Iceland, and Norway firmly in NATO and, if possible, bring Sweden closer to its NATO neighbors. Similarly, the Korean War meant that the Scandinavian countries were faced with a clear choice in the East-West conflict. Unambiguously, they chose the Western side. When the United States brought the issue of Korea to the United Nations, all of Scandinavia (with the exception of Finland, which was not a member) supported the American resolution to send troops to restore the 38th parallel as a border between North and South Korea. Trygve Lie was among the strong supporters of the U.N. intervention on South Korea's behalf, a deed that earned him the enmity of the Soviets. In the summer of 1950, a genuine war scare in Scandinavia pushed these countries closer to the United States. A few months later, after the entrance of the PRC into the conflict, the Scandinavian perception of the Soviet threat reached its zenith.

No wonder, then, that in the wake of the Korean War, both Denmark and Norway became much more eager participants in NATO planning than they were previously. To be sure, the Danes and the Norwegians had signed Mutual Defense Assistance Program agreements already in early 1950. Yet, only in the aftermath of the outbreak of hostilities in Korea did military material begin to flow in significant quantities as both countries embarked on a crash rearmament program in late 1950. In addition, the Americans encouraged the two countries to step up their internal defense programs by allocating more of their national budgets to defense. Accordingly, in the years from 1950 to 1953, defense expenditures more than doubled in Denmark and Norway. The war scare also accelerated the rapid buildup and modernization of the Swedish air force, which had begun in earnest in 1948. Despite Sweden's neutrality, the

United States would soon be willing to furnish certain equipment to that country as well.

In contrast, the Korean War caused the United States to be, if possible, even more cautious in its dealings with Finland, a country likely to experience almost instantly any change in Soviet policy toward northern Europe. Despite the war scare that followed the North Korean attack, American policymakers knew that Finland's special relationship with the USSR did not allow for any U.S. military aid or defensive cooperation. As in the late 1940s, the country was very much on its own, and the American objective was to try and maintain the status quo of the delicate Finno-Soviet relationship by not providing any excuse for the Soviets to make aggressive political moves toward Finland.

Learning the news of the North Korean attack was therefore particularly disconcerting to the Finns. Soon after the war erupted, President Paasikivi told his old friend, and Finnish ambassador to Sweden, Georg A. Gripenberg that he was very disappointed with both the United States and Great Britain, whose policies in Korea he considered "amateurish." Despite full knowledge of North Korean militarization, the Americans had done nothing to increase the strength of South Korean forces and therefore virtually "invited" an attack, Paasikivi complained. The president also admitted that he was afraid of the beginning of a new era in world history: the era of communism. In addition, the war prompted Paasikivi and the newly appointed prime minister, the Agrarian Party leader Urho K. Kekkonen, to order the Finnish military to study necessary changes in Finland's security policy, in case the Soviets were to use the war and the increased international tension as a pretext for demanding military consultations as had been spelled out in Article Two of the 1948 FCMA treaty. Accordingly, in the summer of 1950 Generals Aarne Sihvo (chief of staff) and Erich Heinrichs (commander of the army) prepared elaborate memoranda recommending a large-scale improvement of Finland's defensive capabilities. With the exception of the Law on National Conscription that was sent to the *Eduskunta* on 15 September 1950 and passed on 1 January of the next year, however, these plans were not put into practice because of "political reasons" (i.e., the potential suspicions they might arouse in the USSR). Yet the outbreak of the Korean War had clearly called into question the Finns' ability to retain their independence without a strong defense.[3]

The question of the Soviet role in Korea and its possible impact on Finland perplexed John M. Cabot, who had arrived in Helsinki as the new U.S. minister to Finland in February 1950. Only a year earlier, as a member of the U.S. legation to Shanghai, Cabot had witnessed firsthand the triumph of Mao's communists and, as a result of his experiences, was a strong believer in the thesis of a limitless communist appetite for expansion. He was also a pessimist. "Do we face Munich or war?" Cabot asked his diaries on 26 June 1950. If the choice was, as he apparently believed, between these two options, Cabot saw little hope for Finland: "if war, they're sunk; if Munich, their turn soon." Like Paasikivi, Cabot was worried about the Soviets invoking the consultation clause of the FCMA Treaty. At the same time he was torn between dissatisfaction over the non-Communist Finnish newspapers, which, in his mind, were expressing a "neutral tone" that Cabot considered dangerously misleading to the Finnish public, and his own understanding that if the Soviets pressured Finns into military consultations, the United States could do nothing about it.[4]

In Washington, the Korean conflict brought about a rethinking of American cold war strategies that included a brief discussion of Finland's role as well. In many respects George F. Kennan, at the time a counselor in the State Department, agreed with Cabot's concerns. During a meeting of the advisors to the NSC on 29 June 1950, Kennan went even further by placing Finland "right in the Soviet orbit." The United States "would not want to intervene if the Russians took over in Finland," the father of containment added. Kennan had bluntly expressed what many may have thought already but avoided saying in public: Finland was not worth a fight to the United States.[5] On the other hand, the NSC placed a certain trust in the Finns. "The Finnish people are stubbornly anti-Soviet [and] would not willingly assist the USSR" if they were invaded, NSC 74 stated. Moreover, although the NSC considered the risk of war in Finland possible, it argued that the "advantages of a conquest [to the USSR] are doubtful." In Washington, Finland was not considered such a high-risk item as Turkey and Yugoslavia, where Soviet attack was considered "a definite possibility."[6]

The commencement of the war in Korea had an inevitable and far-reaching effect in Scandinavia and in U.S. policy toward the region. Fears that World War III was about to commence and that Northern Europe would be drawn into an unimaginable vortex of destruction caused the leaders in all five countries to rethink their policies. Although no such aggression materialized, the prospect of it also allowed the United States to establish a permanent presence in Scandinavia.

SECURING THE NORTHERN FLANK

The Korean War and the war scare that it produced—particularly after the Chinese troops crossed the Yalu River in October 1950—led to significant logistical changes in U.S. and NATO strategy. In early 1951 NATO established a unified command structure for Europe with Dwight D. Eisenhower as the first SACEUR (Supreme Allied Commander Europe). Simultaneously, NATO established AFNORTH (Allied Forces Northern Europe) that stationed its headquarters in Kolsås near Oslo. Soviet protests that this move undermined the Norwegian commitment to a "no bases" policy were to no avail. In addition to these organizational changes, however, the Korean War was the prime factor behind securing the continuation of U.S. base rights in Greenland and the return of American soldiers to Iceland.

The Greenland base issue presented no real problems. Although reluctant to negotiate a specific agreement granting the United States bases on the frozen island in the aftermath of World War II, the Copenhagen government had not protested the existence of American military installations since the spring crisis of 1948. Immediately after the founding of NATO in April 1949, the U.S. and Danish governments—formally within the framework of NATO—commenced negotiations for a treaty that would supersede the wartime pact. Yet only after the outbreak of the Korean War, which led to a growing sense of insecurity in Denmark and an urgency to secure the "northern flank" against potential Soviet incursions into the United States, did the two countries agree to a treaty.

The Danish-American Defense Treaty was signed on 27 April 1951. According to its terms, the two governments agreed to jointly defend Greenland for the duration of the NATO alliance. In practice, this meant that the Americans received almost everything they had wanted: extensive freedom of movement within (as well as to and from) Greenland and virtual control over the three defense areas and air bases under U.S. operations in Thule, Søndre Strømfjord, and Narssarsuaq. Of the three, Thule, built in 1951–1952 and located in northern Greenland, soon became the central U.S. base as the significance of polar strategy grew with the advances in submarine technology. At the time the treaty was signed, however, the air base in southern Greenland, Narssarsuaq, was considered significant as a point from which to guarantee the security of transatlantic air routes. By 1958 the stepping stone strategy had lost much of its significance, and the Narssarsuaq base was deactivated.

Although the Soviets protested what was, in essence, an abandonment of the "no-foreign-bases-in-time-of-peace" pledge that Copenhagen had repeatedly made in the late 1940s, the Danes insisted that the Danish-American Defense Agreement of April 1951 did nothing to jeopardize Soviet security. After all, the bases had been there all along, and the frozen island was much closer to North America than to Europe. Nor did it bring NATO bases any closer to the Soviet heartland. The Copenhagen government did, nevertheless, reassure the Soviets that no foreign bases would be allowed in the Danish peninsula—unless there was an attack or an imminent threat of an attack.

Whereas the Danes had only extended a pact that had existed since 1941, Iceland's reversal of its base rights policy was more dramatic. After all, only a few years earlier the *Althing* had seriously debated whether to allow even civilian U.S. operators to run the Keflavík base. But the Cold War had taken its toll already in 1949, and when Iceland joined NATO, the decision was seen as a prelude to accepting foreign troops into a country with no defensive force of its own. On the eve of the North Korean attack, the country's domestic political scene had changed since the Keflavík agreement of 1946 and even since 1949. The communists were clearly on the defensive, and the cabinet that had taken over in March 1950 was organized under the leadership of Steingrimur Steinthorsson and dominated by his generally pro-Western Progressive party.

The decision to accept American troops back to Iceland was, however, mostly a result of the outbreak of the Korean War. Discussions over Iceland's defense started immediately after the North Korean attack and, almost without fail, ended with the conclusion that Iceland needed a protector to deter a possible Soviet invasion. If there was no deterrent and the Soviets did land on the island, many people feared that Iceland would become a battlefield because the Americans could never allow their main enemy to occupy an island so close to North America. The sensationalist Reykjavík paper *Manudagsbladid* asked in July 1950: "Will Iceland Become a Bloody Battlefield?"[7] The politicians, although more reserved in their earlier comments, came to the same type of alarmist conclusion, especially after the Chinese troops crossed the Yalu River to Korea in October 1950.

Pressure was also building from NATO. The Standing Group (SG) of the alliance requested that Iceland rethink her attitude about the presence of foreign troops soon after the hostilities commenced in northeast Asia. In September 1950 Iceland's foreign minister, Bjarni Benediktsson, met with members of the SG and was pressed on the sudden imminence of the Soviet threat to North Atlantic security, the significance of Iceland to NATO defenses, and the need to guarantee the island's security against a potential attack. Early in 1951 the new SACEUR, Dwight D. Eisenhower, made an inspection visit to Iceland, adding fuel to the growing rumors of an impending U.S.-Icelandic defense agreement.

During the spring of 1951 the Icelandic government negotiated a return of the U.S. military to the country. Under the terms of the defense treaty that was signed in Reykjavík on 5 May 1951, the United States, on NATO's behalf, took upon itself the task of defending Iceland. The agreement further stated that either party could at any time request a NATO Council review over the need to continue the pact—a clause the Icelanders would later invoke. Unlike the Greenland treaty signed only a week earlier, the Icelandic defense agreement also gave the Reykjavík government the right to limit the number of U.S. forces, and the Americans agreed to be sensitive regarding Iceland's sparse population and long tradition of being unarmed.

Although the Steinthorsson government did not present the treaty to the *Althing* for ratification until several months later, it had discussed the terms with the representatives of all parties except the communists who, naturally, were outraged when the terms of the pact were made public two days later. On the same day, 7 May 1951, the first U.S. contingent landed in Iceland and proceeded to occupy the Keflavík base. In a few weeks the Icelandic Defense Force (IDF), commanded by General E. J. McGraw, would number approximately 5,000. The Americans were back after a five-year hiatus.

When the defense agreement was finally submitted to the *Althing* for formal approval in October 1951, it passed with flying colors. Only the communists objected. Their spokesman, Einar Olgeirsson, made an impassioned speech in which he disputed the view that the Korean War had decreased Iceland's security. Instead he argued that if a war in northeast Asia was an adequate justification to bring U.S. troops to a small island in the northern Atlantic, the

American troops arriving in May 1951 at Reykjavík's Keflavík Airport
following the conclusion of an Icelandic-U.S. defense agreement that
was part of the increased U.S.-NATO defense commitment in the wake
of the Korean War.
Courtesy of the National Archives.

American troops were likely to stay permanently "because there will always be
struggles on the part of Asian and African nations to throw off the yoke of
American oppression."[8] The speech made no impact; the *Althing* ratified the
treaty by the end of the year.

The quiet compliance of the *Althing* was mostly because the real decisions had already been made. The parliament simply rubber-stamped an
already accomplished fact. Yet there was a stark contrast between the 1951
Defense Agreement and the strong rejection of the idea of an American
base only five years earlier. At least for the moment, the heat of the Korean
War had brought the Icelandic government firmly to America's side in the
Cold War.

The Korean War also seemed to call into question the strongly held views
about the establishment of foreign bases in Norwegian territory during peacetime. For example, the Norwegian defense minister, Jens Christian Hauge,
spelled out a slight modification of his government's defense policy in a speech

to the *Storting* in February 1951, indicating a slight departure from the previous "no-foreign-troops-or-bases-in-peacetime" policy:

> The Norwegian base policy does not prevent Norway from making bases available to Allied armed forces in the event of an armed attack on the North Atlantic area, or at the time when the Norwegian authorities consider themselves exposed to the threat of attack and summon Allied forces to the country. Nor does the Norwegian base policy prevent Norway, in prescribed constitutional forms, from entering into conditional agreements with our Allies, having a situation of this kind in mind. Our base policy cannot prevent Norway from developing her military installations according to a pattern which will make them capable of receiving and effectively maintaining Allied armed forces transferred to Norway in order to assist in the defence of the country. Our base policy cannot prevent Norway from participating in joint Allied exercises or being visited for short periods by the naval and air forces of our Allies, even in peacetime.[9]

The speech was given to the members of the Norwegian parliament, but it was probably also aimed at Moscow and at Norway's NATO allies, particularly the Americans. It clearly captured the Norwegians' growing need for strengthened resolve to deter or counter the possibility of a Soviet maneuver in Europe in the early 1950s with increased defense spending and closer ties to NATO.

The Americans jumped at what seemed like an ideal opportunity to strengthen the exposed Northern Flank. In 1951 Washington suggested the stationing of a tactical airwing with approximately 75 aircraft in Norway. Despite long deliberations and even added pressure from the British, however, the Norwegians eventually rejected the plan at a NATO meeting in Lisbon in February 1952. The need to reassure the Soviets, the fear that a base in Norway would mean hard times in Finno-Soviet relations, the stabilization of the situation in Korea, the continued neutralist tendencies in Norwegian domestic politics, and the reluctance to be closely associated with the Americans (in this context it is significant that the Norwegians specifically requested that the commander of AFNORTH be a British rather than an American officer) combined to enforce the continued negative stand regarding the stationing of foreign troops or the establishment of bases in Norwegian territory.

Nor did the Danes, despite pressure from Washington and a cooperative attitude regarding Greenland, allow foreign troops in the Jutland peninsula. In this case, however, the reasons can be traced back to shifts in domestic politics that occurred in 1952 and 1953. In February 1952 Danish Foreign Minister Otto Kraft had indicated to his American colleague that the Copenhagen government's stand on base rights was potentially flexible, although it was something that could not yet be discussed in public. Three months later he signaled a willingness to enter into secret discussions over the establishment of two NATO air bases in Denmark (at Tirstrup and Vandel) while the government simultaneously launched a campaign in Denmark that was meant to increase public support. Throughout the fall of 1952 Kraft remained optimistic that despite the unclear stand of the major opposition party, the Social Democrats, the conservative-liberal government would eventually be able to guarantee the establishment of two NATO bases with 150 to 200 planes and 4,000 to 5,000 troops. However, in December 1952 he advised the United States that in order to get the necessary support from the Social Democratic party—including its leader, Hans Hedtoft—a list of conditions needed to be met. The most important of these, he maintained, was that the planes stationed in Denmark could not be used to participate in local conflicts outside Danish soil without Copenhagen's explicit approval. The State Department and Pentagon rejected such a condition outright and the base rights issue suffered a sudden death.

The Social Democrats used the public discussion over NATO bases skillfully in the September 1953 parliamentary elections—the first ones held under the new Danish constitution that created a single-chamber parliament, the *Folketing*. Already in January the Social Democrats had launched a new slogan that was to capture the essence of the ambiguity inherent in Danish security policy for years to come. The slogan read: "For the Atlantic Alliance—against yesmen."[10] It would have been a suitable slogan for many other parties among the Scandinavian NATO members as well.

Despite the continued reluctance of Norway and Denmark to comply with foreign bases in their territory (except in Greenland), the Northern Flank seemed secure by the time Eisenhower entered the White House in early 1953. What made the area particularly secure was that the nonaligned part of Scandinavia seemed to effectively deter the possibility of a Soviet attack.

THE FIRST LINE OF DETERRENCE

Finland and Sweden, in the myriad of security policies that touched on their respective territories, had become intricately linked to each other already in the late 1940s. The trend continued during the early 1950s, although the approaches toward the two countries, as well as these countries' foreign and security policies, were dramatically different. From the U.S. perspective, the two countries did, however, constitute a type of first line of defense for NATO's Northern Flank in the midst of the Korean War.

Despite its often critical statements regarding American policies vis-à-vis China and Korea and despite its official policy of neutrality, by 1953 Sweden had effectively become a "latent ally" of the United States. Although Sweden had chosen to remain outside of NATO in 1949, it had not been abandoned. Instead, it became a type of neutral extension of the Western security system that was built in the late 1940s and early 1950s. Because its defensive posture was clearly geared toward an attack coming from the East, the NSC concluded soon after the outbreak of the hostilities in Korea that Swedish neutrality "adversely affects but does not jeopardize the security of the US."

In case of a military conflict, the Americans expected that Sweden would fight against the Soviets and thus vicariously side with NATO.[11] Ensuring that Sweden had an adequate defensive capability was therefore among the primary American objectives in its policy on Scandinavia. The premise underlying this goal was that neutral Sweden should "be in the best possible position to resist Soviet pressure or aggression."[12] That the Swedes themselves believed in a strong military as a precondition for credible neutrality helped matters from the U.S. perspective. As Paul Cole put it, Sweden's desire to maintain a formidable regional defense force while at the same time remaining outside of alliances was "based on the assumption that as the size of the force required to attack Sweden grew, the risk that such an attack would take place diminished."[13] These feelings strengthened after June 1950 and the United States thus found a receptive, if secretive, partner in the Swedish government that looked for Western help in building a strong defensive posture. Such a desire was also instrumental in gaining Sweden's cooperation for economic warfare, because the United States could, in return, offer military equipment that it otherwise sold only to its allies. Sweden's agreement in late December 1951 to participate in export controls against the USSR and Eastern Europe was thus based on a tacit give-and-take: in return the United States made military assistance available for Sweden. A few months later, on 28 February 1952, Sweden became eligible for reimbursable military assistance under the Mutual Defense Assistance Act of 1949, which meant that it could buy military equipment from the United States without too many restrictions. By 1953 Swedish requests for military equipment were routinely approved.[14]

Sweden was also indirectly linked to NATO's military planning. As early as November 1949 Swedes had participated in meetings with Norwegian and Danish officials on technical military cooperation that eventually led to joint covert military planning. By late 1952 the United States and Great Britain were playing a role in these schemes, which led the U.S. Ambassador to Sweden, Walton Butterworth, to consider Swedish neutrality as more of an asset than an obstacle for American security planning.[15]

The same was true of the public views regarding Sweden's role and relationship to NATO defense. For example, an October 1952 article in the U.S. News and World Report described the strong defense buildup in Sweden as follows:

> Sweden [is] arming to the teeth. . . . no country in Europe, with the possible exception of Britain, is as well prepared for trouble or is making a bigger defense effort. And, if trouble comes, NATO commanders count these defenses as an asset on the side of the West. Never neutral in their sympathies, the Swedes have become overwhelming[ly] pro-western in recent months. Sweden still isn't ready to join the Atlantic Pact. But U.S. military men consider her present defense policy the next best thing.[16]

By late 1952 the Swedes had built a remarkable stock of approximately 1,000 tactical planes, had modernized their navy and the equipment used by the army, and had improved the military training of their reserves.

The situation in Finland stood in stark contrast to the highly modernized (and "Westernized") Swedish defense effort. The restrictions mandated in the 1947 Paris Peace Treaty on the equipment of the Finnish military were still in place. The restrictions limited the number of planes the air force could have and the number and types of ships allowed for the navy, put a lid on the number of service personnel allowed in arms at any given year, and prohibited missiles or submarines. In addition, the Soviets still had their naval base in Porkkala (near Helsinki) and were unlikely to give it up during the tense situation in the early 1950s. Clearly, U.S. military aid, direct or indirect, was unavailable to this country, lest the Americans wished to risk a hostile Soviet move. Rather, NSC 121 argued that the "key to U.S. policy is to avoid any steps which would threaten the delicate balance of Finnish-Soviet relations and call forth drastic measures inimical to Finnish independence."[17]

The combination of a low-profile U.S. policy and a conscious effort by the Finns not to give the Soviets any grounds for charging that the Helsinki government was leaning toward the West had so far meant that Finland was not a recipient of Marshall Plan aid while at the same time it was committed to heavy reparations to the USSR. The same policies continued in the early 1950s with, it appears, at least moderate success. That is, despite the tense world situation there was no Soviet "move." Instead, beginning in early 1952, the Finnish leaders—particularly Prime Minister and future President Urho Kekkonen—began to publicly refer to Finland as a neutral country. Perhaps most important in preserving the continued belief in the wisdom of a delicate U.S. policy, however, were two developments that seemed to spell out an improvement in Finland's international status in 1952.

First were the Helsinki Olympics in the summer of 1952. Having the Soviets participate for the first time allowed the Finnish government to try and present Finland as a "neutral meeting place" between East and West. The focus on Helsinki also allowed the Finns to rid themselves of the disturbing image of their country as an Iron Curtain nation. Whereas the euphoria of the Olympics was short-lived and probably enhanced the Finns' self-image more than their position in the world, the end of Finnish reparations to the USSR in September 1952 signaled an end to Finland's painful postwar adjustment and a true beginning of "postwar" Finnish history.

The immediate reaction in the United States to the last reparations shipment on 19 September 1952 was positive. U.S. newspapers were filled with sincere admiration toward Finland—the country that had the mythic, if somewhat misleading, image of being the only country to have paid back World War I debts to the United States—for having completed its reparations to the USSR and maintained its independence. "Did Finland Outsmart Stalin?" one magazine asked. Nor were such feelings limited to the media. On 25 September

1952, George Kennan used Finland as an example of "the loss of Moscow's control," which in his mind indicated that the United States was not losing the Cold War, as the McCarthyites argued at home.[18]

As long as Finland retained its independence, it appeared to be an outpost of Western democracy in northern Europe in the early 1950s. Ideologically and culturally the Finns remained dominantly anti-Soviet despite their "good neighbor" foreign policy. Strategically, notwithstanding the existence of a Soviet naval base in southern Finland, the country was an added cushion between the USSR and NATO in Scandinavia. It was also an inexpensive bulwark; the Finns were not offered, nor did they ask for, ERP or military aid. In a sense, the Americans "got" Finland "for free."

The link between Finland and Sweden was a complex one. On the one hand, it seemed clear that the Soviets would not like to see Sweden join NATO—especially as its air forces became increasingly impressive—and were thus likely to act circumspectly vis-à-vis Finland. On the other hand, the Swedes were not likely to join NATO or move too close to that organization, because that might alarm the Soviets and produce problems for the Finns. Strategically, the optimal policy for the United States in the early 1950s was therefore to help the Swedes build up their defenses while at the same time maintaining an extremely low profile on Finland in order not to alarm the Soviets. Although the end result—in terms of defense postures—was a remarkable disparity between the modern and strong Swedish defense (armed neutrality) and a relatively weak and old-fashioned Finnish force, the combination of the two seemed to both reassure and deter the Soviets.

By 1953 it seemed that all was well in American-Scandinavian relations. Base rights in Iceland and Greenland had been secured, Norway and Denmark were cooperating effectively—if not unambiguously—within NATO, Finland had not been brought under undue pressure from the USSR, and even the Swedes were quietly cooperating with economic warfare. From a military-strategic point of view, the Korean War had been very fruitful for U.S. policy in Norden. Not only that, but economically Northern Europe seemed to provide a showcase of sorts.

SCANDINAVIA REBUILT

In the early 1950s, most Scandinavian countries had little or no unemployment. The Marshall Plan aid given to Norway and Denmark—that respectively totaled $425.7 million and $266 million in grants, conditional aid, and loans—certainly played a role in the recovery process of these countries. It had, for example, helped the Norwegians rebuild their merchant marine, a prime source of the nation's wealth. In the end, however, aside from providing added capital to help in the conversion and modernization of certain industries, the Marshall Plan, which ended in July 1952, alone did not lead to a speedy recovery in Northern Europe. Other factors, including the fact that these countries had suffered physically much less than many continental European nations, were probably more influential. In addition, the stability of the political systems and the flexibility of the type of planned economic systems typical for Scandinavia certainly helped the recovery process. As Littgow Osborne, the U.S. ambassador to Norway from 1945 to 1947, maintained in an article in the *Foreign Policy Bulletin* in late 1952, the Social Democrats had been "the driving force behind return to normalcy."[19]

A part of that "normalcy" was, of course, the fact that the Scandinavian communists had suffered defeat after defeat since 1946–1947. A speedy recovery certainly helped the noncommunist parties in their political campaigns against the communists' gloomy predictions of the upcoming demise of the capitalist system. But rapid economic progress in the aftermath of war did not necessarily guarantee future economic growth. For countries such as the Scandinavian ones, much depended on foreign trade and access to markets, particularly in Western Europe—furiously in the midst of debates regarding potential economic integration. Without continued access to such markets, Scandinavia would either suffer economically (which could undermine political stability) or have to turn elsewhere, perhaps to the Soviet Bloc. That, however, could have significant political consequences. In this regard, Finland seemed to offer a warning.

The satisfaction in the United States over the end of Finland's reparations payments in 1952 soon changed into a concern about growing Soviet economic penetration in that country. Finland was heavily reliant on the USSR for imports of oil, coal, cereals, and fertilizers, and equally dependent on the Soviet Union as a market for the products of its metal and machine tool industries. The prospect of Soviet domination was soon noticed by the American media. An article in *Time* on 29 September 1952 summarized the problem as seen from Washington. "[Finland's] economy is now almost wholly geared to Russia," the article declared, despite the fact that Finland's trade with the Soviet bloc was approximately 18–20 percent of its total foreign trade. The writer further announced that while the "Finns will continue to deliver goods to Russia . . . in exchange they will get whatever goods (wheat, fodder, gasoline, oil, fertilizers) *the Russians see fit [to] spare them.*"[20] The Finns seemed irrevocably in the arms of the Kremlin and on the way to becoming "a Soviet economic serf."[21] When the Finns and the Soviets signed a supplementary trade agreement on 23 September 1952 and a tripartite trade agreement that included Mao's China, the outlook from the U.S. perspective seemed even bleaker.

In contrast, for most Finns the 1952 trade treaty did not mean increased dependence on the USSR, it meant survival. Shipbuilding and other metal industries that had been set up to manufacture the goods for reparations deliveries were not a traditional part of Finland's economy, but an addition of the postwar years. Nevertheless, they employed hundreds of thousands of Finns by 1952, and unless the government wanted to face mass unemployment, it had to find a large market for these goods. Because Finland's metal industries were not geared toward competing in Western markets, the Soviet Union was a natural outlet. Finland's 1952 exports to its largest trading partner, Great Britain, had decreased to almost half the 1951 figures, which led to even more pressure to look for additional trade opportunities in the East.

In the end, Finland was not integrated into a Soviet economic bloc. The increase in Finno-Soviet trade that took place in 1953–1954 was only temporary and largely a result of developments beyond the control of either the Finns or the Soviets. A decline in the prices of wood, paper, and cellulose products in the world market in the second half of 1952 put this part of Finland's economy in major trouble; many factories were forced to close down in late 1952 and throughout 1953. This decline led not only to a decrease in Finland's exports to the West (where the principal market for wood and paper products was located) but also to record-high unemployment in this sector of the Finnish economy. Given that Finland's foreign trade during the first quarter of 1953 featured a 40 percent decrease compared to the first quarter of 1952, it was no wonder that the Finns looked toward increasing Soviet trade as a way of escaping some of their economic distress. But in the long run, the volume of Finno-Soviet trade stabilized and remained at approximately 20 to 25 percent of the country's total foreign trade for the remainder of the Cold War. The proportionally large increase in Finno-Soviet trade in 1953 and thus of Finnish economic reliance on the USSR was a historical accident resulting from the cumulative effect of the end of Finnish reparations, Western economic warfare, reduced world demand for the products of Finland's wood and paper industries, and the need for markets for the Finnish metal industry.

This is not to say that the new American administration did not take the developments in Finno-Soviet economic relations seriously in 1953. Indeed, the new secretary of state, John Foster Dulles, was concerned about the Finnish situation during the first year of his tenure at Foggy Bottom. But he ran into an old American dilemma: how to fight the Soviets in Finland without alarming them? In other words, Dulles was faced with the same problem that had bothered most Americans dealing with Finland and postwar Finno-Soviet relations: Although the secretary of state saw the Soviets as only waiting for a chance to increase their influence over Finland and the upsurge in bilateral trade as a clear indication of that, he was afraid that a large American/Western attempt to change the course of events would be counterproductive. Such a move would allow the Soviets to accuse the Finns of being too close to the West and to use this as an excuse for applying increased political pressure. It was a no-win situation. While Dulles complained that the policy conducted at the time "cannot possibly yield results commensurate with the seriousness of the problem," the secretary of state also maintained that Washington could not change its approach, because "a massive effort aimed at diverting existing Soviet-Finnish trade to Western channels would threaten the delicate balance of Finnish-Soviet relations and call forth drastic Soviet measures affecting Finnish independence." Indeed, Dulles concluded, "a major US initiative ... would incur greater political and military risks than the present situation entails." Instead of direct U.S. involvement, the policy that the NSC adopted in August 1953 can best be characterized as a piecemeal approach, an effort to try and convince other Western powers to increase their trade with Finland.[22]

Although these developments in Finno-Soviet trade were mostly based on a unique set of circumstances, they did raise some broader fears. First, the Soviets appeared eager and increasingly capable of using trade as a means of maintaining influence in a nonbloc country. Second, such an "economic offensive" might be directed westward from Finland, that is, toward Sweden, Norway, and Denmark. Given the Scandinavians' reluctance to participate in the European integration efforts supported by Washington, such Soviet moves, if they did materialize, might indeed prove successful.

THE RELUCTANT EUROPEANS

In his April 1950 article in Foreign Affairs, Norwegian Foreign Minister Halvard Lange had little positive to say about European integration. Instead Lange talked about the Atlantic partnership and Scandinavian cooperation. He pointed out that there was "considerable skepticism among the Norwegian people" concerning Scandinavian customs unions. Because of his country's less developed industrial base when compared to, say, Sweden, he expressed reservations about a closer partnership with continental Europe.[23] The next year, however, in a speech at the Storting, Lange strongly supported Nordic integration in all its forms. Moreover, many other leading politicians in Scandinavia—including Iceland's Foreign Minister Bjarni Benediktsson, Norway's Prime Minister Einar Gerhardsen, and Sweden's Foreign Minister Bo Östen Unden—made known their desire for increased Nordic cooperation in 1951–1952.

This emphasis on Scandinavian cooperation was in some ways a response to the pressures of Western European economic, military, and political integration represented by the ERP, OEEC, NATO, and the failed plan for the European Defense Community (EDC), as well as to the emergence of continental European cooperation in the form of the European Coal and Steel Community (ECSC), founded in 1950, and the agricultural integration ideas—the so-called Green Pool—floated around in the early 1950s. Although there seemed to be general agreement over the need to gradually liberalize, an ongoing debate emphasized two separate ideas on how to achieve that goal: via smaller scale sector integration or via outright unification. The Scandinavians, unlike, for example, the Americans, had little interest in broad integration plans, but remained reluctant Europeans.

One explanation why many Scandinavians rejected the idea of European federalism is a political one. Given their relationship with the USSR, the

Finns, for example, would have little chance to be involved in any kind of unity scheme. Similarly, the Swedes feared the loss of neutrality, and the Danes and Norwegians were inherently suspicious about being bogged down by continental European politics. Still concerned about reassuring the Soviets, the Oslo and Copenhagen governments wished to retain a degree of independence, and were turned off by the strong emphasis on the political aspects of integration embedded in, say, Jean Monnet's visions of a unified Europe.

There was also an economic argument against a broad supranational approach. Given the relatively higher wages and production costs in Northern Europe, these small countries would have little chance of effectively competing in a large free trade area. They might, moreover, be overrun by a large flow of continental laborers in search of higher wages that would result, most likely, in a high degree of unemployment. In short, European federalism represented a profound threat to the welfare state and to the homogeneity of Scandinavian societies. Because of these reasons, during the "grand debate" at the Council of Europe in 1949–1951 over the different approaches to European integration, the Scandinavians tended to align themselves with the British point of view and prefer functionalism to federalism.

The British connection can also be explained by the fact that for all the Nordic countries, that nation had been and still remained the most important trading partner. Most importantly for the future of European unification, however, the Anglo-Scandinavian grouping that emerged in the late 1940s and early 1950s came to represent the other alternative to European trade liberalization that eventually climaxed in the founding of the European Free Trade Association (EFTA) in the late 1950s. However, the combination of the rejection of a supranationalist (and pan-European) approach—something that was regretted in the United States—and a search for trade liberalization also strengthened pan-Scandinavian ties in the early 1950s.

COBWEB INTEGRATION

The question in the early 1950s was not so much whether there would be any regional cooperation, but rather when and under whose auspices it would occur. The establishment of the Nordic Council in 1952–1953 and the different forms of Scandinavian cooperation that it supported were symptoms of the reluctance of Northern Europeans to be too closely integrated to the affairs of the continent and of the desire to support and preserve a pan-Scandinavian option, a Nordic Model, in the heat of the Cold War. At no point, however, was integration in the sense of an economic union considered. What northern Europeans aspired to was increased cooperation in a wide range of fields, at times characterized as "cobweb integration."

Prior to World War II, a number of intra-Nordic associations and assemblies, including trade associations, the Norden Association (which promoted increased cultural contacts among the Scandinavians), and formal as well as informal labor union cooperation, existed. Although the war hindered the development of such cooperation, much of it was revitalized in the mid- and late 1940s. By the 1950s, for example, the Norden Association had 500 local branches spread around the five countries; it was publishing various periodicals and actively promoting lecture tours and exchange visits between "sister" branches in the other Nordic nations.

Prior to the early 1950s, this activity received little or no public funding and was limited to nongovernmental levels. There were, for example, no official interparliamentary meetings, although a Northern Interparliamentary Union (NIU), a private group of Scandinavian parliamentarians, had been founded in 1907. It was this informal body that served as the springboard for the founding of the Nordic Council (NC) in 1952.

The origins of the NC go back to the prewar years. In 1938 Danish Foreign Minister Peter Munch suggested the establishment of a joint body of Scandinavian parliamentarians that would hold meetings on all matters of common interest. Even the outbreak of World War II had not completely disillusioned the supporters of such ideas. For example, Swedish Prime Minister Per Albin Hansson raised the idea of interparliamentary meetings several times in the early 1940s, notwithstanding the fact that two countries were under German and one under American occupation, and that the Finns were actively fighting alongside the Third Reich. The failed SDU talks of 1948–1949 also had the paradoxical result of increasing the momentum for Scandinavian cooperation in nonmilitary fields, something that was evident in Norwegian Prime Minister Einar Gerhardsen's musings in late 1950. It took almost another year, however, for a concrete proposal to be presented.

This happened in August 1951 at the NIU's 28th delegate meeting in Stockholm. The Danish Social Democratic Party's leader and former (as well as future) prime minister, Hans Hedtoft, made an initiative to create an official joint body that would meet regularly and start molding Scandinavian cooperation in various fields. The reception was nothing short of enthusiastic. Draft statutes were quickly drawn up by a committee with representatives from all five countries. (In addition to Denmark's Hedtoft, other representatives were Oscar Torp for Norway, K. -A. Fagerholm for Finland, Sigurdur Bjarnason for Iceland, and Nils Herlitz for Sweden). Although it soon became clear that Soviet objections would keep the Finns outside the organization, the plans developed rapidly. Draft statutes were accepted in February 1952 at a meeting in Stockholm, and during a meeting in Copenhagen a month later, the Danish, Icelandic, Norwegian, and Swedish foreign ministers agreed to submit proposals to their respective parliaments. These were approved with wide margins in May and June 1952. Vocal opposition in the countries came from two principal sources. In Denmark and Sweden, the local communists echoed Moscow's views by opposing any supranational cooperation agreements as being a vehicle of NATO and the United States. In Norway, by contrast, most nonsocialists—in the opposition at the time—voted against the

NC. In Iceland, a mixture of communists and Independence Party members reacted in the same way. In both cases, the opposition seemed based on nationalistic arguments that presented the founding of a regional supranational organization as a way to undermine the national sovereignty of Norway and Iceland.

There was also an economic side to the anticooperative sentiments, particularly in Norway. While both the Danes and Swedes were enthusiastic about the possibilities for closer economic cooperation, the economically weaker and less industrialized Norwegians saw in it a threat of being overrun by their more affluent neighbors. Thus, the same concerns that would later work against Norwegian membership in the European Economic Community and the European Union in the 1970s and 1990s were already present in the 1950s, hindering the chances of integration among the Scandinavians. As a result, particularly in the first years of its operation, the four-nation NC that began its operation in 1953 (Finland was to join three years later) focused on issues linked to "cooperation" rather than "integration."

The NC started out as an interparliamentary body to which each member country elected representatives from within its own legislatures. From early on, the NC's strengths and weaknesses were a result of its extraordinarily broad membership. A specific stipulation of the statutes passed by the Scandinavian legislators stated that the representatives of each country should be drawn from different political parties—thus members of opposition in their own countries actually got to participate in intergovernmental work that was otherwise reserved for majority parties. The strength of such a decree was that the NC represented a true cross section of Scandinavian political ideologies; the negative result was that the NC's recommendations did not necessarily represent the views of each and every national government, and their implementation could be compromised at the local level. To prevent that from happening, each government was allowed to send to the NC meetings as many of their cabinet members as they considered necessary; although these representatives could not vote on resolutions, they could voice their views. The number of parliamentary representatives mirrored the political strength of the four countries: while all others could send 16 members to the NC, Iceland—because of its small population—could only send 6.

The NC's founding resolutions set clear limits to the type of issues that the new organization could be involved in. It would have no right to meddle with military questions or with the member countries' relations with countries outside Scandinavia. The council was, in short, set up as an advisory body, devoid of any power to impose its will on national governments. However, given its composition, the NC's recommendations usually did meet support when put to a vote at the *Riksdag* in Stockholm, for example, or the *Althing* in Reykjavík. Some of the most significant early examples of such resolutions included a virtual freedom of movement across the national boundaries in Scandinavia without passports (approved in 1954) and the establishment of a common labor market for most professions in 1954. The 1956 common pension plan meant that, for example, Swedes living in Copenhagen could draw their Swedish pension as though they were actually living in their native country.

This successful cooperation among the Nordic countries with such remarkable ease was undoubtedly due to their uncharacteristically high level of uniformity toward political values and institutions, social programs, economic statuses, and cultural identities. Yet it would take a long time to make any significant steps from cooperation to integration, a goal that the United States was strongly supporting on a much larger scale in Western Europe. An article in *Newsweek* on 21 March 1955 noted that while the establishment of a common labor market and a system of reciprocal social benefits were remarkable, "anything so sweeping as a genuine customs union is probably at least five, more likely ten, years in the future." The essay maintained, however, that "cooperation on individual projects within clearly defined limits will increase. The future of Scandinavian regional cooperation lies in the step-by-step technique."[24]

So it would. The economic integration of Scandinavia would remain a distant dream for the time being, in part for nationalistic, in part for economic reasons. The same reasons that made the Scandinavians reluctant partners in broader schemes of a united Europe kept Nordic cooperation limited to cobweb integration.

MCCARTHYISM'S DISCONTENTS

Although the Scandinavians generally pledged their support for the militarization of containment in the early 1950s and attached themselves more firmly to the West, these actions did not necessarily translate into outright approval of all things American. For example, from the Scandinavians' viewpoint, which is generally oriented toward a "mixed" economy such as their own, in which government plays a decisive role, the victory of the Republicans in the November 1952 presidential elections was a victory for the interests of big business and the type of "vulgar capitalism" rejected by most Nordics. Since Franklin D. Roosevelt had launched his New Deal in the 1930s, the Democrats had been viewed as the party more oriented toward, albeit by no means adopting the principles of, social democracy, the dominant ideology in Northern Europe. For the distant observer in Stockholm, Copenhagen, or Oslo, the Republican victory—combined with the outburst of McCarthyism in the early 1950s—seemed to be another signal of the victory of right-wing extremism over reason.

A certain ambivalence had always existed in American and Scandinavian perceptions of each other. On the one hand were the positive images based on similar values: many Americans and Scandinavians perceived each other and themselves as hard workers and believers in democratic ideals and the rights of the individual. That the Scandinavian immigrants to the United States had been able to blend easily into the dominant white culture had much to do with such positive notions. The relationship, however, had another aspect, one that stressed the harshness of the unlimited individualism in the United States and the racial and ethnic inequalities considered so "American" by the Scandinavians living in their homogenous societies in northern Europe. In contrast, the traditionally antiestablishment character of American political rhetoric (or mythology) found something very unappealing in the strong traditions of state intervention in the Scandinavian brand of social democracy, even though the Scandinavians thought that American character had been somewhat tempered by the experiences of the Great Depression. Nevertheless, while the average American was extremely distrustful of government as an agent hindering his or her individual freedom, the Scandinavians were far more willing to compromise some of their liberties for the common good and use the government as an agent of social change.

During the late 1940s, the negative attitudes had been largely hidden beneath the surface. Scandinavians believed that most of what the Americans did was positive—whether it be the inception of containment, the racial integration of the U.S. armed forces, or the launching of the Fair Deal. When American policy affected Scandinavia, as with the Marshall Plan or the negotiations that led to the establishment of NATO, the United States was rarely seen as imposing its will. But in the early 1950s, things changed. What had previously been reason now appeared to be hysteria. The age of McCarthyism did severe damage to the image of the United States.

Much of this climaxed during the first year of President Dwight D. Eisenhower's administration when such actions as the efforts to ban "communist" books (a category that included such authors as W. E. B. DuBois and Agnes Smedley) from the United States Information Service libraries abroad, the Rosenberg trial and execution, and President Eisenhower's apparent sheepishness in dealing with the junior senator from Wisconsin did little to improve the Europeans' trust in effective and reliable American leadership. Charges of "creeping American fascism" were widespread throughout the summer of 1953. By July, Eisenhower had become so concerned over the effects of McCarthyism that he stated at an NSC meeting that "he was much disturbed and concerned that so many of our allies seemed frightened of what they imagine the United States government is up to. It is a sad fact, said the President, that every returning traveller whom he talked to stated that the people of Europe were vastly confused about the objectives and programs of the Republican administration. The name of McCarthy was on everyone's lips and he was constantly compared to Adolf Hitler."[25]

Such concern eventually prompted Secretary of State John Foster Dulles to send a query to all the chiefs of missions at NATO countries, asking for a full estimation of the reasons behind the growing doubts expressed about U.S. leadership.[26] The answers he received were indicative of the general opinion not only in Europe but also Scandinavia (although only the embassies in Norway, Denmark, and Iceland had been asked to contribute). In a memorandum dated 24 August 1953, Assistant Secretary of State for Europe Livingston Merchant summarized the answers to Dulles's query. Merchant explained that "[s]everal of our Mission Chiefs report that the domestic political phenomenon known as 'McCarthyism' has done more to weaken American prestige and tarnish American leadership than any other single development." In addition, he referred to the commonplace European perception, evident at least as far back as the days of Tocqueville, that the Americans were "politically immature." Wrote Merchant: "the controversy over United States libraries abroad has made the American Government appear ridiculous and childish in foreign eyes." The same applied to McCarthy's abusive behavior in Congressional hearings. As a result, McCarthyism seemed to be "regarded by some European leaders as Communism's greatest present asset in Europe." What did they mean by this? Simply put, Merchant wrote: "The effects of 'McCarthyism' are particularly serious among European Socialists and other non-communist leftists who fear that American thinking tends to 'lump together' communism, socialism and all other unorthodox philosophies. In conjunction with obvious and energetic Soviet efforts to revive a 'popular front' spirit among European leftists, it is possible that 'McCarthyism' will alienate a vital segment of European public opinion and thereby diminish the prospects of maintaining middle-of-the-road coalition governments sympathetic to American objectives." Thus, the report concluded:

> perhaps the gravest danger now apparent is that growing anti-American sentiment may tempt the non-Communist left in Europe, principally the European Socialists, to depart from their postwar policy of cooperation against communism and move toward a neutralist position . . . With the Soviet Union now making obvious and intensive efforts to consolidate leftist sentiment against the United States, the danger that the non-Communist left may succumb to an anti-American virus is very grave.[27]

In Northern Europe, where the socialist, or social democratic, parties had long been in powerful positions (either in government or as a major opposition force), this development was not only a disheartening prospect, but an acute possibility. The Scandinavians resented McCarthyism strongly, finding it a disturbing indication of political perversion in freedom's land.

In Norway, McCarthyism was resented as a movement of extremists. The activities of the House Un-American Activities Committee (HUAAC) were considered a witch-hunt that victimized liberals and undermined the traditions of liberty and freedom, which were the benchmarks of Scandinavian admiration of American society. As one paper put it, the McCarthyite extremism did more damage to U.S. credibility around the world than any "Commie spy or traitor."[28] Indeed, when Trygve Lie announced his resignation as secretary general of the United Nations in the fall of 1952, some Norwegian papers argued

Norwegian Trygve Lie, the first U.N. secretary general, giving a radio address in June 1951 on the possibility of a negotiated peace in Korea. Despite his strenuous efforts, Lie was unsuccessful in his mediation attempts.
Courtesy of the National Archives.

that this was partly due to the mounting criticism directed toward the United Nations by the "primitives" in the American press as well as by the so-called McCarran committee in Congress. "[T]he names 'McCarthy' and 'McCarran,' " Ambassador Charles U. Bay wrote from Oslo in late July 1953, "symbolize a disconcerting development of undemocratic and irresponsible forces within [the United States]."[29]

A similar pattern could be found in Denmark. "There is no doubt that the feeling of the vast majority of Danish Government officials and the Danish people is one of revulsion," John O. Bell of the U.S. embassy in Copenhagen wrote in July 1953. The word "McCarthyism," Bell added, "connotes a sort of neo-fascism which they both fear and despise." What was particularly disconcerting to the Danes, moreover, was the timidity of both the Truman and Eisenhower administrations in their dealings with the senator from Wisconsin, which seemed symptomatic of the potentially erratic and unpredictable nature of American policies in general.[30]

In addition to its impact on U.S. foreign policy, McCarthyism clearly represented to Northern Europeans the worst in American culture: nativism and racism. This view was evident in an article in the Finnish journal *Suomalainen Suomi* in March 1954. Noting first that according to a recent Gallup poll, every other American accepted McCarthy's actions despite the fact that the press and intellectuals had repeatedly refuted many of his wild accusations, the article then lamented: "This is mass psychosis at its strongest, and it will not whither away without a fight . . . Not that McCarthy is attacking minorities or even pressuring labor unions. Rather, McCarthy's actions have created an atmosphere in which all kinds of anger, fear and prejudice against *all* intolerable ideas can be organized together. 'Subversive' is a great magic word, which makes everyone shudder. 'Revolutionary' can mean anything progressive." The author went on to speculate about the meaning of McCarthyism's popularity: "It is hard to know what it is that makes the American mind so easily organized toward collective action in good and bad. One can find an eager group to support any given cause, whether it was sending clothes to Korean children or lynching negroes. Some say this is a childish people, others that it is an uneducated one. Whatever the answer is, the most significant thing from McCarthy's point of view is that the tendency [toward collective action] exists."[31]

The Swedes, not unexpectedly, found McCarthyism equally disturbing. *Svensk Tidskrift*, for example, wrote in 1953 that "Goebbels would have envied McCarthy's methods" and added that "the thought that Joe McCarthy could have a chance [which the journal considered extremely slim] of reaching [the presidency] is scary." A year later the same journal was predicting that, given his attacks on the army, McCarthy was bound to decline in popularity. Yet, the respected conservative Swedish journal added, "the damage that he has done to the United States' outlook and leadership standing in the western world is incalculable."[32]

Happily, the Swedish paper was correct in its estimation about McCarthy's forthcoming demise. Yet there was no question that his actions had inflicted a long-lasting stain on the general European and Scandinavian perception of Americans as a people. McCarthyism was not, however, the only determinant in the context of image-building that lay a basis for the stereotypes of what an "American," "Finn," "Swede," or "Scandinavian" is.

POSITIVE IMAGES AND NEGATIVE STEREOTYPES

What were the American attitudes about Scandinavia and Scandinavians in the early 1950s? Such views are, unfortunately, far less well documented than those from the other side. In large part, this is probably due to the small size of the five countries and their long distance from the United States. The relative inattention of Americans to things Scandinavian can also be explained by reference to the very stability of Northern Europe, to its status as, in the words of *Harper's Magazine*'s George Soloveytchik, "Europe's Quiet Corner."[33] The last Northern European country to make American headlines was Finland during the Winter War of 1939–1940. The next time it would happen would be when Swedish Prime Minister Olof Palme launched his severe criticism of American policy by comparing the 1972 Christmas Bombings to the Holocaust and caused a virtual break in American-Swedish diplomatic relations (see chapter 5).

In any case, it was probably the visions of Sweden, the most populous of the Scandinavian countries, that played the largest role in the American view of Scandinavia in general. Although Americans held no great antipathy toward Sweden, its neutrality and its long legacy of progressive welfare policies certainly had made their marks. In a late December 1951 article on Sweden by one of *Time*'s senior editors, Henry A. Grunwald, the country was bluntly characterized as a "Well-Stocked Cellar." In referring to Sweden's neutrality, Grunwald described the country as a "determined abstainer from Europe's common effort to ward off a third [world war]". He also argued that Sweden was a country ruled by "benevolent despo-socialism." And, in a paragraph that neatly summarized the negative stereotypes that were held about the Swedish welfare state, Grunwald further lamented:

> Swedish life is controlled and regulated to a degree difficult for an American to imagine; not that these people are not free, but they have a polite and padded kind of freedom . . . The Swedish welfare state takes care of its citizens from the womb (prenatal benefits to mothers), to birth (maternity hospitals), to infanthood (home assistants to young mothers), through school (free lunches), to jobs (vocational training), through sickness (next-to-free hospitals), through accidents (invalid insurance), through mental troubles (free psychiatric advice), through old age (old-age pensions), to the tomb (funeral benefits), to salvation, if possible (state-paid preachers).

What was it that Grunwald found so wrong about all these benefits? In his mind, they were responsible for "a deep undercurrent of emotional unrest" that was evident in the rise in divorce and illegitimacy rates, alcoholism, juvenile delinquency (consisting mostly of car and motorcycle thefts, "done for the hell of it," as Grunwald put it), and the lack of interest in religion—all, of course, uniquely Swedish, or at least non-American, phenomena. Grunwald closed his brief account by asking if the Swedes were "a happy people." Although admitting that the natives themselves would likely answer in the affirmative, he suggested that "the panorama of Swedish life seems to say no. An invisible wall seems to divide them from each other and from the world. Each sits in his own little cellar, inattentive to the world and determined to enjoy his own Golden Peace which—he feels—hard work, right thinking, progressive sewage disposal and a little luck have earned them."[34]

A less negative view could be found in an article in *Harper's Magazine* in February 1953 by George Soloveytchik. The author (who did not include Iceland in the article) expressed his continued amazement over "how these curious people manage to combine progressive democracy with monarchy (except in Finland) and with old-world tradition; how they run their highly efficient co-operative movements on purely capitalistic lines; and how their Labor or semi-Labor governments practice their peculiar form of socialism without nationalizing anything and without upsetting in any very noticeable way the existing social order."[35] It was a bewildering state of affairs indeed.

Although snapshots such as these two articles presented the American public with a necessarily skewed view of the Scandinavians, there was, starting in the late 1940s and early 1950s, a new significant vehicle to broaden cross-cultural understanding. The so-called Fulbright agreements—educational exchange programs that gave numerous foreigners an opportunity to spend a year or more as a student in an American university and in return allowed students from the United States to spend a year abroad—served to increase awareness of at least some aspects of American and Scandinavian societies. By the early 1950s, all Scandinavian countries were taking part in the Fulbright program, the impact of which was studied as early as 1954.

In William H. Sewell, Richard T. Morris, and Oluf M. Davidsen's "Scandinavian Students' Images of the United States: A Study in Cross-Cultural Education," the authors discussed many of their findings, which were based on extensive interviews with Fulbright scholars and students from Denmark, Norway, Sweden, and Finland (even though Finland had concluded its agreement in 1952, it was included in this particular study). Their findings, although hardly conclusive, offer an interesting insight into the cultural side of the American-Scandinavian relationship.

In general, the Scandinavians seemed to have experienced a gradual learning process. They initially appreciated "the American personality" for its frankness and openness, but after a few months tended to complain about the "superficial nature of American friendliness" and "the seeming shallowness of friendships." Although they adjusted to the American society quite easily, the Scandinavians were shocked by the importance of religion in people's lives and the obvious prevalence of ethnic and racial tensions. The "pre-contact" picture of a nation where "individualism flourished, where strong opinions were strongly voiced, and where mobility and lawlessness were pronounced" was almost completely reversed. Instead of strong individualism, the students found "a mass culture which implacably forces every individual into a mold of conforming behavior." As the surveyors described it: "The American code seems to the Scandinavian student to be: Do not be different, but if you have to, be different together." In addition, in a shocking revelation to anyone with the image of Scandinavia as the law-abiding bird's nest where the government takes care of its citizens from cradle to grave, these Scandinavian students found that there were "too many laws" in the United States and that "police interfere in too many spheres of private life." One student added: "Political ideas all come from newspapers. Americans are like a flock of sheep. They don't think for themselves." And lastly, the ultimate insult from the students from countries with state-run Lutheran churches: "Religion [in the United States] is external. They go to church, but they aren't really religious in the way they choose to act." In short, Scandinavian students saw the United States not as a land of uninhibited individualism, but one of conformity, albeit conformity not perpetrated by the government but rather by the marketplace.

Was it all bad? No. In the end, the Fulbright experiments seemed to serve their purpose extremely well by spreading a largely positive image of the United States to Northern Europe. As the follow-up interviews indicated, most negative images reflected a type of cultural defense mechanism that made the Scandinavians (and probably most other exchange visitors) defensive of their own heritage, culture, and society and more prone to criticize things "American." The positive aspects of the United States surfaced more frequently after the experience was over and the exchange students returned to their native countries. Said one exchange student: "When you get home, you forget the bad things and remember only the good things about America." The "good things" ranged from friendliness and camaraderie as opposed to the reservedness of Scandinavian cultural and societal norms, to the accessibility of material goods and opportunities for achieving material benefits as a result of hard work that seemed to outweigh those available at home.[36]

Franklin D. Scott, a leading U.S. scholar of Scandinavian history and culture, was also fascinated by the Swedish exchange students' attitudes about America. He found a dominantly positive reaction—again regarding Americans' friendliness, self-confidence, optimism, capacity for teamwork, and so on. However, this positive view was marred by a few notable complaints. McCarthyism naturally shocked the Swedes, who were "astounded that a liberty-loving people will tolerate deceitful exaggeration and browbeating." In addition, the Swedes found American culture "nonexisting." Finally, they zeroed in on the Americans' attitudes regarding religion and morality. Wrote Scott: "The Swede is likely to pride himself on the fact that he has accepted sex as one of the natural facts of life; he finds American attempts to deny freedom in sex an abomination. This is the aspect of American life in which he finds the greatest hypocrisy."

Much like Sewell and his coauthors, Scott praised the positive significance that the program had for the American image abroad. He argued that "a few words from a returnee have more impact than hours of propaganda out of either Washington or Moscow." In a summation that captures the subtleness of the cultural and educational impact of such visitors upon return, the author maintained that the Swedes "have not [a] fear of American imperialism, no sense of cultural inferiority, no deep-seated historical resentments; they are free psychologically and actually to choose or to reject, to accept and modify what and when they will. They use their American experience, therefore, not as disciples of America, but as discoverers for Sweden."[37]

The most accurate summarization of the American and Scandinavian views of each other in the 1950s would probably be "shared ambivalence." The negative stereotypes—Americans as narrow-minded, uncultured, and too easily mobilized for reactionary causes; Scandinavians as, ironically, narrow-minded, monotone, and technocratic—were balanced by the positive images of each other as people who shared the basic values of democracy, hard work, and resentment toward totalitarianism in all its forms. There was not a noticeable "cultural conflict." Instead, disagreements tended to arise in other arenas: economic, political, and strategic. Often the disagreements were results of the changing dynamics in the broader international framework.

BLUEBEARD'S DEATH

The spring of 1953 was a key period for Northern Europe's role in the East-West conflict. The inauguration of Eisenhower in January and the coinciding shift in American and NATO strategy toward increased reliance on nuclear weapons—the New Look and Massive Retaliation—meant a gradual increase in the significance of the Northern Flank for U.S. hemispheric and Atlantic defense. In particular, the shift in U.S. strategy would gradually increase the role of Norway in strategic calculations and eventually bring back the issue of Spitzbergen. Yet much of this shift would take place gradually and became evident only in the late 1950s. The more immediate change in Scandinavia's position in the years 1953–1955 was political in nature, brought on not by the results of Ike's victory, but by the more dramatic changes that took place in the Soviet Union.

On 4 March 1953, Stalin died. A new era in Soviet foreign policy and in East-West relations finally seemed possible. Already on 15 March, Grigori Malenkov announced that there was no dispute between the Americans and the Soviets that could not be decided by peaceful means. Two weeks later the Soviets agreed to the nomination of Sweden's Dag Hammarskjöld, whom they had previously rejected as too pro-Western, as secretary general of the United Nations. In the summer of that year, the new Soviet leadership also began to move toward a more compromising direction regarding Austria and Korea. Something that the Soviets referred to as the "thaw" and the Westerners as the "Malenkov peace offensive" had begun.

The months and years that followed were filled with false starts and unmet expectations, but also with several significant steps that signaled the coming of a more normal international atmosphere. For example, the Korean War was brought to a close in 1954 and a genuine dialogue appeared to be emerging, if only gradually, between the United States and the Soviet Union. The French National Assembly rejected the EDC proposal, but this setback to Western defensive planning was soon corrected when West Germany joined NATO in 1954. Any hope of minimizing the division of the European continent into two hostile blocs seemed futile—especially when the Soviets responded by creating the Warsaw Pact in 1955, thus providing an appearance of legitimacy for the continued presence of Soviet troops in Eastern Europe. The Cold War was by no means over, but it was clearly entering a new phase. In 1955 the thaw would have as its concrete result the neutralization and unification of Austria and would be symbolized by the so-called spirit of Geneva.

These changes in Soviet policy and superpower relations also meant that the Scandinavians felt less threatened by the prospect of a military conflict in their region. The oft-quoted phrase "peaceful coexistence" seemed to offer hope for a brighter future for small countries not capable of defending themselves on their own, yet geographically unable to escape being drawn into the strategic calculations of larger powers. Although the NSC maintained in late 1954 that "despite the talk of 'coexistence,' the communist powers will continue strenuous efforts to weaken and disrupt free-world strength and unity and to expand the area of their control,"[38] the Scandinavians were becoming cautiously optimistic about the future. A more relaxed international atmosphere decreased threat perceptions in Scandinavia, but as some of these countries experienced new economic problems, trouble seemed to be ahead for Scandinavian-American relations. This trouble was reflected in the gradual rise of neutralist sentiments in the three allied countries.

THAW COMES TO SCANDINAVIA

In Denmark, the end of the Korean War prompted the Hedtoft government to cut defense spending by 25 percent in the fall of 1954 and to cut the number of months required for military service from 18 to 12. The decision was influenced in part by an economic crisis that hit Denmark in 1953–1954. Dwindling exports of foodstuffs and rising imports of consumer goods, particularly cars from West Germany, had reversed the postwar trends in Danish foreign trade—between 1947 and 1951 exports had tripled, but then stagnated and even turned to a gradual decline. By 1954 the Danish government suffered from a serious foreign exchange crisis that forced it to add new excise taxes and make serious cuts in the national budget—not only in defense, but also in government support for housing projects and education. Nevertheless, the Social Democrats came to power in 1953 supported by a marked rise in neutralist sentiments after Stalin's death, a trend that continued following the end of the Korean War. As the war scare withered away and economic difficulties mounted, the Danish commitment to build up their defenses, despite NATO and U.S. protests, was clearly on the decline.

A similar trend was apparent in Norway, where the Labor Party's Einar Gerhardsen had regained the premiership in early 1953. A prolonged debate over cutbacks in defense expenditures started soon after Stalin's death, although the first major reductions would have to wait until 1956. Like Denmark, Norway was also experiencing economic difficulties that put budgetary constraints on, for example, the planned expansion of the Royal Norwegian Air Force (RNAF). In 1954 the Norwegian government opted to expand the RNAF by only one squadron (25 aircraft) instead of three, even though the United States offered to provide the necessary material free of charge. As a July 1955 report from the American Embassy in Oslo put it: "the internal economic strains, the 'co-existence' blandishments of the Soviet Union, the cutback examples of Norway's allies and the mysticism of the 'new look' have created a milieu which has exposed the defense build-up to closer scrutiny and sharper criticism."[39]

In neutral Sweden, the post-Stalin era was welcomed with some reservations. For example, military buildup continued at the same pace as before; approximately 5 percent of the GNP was spent on defense throughout the 1950s and 1960s. Nor was there any rush to greet the new Soviet leadership with open arms. Instead, in 1954 the Swedes began a prolonged (five-year) debate over whether to add nuclear weapons to the nation's military arsenal. Nevertheless, Dag Hammarskjöld's election as the secretary general of the United Nations gave the Swedes a voice to be heard in international affairs. During Hammarskjöld's tenure, which lasted until his tragic death in 1961, the former member of the Swedish foreign service would, indeed, be an active mediator—with limited success—of international crises from Africa to Southeast Asia. Although he was not, of course, an official representative of Swedish foreign policy, Hammarskjöld did raise the profile of Sweden's neutrality and thereby of the image and possibilities of "bridge building" by nonaligned and neutral countries. Thus, while retaining the strong tradition of "armed neutrality," Sweden's foreign policy began to move increasingly toward "active neutrality" during the thaw.

Stalin's death also called for reconsideration of Iceland's decision to seek American military protection after the outbreak of the war in Korea. After long negotiations, however, a supplementary agreement to the 1951 U.S.-Icelandic defense agreement was signed on 25 May 1954. It raised the number of authorized American personnel in Iceland, permitted rotational training of air units, made a provision for antiaircraft artillery and gave the United States the right to build a port. At the same time, this agreement also met some Icelandic concerns by providing for stricter regulation of the activities and movements of American troops and by providing for Icelandic participation in the construction programs. Such conditions addressed a serious socioeconomic problem already evident during World War II. Although concerned about the presence of foreign troops, Icelanders were even more opposed to the use of American civilian workers in the construction of the Keflavík base. Indeed, in

1951–1955, 20 percent of Iceland's national income came from the base, which also employed 4 percent of the country's population. The 1954 agreement was, therefore, as the NSC put it, "designed to assist in alleviating Icelandic dissatisfaction."[40]

Notwithstanding these efforts, trouble was ahead for U.S. base rights in Iceland. Latent anti-Americanism and neutralist sentiments continued to increase after the end of the Korean War. Added to these sentiments was the Icelandic belief that with West Germany's accession to NATO in 1954, a more effective "continental shield" was developing to contain any possible Soviet offensives—an argument that Americans inverted by saying that the continental shield in fact left the North Atlantic a more desirable route via which the Soviets would plan an attack. That twist did not convince many Icelanders. Instead, as an article in *U.S. News and World Report* in June 1954 maintained, there was an "[a]lmost universal resentment toward the stationing of foreign troops [in Iceland, which] helps the Communists campaign to undermine the U.S. position here."[41] To counter this resentment, the United States Information Agency began a major propaganda offensive in Iceland in late 1954. But the fear remained. In that same article, "one of the best-informed foreign observers," when asked whether American troops would be removed under Icelandic demand, responded, "Not this year. Maybe not next year. But in time it's far from impossible."[42]

In the end, the most dramatic impact of the changes in Soviet rhetoric and policy would be felt in Finland, where it provided an opportunity for the country to look forward to some concrete benefits. In particular, the time seemed right for the foreign policy establishment in Helsinki to begin constructing a neutral profile for Finland, something that the Finnish prime minister (five cabinets in 1950–1956) and future president (1956–1981), AP leader Urho K. Kekkonen, had attempted as early as 1952. The problem from the American point of view was that Kekkonen's policies were not just confined to the improvements in Finland's image. In 1952 he had also proposed (as he would repeatedly throughout his remaining political career) that the expansion of neutrality westward—to Norway and Denmark—would be in the general interest of Finnish security because it would minimize the Soviet perception of a threat emanating from Northern Europe. In his so-called pajama speech that was published in the AP's newspaper *Maakansa* on 23 January 1952,[43] Kekkonen reasoned that large-scale "Scandinavian neutrality—such as Sweden has followed for almost one and a half centuries—would be in Finland's interest because it would remove even the theoretical threat of an attack against the USSR via Finland." Thus, Kekkonen continued, the Soviets would have no reason (or excuse) to demand military consultations by referring to the 1948 Finno-Soviet FCMA Treaty. Moreover, Kekkonen argued that the pact "presupposes a kind of neutrality for Finland because it spells out Finland's desire to remain outside big power conflicts."[44]

Although it took a few years—and the induction of a new leadership in the Kremlin—before the Soviets capitalized on Kekkonen's statements in their Scandinavian policy, and although such "expansive" statements regarding neutrality caused much concern in the United States throughout the 1950s, the Finns were, clearly, eager to improve their international position. Hungrily hoping to break away from the virtual isolation to which they had been confined since World War II, the Finnish foreign policy leadership had much to benefit from the doctrine of peaceful coexistence and from a substantive claim to "a kind of neutrality." This was the case particularly after an agreement on the Austrian solution and neutralization was reached in the spring of 1955. Max Jakobson, the press secretary of the Finnish embassy in Washington and later Finland's ambassador to the United Nations, captured the Finnish expectations in a cable from the United States in May 1955: "We have reason to hope that [because of Austria] the Soviet Union would recognize our neutrality more clearly than it has . . . we might gain from the current situation if we could show the Soviets that strengthening Finland's neutrality would benefit their general goals."[45]

It was to happen soon enough.

chapter 4

THE SPECTER OF COEXISTENCE, 1955–1961

In November 1955, Einar Gerhardsen became the first non-Finnish Scandinavian prime minister to visit the post-Stalin Soviet Union. It was the Norwegian's third trip to the USSR. He had been in Moscow during the 1920 Comintern meeting as the representative of the Norwegian Social Democrats' Youth League. In 1936 Gerhardsen had visited Leningrad and Moscow as a member of a labor union delegation. During the first trip, he wrote in his memoirs, Gerhardsen had been "full of admiration for the Russian Revolution and everything it stood for." In 1936 he remembers having "a critical view regarding everything we saw and heard." And in 1955? Gerhardsen had few illusions about how the Soviets were trying to impress him by showing off their great accomplishments, by pointing out their military might, and by assuring him that Norway had no reason to remain a member of NATO. While the tall and lean 58-year-old Norwegian was cynical of the apparent effort to take him for a ride, he remained hopeful that the new Soviet leadership—Khrushchev and Bulganin in particular—meant business when they repeatedly uttered the new favorite phrase of Soviet diplomacy, "peaceful coexistence." Gerhardsen agreed to a final communique that, in addition to making points about increasing cultural and economic contacts, restated Norway's stand that it would not allow the stationing of foreign troops or the establishment of foreign bases in its territory in peacetime.[1]

In early 1956, Swedish Prime Minister Tage Erlander and his Danish counterpart Hans Christian Hansen (Hedtoft died in January 1955) followed suit, visiting the USSR equally hopeful about, yet similarly lacking in any illusions regarding, post-Stalin Soviet foreign policy. While Hansen's visit did not produce a statement about Denmark's basing policy, it resulted in a bilateral trade agreement later in 1956. Erlander, in contrast, won Moscow's positive

Dag Hammarskjöld, a former official at the Swedish foreign ministry, became secretary general of the United Nations in 1953. Here he is shaking hands with President Dwight D. Eisenhower in their first meeting at the White House in 1953 while Secretary of State John Foster Dulles looks on.
Courtesy of AP/World Wide Photos (used with permission, photograph provided by Eisenhower Library).

endorsement of Sweden's neutrality in March 1956, although the Soviets also encouraged the Swedes to be more active in their foreign policy and contribute more to a general relaxation of international tensions. Indirectly, Khrushchev and Bulganin encouraged Erlander to advertise the gospel of neutrality to the Norwegians and Danes.

The years 1955–1956 were, indeed, a period of high hopes among many Scandinavians regarding the international situation. After the death of Stalin, the Soviets seemed to have mellowed. The return of the Porkkala naval base to Finland in early 1956 (negotiated in the fall of 1955) seemed to be a concrete example of the possibility that a tentative thaw had changed into a true détente. With Finland joining the NC in late 1955, the possibilities for Nordic cooperation widened. Many Scandinavians began to view the Cold War as an aberration and the division between East and West as arbitrary. As neutralism gained ground in the mid-1950s, Americans worried that it would forge political pressures within Norway and Denmark to loosen their ties with NATO. In addition, Washington expressed some concern over the activism of Dag Hammarskjöld.

The second secretary general of the United Nations was, most scholars seem to agree, the most effective and—disturbingly to some, delightfully to others—impartial holder of that post. The son of a former prime minister of Sweden, Hammarskjöld had received his Ph.D. in economics from Uppsala University in 1934 (at the age of 29), where one of his major professors had been that unrelenting critic of race relations in the United States, Gunnar Myrdal. Hammarskjöld then joined the Swedish Ministry of Finance as an under secretary while serving jointly as the governor of the Bank of Sweden. Never a member of any political party, the perennial bachelor moved to the Swedish Foreign Office (SFO) in 1947 as under secretary for the Division of Economic Affairs, and in 1949, became the secretary general of the SFO and, in effect, the second in command after Foreign Minister Bo Östen Unden.

In the late 1940s and early 1950s, Hammarskjöld thus had a close working relationship with Unden and was keenly involved in defining the Swedish neutrality doctrine in its postwar form. Later on, as the secretary general of the United Nations, he often used the "Swedish channel" as a way of conveying diplomatic messages to parties otherwise ostracized from the world community (such as the PRC). Hammarskjöld was also a darling of the neutralists in the developing world and presided over the inclusion of many new members to the United Nations from the southern hemisphere, which transformed the East-West membership balance (to the West's advantage) in the first decade of the world organization. He also recommended the establishment of the United Nations Emergency Force in 1956 to resolve the Suez crisis. This action, as Robert Jordan wrote, "elevated Hammarskjöld's office to a leading position in international affairs. No longer could the office be compared to the Pope's as consisting of moral authority, but without the terrestrial means to change the course of history."[2] The United Nations was not in a position to dictate anything to the superpowers, but its capability to use peacekeeping forces has certainly played a significant role in preventing many crises from becoming vortexes of destruction—the speedy solution of the 1958 Lebanon crisis stands out as the best known example. An independent mystic who was willing to criticize both the East and the West, Hammarskjöld elevated the profile of not only the U.N.'s secretary general, but, vicariously, that of his own country's foreign policy as well. Along the way he upset most important leaders of his time including, no doubt, Dwight Eisenhower and Nikita Khrushchev. The quest for peace that the Swede so forcefully executed allowed little room for the moral distinctions needed to drum up support for American leadership in the West. From Washington's perspective, Hammarskjöld was, therefore, another force potentially increasing the popularity of neutralism.

In the end, Washington had little reason to be upset about Hammarskjöld or the phenomenon of neutralism in general. Khrushchev's talk of peaceful coexistence contrasted sharply with Dulles's ruminations about rollback, especially when these ruminations combined with the excesses of McCarthyism to cause a momentary shift in Scandinavian (and general European) attitudes during the first years of the Eisenhower administration. The Soviets, however, concretely proved the hollowness of their rhetoric by their actions in 1956. In particular, the suppression of Hungary in October 1956 struck a devastating blow to what can be characterized as a "neutralist moment" in Scandinavia and largely returned the situation to what it was at the time of Stalin's death. The Nordic Balance was not to be shaken by the promises of coexistence. Instead, in the early 1960s, when new international crises appeared—from the U-2 incident to the strains over Berlin—the Scandinavians were as committed as ever to the foreign and security policies they had defined for themselves in the late 1940s. Any noticeable conflict in American-Scandinavian relations during the Eisenhower presidency was linked to the differences between the domestic systems in the United States and Northern Europe; the Middle Way was to become one of the whipping boys of Republican politicians when they tried to warn the American public about the Democrats' "welfare state leanings." But with the triumph of Kennedy and the demise of Nixon that, too, seemed like a minor conflict.

THE APPEAL OF NEUTRALITY

The unexpected Soviet moves that began with the decoupling of the Austrian and German questions in February 1955 and led to the signing of the Austrian State Treaty in May and the Geneva four-power summit later in July caused widespread speculation in Scandinavia. For example, the Finns looked for ways in which they might benefit from the Austrian "example" and from what appeared to be a general shift in Soviet foreign policy. Nor was Prime Minister Kekkonen shy in making these sentiments public. He was particularly intrigued by the potential expansion of neutrality to western Scandinavia. In an interview with the German newspaper *Die Welt* on 23 April 1955, for example, Kekkonen openly argued that, "In my opinion international politics have reached a juncture in which true neutrality has become a viable option. One can say for certain that it would benefit the cause of peace in Europe. In 1952 I took the liberty to recommend this type of policy for Scandinavia. Now I might dare to think that it could be realized in an even larger scale."[3]

Kekkonen's activism in this field and his increased efforts during 1955 to promote Finland's membership in the NC were partly linked to the opening of the 1956 presidential campaign that would pit him against the former prime minister and speaker of the *Eduskunta*, Social Democrat K.-A. Fagerholm. Much of the debate between the two leading candidates focused on foreign policy and on which of them was the truer disciple of Paasikivi. At the same time, Kekkonen's statements were consistent with his previous policies, specifically with his 1952 pajama speech. They would become a trademark of Finnish foreign policy during Kekkonen's presidency (1956–1981) and, much like the pajama speech, would add further stigma to his already negative image in the West.

Kekkonen was, clearly, capitalizing on the neutralist moment in the mid-1950s. With the Austrian State Treaty, neutrality had become a key issue in European politics. The idea of a neutral belt between Eastern and Western Europe—inclusive of a unified, neutral Germany—was taken seriously even by the father of containment, George F. Kennan. In some ways, the neutralist moment can even be seen as a harbinger of the détente of the 1960s and a successful example of how the divergent interests of the two superpowers could be compromised in a given situation. The Austrian solution thus gave hope to those looking for a third way. The Swedes, the champions of the Middle Way, along with reluctant NATO partners Denmark, Norway, and Iceland, believed they would benefit from the reduction of Cold War tensions.

While such small powers as Finland and Austria may have viewed neutrality as a respectable national security policy, the United States and the USSR viewed these concepts mostly as tools of their foreign policies. For example, although the Soviets would have preferred a unified and neutral Germany to a divided one—even if the eastern half was under Soviet rule—they were not supportive of neutrality as a general rule. Moscow placed strict limits as to where neutrality was acceptable. It was not allowed in the Soviet bloc and the Kremlin made no apologies for that. When John Foster Dulles suggested to Nikolai Bulganin during the July 1955 Geneva Summit that Finland be an example of how the Soviets should arrange their relations with Eastern Europe, the Soviet leader reportedly "froze up." Later, Bulganin denied that Finland was a "realistic example" in this context.

In Washington, the specter of neutralism did cause some headaches. Before the July 1955 Geneva summit, the National Security Council prepared a major report on the challenges and prospects of neutralism in Europe, a report that became the basis for American policy toward neutrality as it was spelled out in NSC 5602 in February 1956. It turned out to be a complex issue. To begin with, finding a proper definition of the concept was not easy. After distinguishing neutralism, "an attitude or psychological tendency," from such concepts as neutrality ("the actual status of a nation in foreign relationships") and neutralization ("the process by which a particular country or area assumes . . . a status of neutrality"), the NSC went on to spell out "a pragmatic 'working' definition of neutralism" as "any attitude which involves *a disinclination to cooperate with U.S. objectives in the cold war* and in a possible hot war combined with either a similar disinclination or, at worst, a hesitation to go so far as to cooperate with USSR objectives."[4] Neutralist sentiments were, to say the least, considered negative from the American point of view. The definition, moreover, was inclusive enough to make almost anything that did not comply with American or Soviet foreign policy a "neutralist" sentiment. Accordingly, the NSC pointed out that "resistance to neutralism is usually in accord with U.S. interests [and] the U.S. needs to be alert to the dangers of neutralism." The NSC felt this was especially necessary because the USSR and the communist parties of western Europe had "repeatedly demonstrated their willingness to utilize both the concept of neutrality and neutralist attitudes in pursuit of their objectives." Indeed, as the NSC pointed out, a 1954 Soviet *Encyclopedia* even recognized that the Kremlin had used neutrality "as a means of strengthening its own security and universal peace."[5]

What did the Soviets think they could gain by pursuing such policies? Why were they making the spread of neutralism the "principal immediate goal of Soviet policy in Europe," as it seemed to Washington in the summer of 1955?[6]

The NSC's answer was simple: a change of strategy. The Soviets had not abandoned their expansionist goals. Instead, the Soviets were attempting to crack the unity of the free world. Khrushchev and the rest of the Kremlin leadership were

> approaching the conclusion that their ultimate goal of a Communist Europe cannot be profitably pursued at this time either through military aggression or through direct efforts to convert Europeans to Communism, and that their best current opportunities for progress are to be found in pursuing the intermediate goal of separating the European nations from the U.S.[7]

In this context, Soviet overtures to Scandinavia gained added importance. After all, with the strong tradition of neutrality and the reluctance of Norway and Denmark to become full-fledged NATO partners even at the time of heated East-West tensions—such as during the Korean War—these countries appeared prone to embrace the notion of coexistence. Furthermore, the eastern outpost of Scandinavia, Finland, was eager to seek material benefits from the changes in Soviet policy. Such benefits might have a spillover effect to Finland's western neighbors and undermine their support for NATO. In the fall of 1955 this was exactly what seemed to be taking place.

THE SPIRIT OF PORKKALA AND THE NEUTRALIST MOMENT

Rumors that the Soviets were considering the return of the Porkkala naval base to Finland were rampant in the summer of 1955. The common feeling in diplomatic circles was that if the Soviets were seriously pushing for a neutral zone in Europe, or at least in Scandinavia, they could best promote this effort by retreating, at least militarily, from Finland. Since the Soviet withdrawal from Port Arthur on 1 May 1955, Porkkala was the only remaining Soviet military base outside of Eastern Europe. At the Geneva summit in 18–25 July 1955, the Soviets also demanded the withdrawal of all foreign troops from Europe, criticizing specifically the placement of American troops on the continent under the auspices of NATO. Withdrawing from Porkkala—a base with little strategic significance in the nuclear age—would naturally make their case for such action more credible. At the same time the Finnish papers were carrying on a heated discussion about the impact of the spirit of Geneva on Finland. On top of the list was, naturally, the return of Porkkala and the lost territories of eastern Karelia, which the Soviets had seized in 1944. In addition, some editorials contemplated the question of Finnish membership in the Nordic Council.

According to Khrushchev's memoirs, the return of the Porkkala naval base became part of his policy as early as July 1955, during the Geneva Conference. Khrushchev later remembered discussing the issue with Nikolai Bulganin and pointing out that, "It was high time to demonstrate that we had no intention of forcing socialism on the Finns at bayonet point. We had to make clear our foreign policy was guided by the principle of peaceful coexistence." Bulganin reportedly agreed.[8] Thus, on 17 August 1955, Soviet Ambassador to Finland Viktor Lebedev brought President Paasikivi a letter from Marshall Voroshilov, inviting the president to Moscow to negotiate the continuation of the 1948 FCMA Treaty that was about to expire in 1958. More importantly to Paasikivi, Lebedev told him that the Soviet Union was ready to renounce its rights to the Porkkala base.

The negotiations commenced in Moscow on 15 September 1955 and led to the signing of two documents four days later. The first one simply prolonged the FCMA Treaty by 20 years (until 1975) without making any changes in the original text. In the other treaty, the Soviets agreed to a complete withdrawal from the Porkkala base by the end of January 1956. In addition, Khrushchev indicated to Prime Minister Kekkonen—who emerged as the true leader of the Finnish delegation despite the presence of the 85-year-old Paasikivi—that he had nothing against Finland's joining the NC, something the Soviets had previously considered a hostile act, virtually analogous to siding with the West. As a result, Finland applied for NC membership soon after the Moscow negotiations ended and attended its first meeting in January 1956.

In the West the reaction to the return of Porkkala was mixed. While expressing their satisfaction that Finland was about to rid itself of the Soviet base, most NATO countries were concerned about Porkkala's use as a propaganda weapon. The Soviet action could certainly be used as an argument to demand the withdrawal of American bases in, say, Iceland. In addition, it might be used as a propaganda weapon directed against Scandinavian affiliation with NATO. The return of the Porkkala base thus created certain new challenges to American policy toward Scandinavia. The main question was, simply, what did, or should, Finland and Finno-Soviet relations symbolize?

Peaceful coexistence between socialist and nonsocialist countries? This was, of course, what the Soviets wanted the spirit of Porkkala to advance.

The Americans, however, turned the Soviet argument on its head. As Max Jakobson, the press secretary of the Finnish embassy in Washington, noted in late September 1955, many American writers challenged the Soviet Union to make their relations with Finland a true example of their foreign policy "by applying it to its other neighbors." Jakobson found a curious situation in which "Finland has become a unique source of debate between east and west, a debate in which both sides accept the exemplary nature of Finno-Soviet relations as a premise. The disagreement is over which side should follow this example."[9]

In the mid-1950s, U.S. officials seem to have felt that the easiest way out of any public complications that the return of Porkkala could produce was to officially ignore the subject. Although the United States assured the Finns through diplomatic channels that they were quite pleased with the way things turned out, they issued virtually no public statements about Porkkala's return. Nor did the Soviet action seem to promote changes in general American policy toward Europe or Scandinavia. Judging by this lack of public attention, the possibility that the Soviets might be successful in bootlegging neutralism to western Scandinavia by using Finland as a lever seems to have been limited.

The evidence does suggest, however, that American officials considered the prospect of Scandinavian neutrality more than purely academic. The sudden Finnish interest in joining the NC—that evidently resulted from the Soviets' dropping charges that the organization was pro-NATO and anti-Soviet—appeared to reflect, as the Moscow Embassy argued, a Soviet belief that "Finnish membership may serve in [the] long run to dilute Norwegian, Danish, and Icelandic attachment to NATO."[10] Similarly, the Northern European Chiefs of Mission conference held in London in late September 1955 concluded that "Soviet policies have made a deep impression on public opinion [in] all Scandinavian countries which uncritically welcomes apparent lessening of war danger." In the long run, the summary added, the combination of the spirits of Geneva and Porkkala, combined with internal economic pressures, "may lead to irresistible pressures to reduce defense expenditures."[11] Moreover, despite both Finnish and Norwegian claims to the contrary, Finland's membership could, the NSC argued, "add strength to the neutralist tendencies in the [Nordic] Council which are led by Sweden and are influential in Iceland and Denmark."[12]

Such a scenario was especially troubling because of the strong connection that Americans thought existed between the spread of neutralism and communism. After all, the NSC maintained, neutralists were much more "exposed" to communist pressure than those with strong ties to the West. This, in turn, served to make neutral countries prone to be " 'neutral' against the U.S." In the context of the Soviet-American confrontation, therefore, the spread of neutralist sentiments from Finland and Sweden to the rest of Scandinavia would mean a net loss to the United States and a net gain for the

USSR.[13] In addition, the spread of neutrality was also a strategic threat. As Secretary of State Dulles said in an address to the American Legion in Miami, Florida, on 10 October 1955: "Soviet rulers advocate to others what they call 'neutrality': By this they mean that each nation should have the weakness which is inevitable when each depends on itself alone."[14] It seemed important to stress to the NATO partners of Scandinavia, as American representatives did during the organization's meeting in Paris in December 1955, that the Soviets had not returned all their foreign bases, but still held firm positions in, for example, the Baltic countries.[15]

Such concern grew in 1956. Finland's accession to the Nordic Council, which meant that the FCP would have to be included in the delegation representing Finland (the exact number depended on their proportion of seats in the *Eduskunta* at any given moment), not only increased the communist presence in the organization, but, given Finland's cordial relationship with the Soviets, raised the possibility that other Scandinavians might gradually drift toward nonalignment. As CIA Director Allen Dulles stated: "the Soviet Union was trying to use Finland as a lever to create a [neutral] Scandinavian Federation."[16] Similarly, an article in *Foreign Affairs* argued in October 1956: "The Soviet evacuation of Porkkala and the granting of permission for Finland to enter the Nordic Council were clearly designed to create neutralist sentiment in Scandinavia and to weaken the existing strength of NATO. Finland *in* the Council can do more to pull Denmark, Norway and Iceland away from their NATO ties than Finland *out* of the Council."[17] In other words, Finland had become the Kremlin's tool; an instrument to be used to expand neutralism in Scandinavia. This strategy clearly lay behind Soviet thinking when they invited Gerhardsen, Erlander, and Hansen to the Soviet Union in late 1955 and early 1956.

Nor was it an accident that a few weeks before the commencement of Kekkonen's first term as Finland's president in March 1956—he overcame K.-A. Fagerholm by the narrowest of margins (151–149) in the electoral college in February—in a speech to the Twentieth Soviet Communist Party Congress, Nikita Khrushchev included Finland for the first time among the European neutral countries (along with Austria, Sweden, and Switzerland). A few months later a pamphlet published in Moscow on Finno-Soviet relations went even further. The author of the text, Yevgeni Arsakovits Ambartsum, identified the Finnish strand of neutrality as perfectly in line with the cooperation between Finland and the USSR that was based on the 1948 FCMA Treaty. He argued that Finland's "friendship" with the Soviet Union could only improve the possibilities of Finnish cooperation with Scandinavian countries. Ambartsum maintained that

> the Scandinavian countries regard Finno-Soviet relations with approval
> mainly because Finland, while enjoying the benefits of cooperation with
> the USSR has not only maintained and strengthened its independence, but

also refrained from joining military alliances, and thus gained a neutral position. And neutrality is regarded positively among the Scandinavian countries not only because of their geographic position, but also due to their historical traditions. After all, neutrality was the official principle of these countries' foreign policy until World War II.[18]

With the Soviets stressing peaceful coexistence and with Nikita Khrushchev talking about a worldwide "zone of peace" that included (in addition, naturally, to the socialist states) the neutral and nonaligned countries, the possibility that allied countries beyond Scandinavia might be lured into thinking that the time of confrontation should give way to a period of accommodation appeared to be a potential threat to Western unity. In other words, while neutrality as an official foreign policy of such countries as Sweden or Switzerland was not necessarily a threatening phenomenon, the possibility that it might hold appeal among NATO nations made neutrality a potential springboard of sorts toward Western disintegration and a vehicle in the USSR's efforts to create wedges within the alliance. It was in this context of changed Soviet tactics and strategies that neutrality became a threat to U.S. policy in Scandinavia.

Neutralism and coexistence were on the agenda in the May 1956 NATO meeting in Paris. The governments included in the talks had few illusions about the Soviet shift in strategy. Great Britain's Sellwyn Lloyd, for example, stressed that in his government's opinion, the "objective of communist domination of the world remains the same [although] tactics [have] changed." Thus he concluded that the need for NATO and Western unity was greater than ever. Turkey's representative Koprulu even maintained that "peaceful coexistence is a Stalinist conception" and that the Western nations should never forget that the "aim of communism always remains same." To combat such duplicity, the NATO countries must, Koprulu added, "strive to establish as close political coordination as possible." The Belgians and the French agreed, stressing that internal changes in the Soviet Union (i.e., anti-Stalinism) did not mean any changes in the Kremlin's foreign policy objectives. The Italians further questioned the wisdom of East-West contacts for countries with strong communist parties, such as Italy, and maintained that even the general improvement in East-West relations might give the impression that the West had abandoned the hope of finding a solution to such issues as the division of Germany.

A slight but significant exception in the context of the Soviet "neutrality offensive" was the attitude of the Scandinavian NATO partners. Denmark's Prime Minister Hans Christian Hansen, who had visited Moscow in early March of 1956, said that Khrushchev had been quite frank with him regarding the Soviet hope of dismembering NATO, and that as long as the "West does not lose sight [of the] real motives behind Soviet readiness to be on 'speaking terms' with the West, East-West contacts could be continued and . . . the scales might be turned in favor [of the] West." Norway's Halvard M. Lange speculated that "Soviet leaders may be groping for a way out of complete isolation and may have sincere desire [to] lessen tension[s]." If this was the case, Lange added, a "completely negative Western attitude might strengthen elements in Russia seeking [a] return [to] hard Stalinist policies." Lange recommended that while little could be expected from the Russians in such fields as disarmament, they "should be tried out on other questions, such as trade. Expanded trade contacts with [the Soviet] Bloc might encourage the Russians to relax [their] grip on satellites."[19]

From John Foster Dulles's point of view, the NATO meeting was far from satisfactory. He had clearly hoped to obtain a unified policy vis-à-vis the USSR and the role of neutrality. It had not happened. Instead, the Scandinavians in particular seemed to have been quite interested in exploring the possibilities of coexistence. The secretary of state and President Eisenhower thus set out to clarify publicly the U.S. position on neutrality during a series of speeches and press conferences in the summer of 1956. The end result—by design or not—was confusion.

On 6 June 1956, President Dwight D. Eisenhower proclaimed during a press conference that in his mind neutrality and neutralism were not necessarily the terrible concepts that some proclaimed them to be. After all, Ike reminded his audience, "We were a young country once, and our whole policy for the first hundred years was, or more, 150, we were neutral. We constantly asserted we were neutral in the wars of the world and wars in Europe and antagonisms." This quote, an example of Eisenhower's less than perfect syntax, made front page news. The *New York Times*' headline the next day read: "Eisenhower Sees Merit in Attitude of Neutral Lands." Ike had opened a can of worms. How could the leader of the Western Alliance, the free world, who repeatedly stressed the evil nature of the Soviet Union and the necessity of free people to unite against that threat, see merit in a policy that did not condemn the USSR outright? If this were acceptable, then the NATO allies might indeed choose to become neutral without any moral qualms if they saw it as a less expensive option than alliance. The confusion did not go unnoticed by the press as articles about neutrality and neutralism appeared at a hectic frequency in the summer of 1956. Suddenly the American public was introduced to the notion that, as an article in *Newsweek* on 18 June 1956 maintained, "[the] chief targets in the struggle for men's minds are the world's neutrals."[20] Much of the initial interest was, however, sparked by the apparent contradiction between Eisenhower's and Secretary of State Dulles's statements.

Three days after Ike's press conference, Dulles took the podium at Ames, Iowa, apparently with the intention of setting the record straight on official American policy toward the neutrals. "The principle of neutrality," Dulles maintained in his speech at Iowa State University, "pretends that a nation can best gain safety for itself by being indifferent to the fate of others." Speaking further about the multitude of security and alliance pacts that the United

States had signed since 1945, Dulles argued that the principle of neutrality had become an obsolete conception and "except under very exceptional circumstances, is an immoral and shortsighted conception." What were these circumstances and was Dulles not contradicting his boss, he was asked three days later. While maintaining that no differences existed between the White House and Foggy Bottom on the issue of neutrality, the secretary of state used Switzerland as an example of the type of neutrality he had referred to, then refused to comment further.[21]

Indeed, Dulles was probably right in maintaining that he and Ike had no significant differences regarding neutrality. Both preferred allied nations to neutral ones and were probably as confused as most of the American public about the meaning of neutrality and neutralism, the two terms thrown around freely in public speeches without adequate distinction. In the private confines of the NSC, moreover, Ike in particular and without meeting significant opposition from his secretary of state, had expressed the same type of sympathy to neutral countries, maintaining that militarily allied nations put themselves in harm's way and that remaining neutral could be considered a way of simply safeguarding one's security interests. In other words, Ike thought that the meaning of neutrality needed to be redefined to mean, as he had put it already in February 1956: "a moral, spiritual and, possibly, a political commitment to our side, but not necessarily a military commitment."[22] But the confusion remained. With the bafflement—what was collectively referred to as the "neutrality muddle"—so evident in their statements, neither Ike nor Dulles could convince very many that the need for the West to stand united in the face of the Soviets was as strong as it had been since the onset of the Cold War. Least convinced were the Icelanders.

ICY WINDS

The Icelanders' wish to send the American troops packing was not new. Since World War II, nationalist sentiments had been high in the young island republic and directed against the U.S. presence. This attitude had invariably been exploited in the electoral campaigns of not only the communists but several other political parties as well. Nor had Iceland's economic woes been extinguished by the hiring of native labor in the construction projects at the Keflavík base after the 1954 supplementary defense agreement.

More disturbingly, the unilateral extension of Iceland's fishing boundaries from three to four miles and a British boycott in October 1952 had led to a remarkable change in Icelandic foreign trade patterns. Icelandic fishermen's exclusive rights to conduct their trade off their coast had been gradually jeopardized by the development of distant-water fishing. In the seventeenth century, a limit of 24 miles off the island's coastline had been set for foreign vessels, and they were prohibited to enter any bays. By the nineteenth century, the limit had been forced back to only four miles, and in 1901 the Danish and

British governments signed a 50-year treaty that not only pushed the limit to three miles, but also opened up major Icelandic bays. In a country whose exports were almost exclusively (90–95 percent) fish, such a pact was naturally unpopular, and a strong movement to drive the foreigners further away in order to prevent overfishing was already underway when Iceland achieved its independence in 1944. The movement had grown even more by the time the 1901 treaty ended in 1952.

Prompted by popular demand and with support from a Hague International Court ruling, the Icelandic government issued a new fisheries limit at four miles and banned foreign fishing in bays. But the British trawler owners—without official support from London—retaliated. They effectively closed the British market (the largest one for Icelandic fish) by issuing a landing ban for Icelandic vessels. Because the Brits bought approximately a quarter of Iceland's fish, the Reykjavík government quickly faced an economic crisis. The answer? Before they were even asked, the Soviets, in March 1953, offered to buy large quantities of Icelandic fish. By 1956, almost 20 percent of Iceland's exports went to the USSR (30 percent to the entire East Bloc), a remarkable change considering that in 1952 the figure had been less than 1 percent.[23]

In addition to the antipathy felt toward the British and to the sudden reemergence of the Iceland-Soviet trade relationship, the Icelanders' threat perceptions were certainly affected by developments in international relations after Stalin's death. As neutralism and nationalism gained popularity, the perceived need to have a U.S. presence declined, a trend that climaxed in early 1956. Perhaps further affected by the Soviet removal of their troops in Porkkala and the impending parliamentary elections, the Social Democrats (in opposition) and the Progressives (in a coalition government with the Independence Party) joined forces in the foreign relations committee of the *Althing* and drafted a resolution that stated that

> In view of changed conditions since the Defence Treaty of 1951 was concluded, and in view of declarations that foreign troops shall not be stationed in Iceland in peacetime, revision of the system then adopted shall immediately be initiated with the purpose that the Defence Force be withdrawn, and Icelanders shall themselves undertake care and maintenance of the defensive installations, other than military duties. If an agreement to this effect is not reached, the Defence Treaty shall be terminated.[24]

It was a strong message. American fears that the Soviets were succeeding in their attempt to foster NATO's gradual disintegration soon appeared. An article in *U.S. News and World Report* pointed out alarmingly in April 1956: "Russia is trying to break the NATO alliance wide open. In Iceland, Soviet plans are found to be gaining ground."[25] "Icy winds from Iceland," announced the *Scholastic*.[26] *Time*'s spin on the matter was slightly different. The *Althing*'s move represented, said an editorial, a typical "Scandinavian distaste for the presence of foreign troops in peacetime." However, the same article argued cynically, "Iceland is willing to stay in NATO, but is not eager to share the burdens of collective security."[27]

To be sure, the extreme views against the presence of American troops did not translate into a landslide victory for the Icelandic Social Democrats and Progressives. The end result, however, was even more disturbing from the U.S. perspective. In the June 1956 *Althing* elections, these two parties did not succeed in getting a majority. To form a new cabinet, the Progressives under Hermann Jonasson (who became the prime minister) and the Social Democrats under Gudmundur Gudmundsson (the new foreign minister) allied themselves with the communists, who had renamed their party the People's Alliance prior to the June elections in which they had scored a significant victory. Discussions with the United States on the future of the Keflavík base began soon after. The future of the IDF looked bleak indeed.

In the November 1956 issue of *Current History*, Columbia University's history professor and chairman John Wuorinen reflected on the developments in Iceland and the potential impact of the growing appeal of neutralism in Norway and Denmark. The Finnish-born former chief of the Scandinavian-Baltic section of the Office of Strategic Services argued that, "There is good reason for surmising that the commitments inherent in NATO membership will not be indefinitely continued, that neutralism will gain ground—unless the international situation markedly worsens."[28] Just after Wuorinen wrote these words, the "unless" occurred as the Soviet neutrality campaign suffered an almost mortal blow in the streets of Budapest.

HUNGARY'S SHADOW: AN END TO ILLUSIONS

The events in Hungary in the fall of 1956 affected Scandinavia in much the same way as did the outbreak of the Korean War in the summer of 1950. If Korea had come to "save" NSC 68, the Hungarian revolution rescued the concern over the potential spread of neutralism into western Europe and did perhaps irreparable harm to the future credibility of the Soviet doctrine of coexistence. The revolution in Hungary was not an isolated occurrence, however, but took place during a year when a number of serious crises that challenged the Cold War order erupted both in other parts of Eastern Europe and in the Middle East.

The Hungarian events were preceded by and coincided with another major crisis that was also related to the principle of nonalignment. Gamal Abdel Nasser, the Egyptian champion of Arab nationalism and one of the leaders of the nonaligned movement (along with India's Jawaharlal Nehru and Yugoslavia's Marshal Tito) had pledged to eliminate foreign control of the Suez canal when he took power from King Farouk in 1952. In 1954 Nasser obtained an agreement that provided for a phased withdrawal of British troops from Egyptian territory, but a combination of Arab-Israeli hostilities, an

American effort to win more Middle Eastern countries behind the Baghdad Pact, and an Anglo-French wish to retain their relative influence in the region, helped create a severe crisis in the fall of 1956. The immediate catalyst was an Egyptian arms deal with Czechoslovakia that prompted Secretary of State Dulles to try and lure Nasser back to the Western camp with promises of large amounts of financial aid from the World Bank that were to be used to develop the Aswan Dam. When this carrot changed to a stick in July 1956 when the offer was suddenly withdrawn, Nasser did not blink. Instead, he seized the Suez canal and announced that he would use the profits from it ($25 million annually) to build the Aswan Dam. In late October and early November, a combination of British, French, and Israeli troops, without American approval, attacked Egypt, but fell short of capturing the canal. Eisenhower, furious at the British in particular, did not support the invasion, but instructed the U.S. delegation in the United Nations to introduce a resolution calling for immediate withdrawal of the invaders. The resolution passed on 2 November 1956 and the troops left Egyptian territory by the end of the year.

The Suez crisis left many legacies, including the establishment of a United Nations Emergency Force by Dag Hammarskjöld and a severe deterioration in Anglo-American and Franco-American relations that strained the Western alliance for years to come. Although the United States did not send troops into the Middle East at this point, American interest in the region was growing; less than two years later, Eisenhower sent marines into Lebanon. But, most interestingly, the United States had also expressed clear antipathy toward nonalignment, particularly when a nation of such persuasion (in this case Egypt) was bold enough to buy weapons from the Eastern bloc. Washington did not look favorably on the type of neutralism that Nasser represented—clearly anti-Western and nationalist. After all, few benefits could be derived for American interests from the "Nasserites" in the broader schemes of the Cold War. On the contrary, prior to Nasser, Egypt had at least been tied to the Western world via its links to Britain. Now all bets were off, and the odds were not good, as the Czech arms deal seemed to indicate. Thus, in some ways, the Suez crisis represented an interesting mirror image of the coinciding events in Hungary.

Although the Suez crisis had little immediate bearing on the Hungarians, events in Poland in the summer of 1956 were a different story. A labor dispute that had begun in the industrial city of Poznan in June 1956 erupted into a large-scale revolt against Soviet rule during the trials against the strikers in October. Unlike the leaders in Hungary a short time later, the Poles eventually received a compromise solution: the Soviets agreed that Wladyslaw Gomulka, considered "Titoist" during the Stalin years and readmitted to the party only in August 1956, was to become the chairman of the Polish communist party and thus the country's leader. Secretary of State Dulles was quite excited about the Polish events and even predicted during a telephone conversation on 22 October 1956 that the sequence of events in Poland "will ultimately lead to free elections." Liberation seemed to be just around the corner.[29]

Hungary broke this illusion. Encouraged by events in Poland, Hungarian students and other members of the intelligentsia spearheaded an anti-Soviet revolt. By 23 October 1956, their demands included the withdrawal of Soviet troops from Hungary and free elections. During the next 13 days, a hectic chain of events progressed from armed conflict and attempts to consolidate democratic gains to repression by Warsaw Pact troops. Under Imre Nagy's premiership (he represented the "liberal" faction within the Hungarian communist party) and severe popular pressure, the new government announced its intention to remove Hungary from the Warsaw Pact and thus become neutral. This time the Soviets—confident that the West would not interfere and pressured by neighboring satellite leaders—crushed the revolt with brutal force. Their troops moved into Budapest on 4 November 1956. Approximately 200,000 Hungarians fled the country, causing a refugee crisis in neighboring Austria. Nagy was eventually executed (in 1958), and Janos Kadar took over the leadership and rebuilt the defunct Hungarian communist party.

What were the lessons of the Hungarian events of 1956? What, in particular, did the Soviet strong-arm tactics and the relatively meager response from Western powers mean for the appeal of neutralism in Scandinavia?

For one thing, it was clear that the nonintervention of the United States proved how hollow the rhetoric of liberation was. To be sure, the United States and its major allies were at the time bogged down in trying to solve the Suez crisis, a fact the Soviets certainly took into account when opting for intervention. The location of Hungary, the rapidity of events, the particularly bold Soviet decision to intervene, and the probability that a Western intervention would only have widened the crisis were sufficient deterrents against any American military action. Once the Soviet attack got under way, however, the Hungarian government pleaded with President Eisenhower to press for a simultaneous withdrawal of foreign troops from Hungary and the Middle East. Fearing that the Soviets were in a "most dangerous state of mind," Eisenhower ruled out even overt diplomatic pressure and instead opted to show moral support to the Hungarian refugees by generous aid and by taking the case to the United Nations. The reaction was much the same from most people except, perhaps, those in Eastern Europe. Even Dag Hammarskjöld, otherwise an extremely active U.N. secretary general, admitted his post's limited power by remaining virtually quiet on the Hungarian issue.[30]

The events in Hungary broke yet another illusion. They provided clear evidence that the Soviet doctrine of coexistence and the favorable phrases regarding neutrality that had been heard from the Kremlin in the past year were, at best, overstatements. Indeed, the Soviets shot themselves in the foot by invading Hungary in 1956, making it clear that while neutrality, in the Soviet mindset, was an acceptable policy for countries west of the Iron Curtain, it had little place east of that line. While calling for the dismantlement of NATO bases and the neutralization of Germany, the Kremlin had no interest in discussing any changes in the status quo of Eastern Europe. As long as Moscow was unwilling to do that, the policy of promoting neutrality and the talk about peaceful coexistence would be viewed, justifiably and logically so, as a smokescreen used to cover the true Soviet design. And those who benefited from and relied on the new Soviet policy, as Finland clearly did, were seen as building their fortunes on hollow ground.

The Scandinavians, some of them targets of Moscow's coexistence-neutralism offensive in 1955–1956, reacted predictably. They condemned the Soviets in the United Nations—except for the Finns, who refrained from taking a stand. The U.S.-Icelandic discussions on the future of the IDF that were taking place in Reykjavík at the time of the Suez and Hungarian crises ended in a December 1956 agreement that, to Washington's relief, supported the status quo. After a few years of gradual decline, the support for NATO membership went up in Norway and Denmark. Shocked by the contrast between the smooth talk of coexistence and the brutality of the crackdown in Hungary, the Norwegians, Danes, and Swedes also refrained from inviting Khrushchev and Bulganin for a return visit. In Finland a voluminous protest was launched when President Kekkonen directed the country's U.N. representative, Georg A. Gripenberg, not to take a firm stand. Yet the Finnish government did not feel it could afford to take a belligerent stand, and the Social Democratic Prime Minister K.-A. Fagerholm did pay a visit to Moscow in early 1957. If anything, the Finns felt they needed to be even more cautious in their dealings with the Soviets.

Although hardly a death blow to Khrushchev's plans of coexistence, Hungary did mean an end to any plans of speedily expanding neutrality to western Scandinavia. It would take time and considerable effort on the part of the Soviets before their northern European neighbors would again talk to them as though they were reliable partners. All this was noticed with satisfaction in the United States. When the Northern European Chiefs of Mission Conference held in London in September 1957 concluded, Denmark, Iceland, and Norway remained committed to NATO membership, and neutralist sentiments, often linked with general pacifism, were only "latent." Nor had the situation changed significantly regarding Finland and Sweden, both of which were perceived as "anti-Russian" and sympathetic to the West.[31]

But all was not good. At the same meeting, Deputy Assistant Secretary of State John Wesley Jones pointed out the problem that Congress's cuts to funding for USIS programs in friendly countries created the potential for American-Scandinavian misunderstandings. The consensus among American ambassadors was that there existed "a continuing need for adequate information and cultural programs in all of Northern Europe," and that it was "unrealistic to assume that because these countries have basically friendly and stable governments [cultural] programs are unnecessary."[32]

Such programs would have been particularly welcome at a time when the stereotype of the United States as a country full of contradictions—between democratic ideals and sanctioned racism, between rich and poor, and so on— was a commonplace notion in Scandinavia and did little to help U.S. foreign or security policy in that region. Indeed, in the late 1950s the Scandinavian view of the United States held a certain disdain. As Robert Coe of the embassy in Copenhagen stated in May 1957, there was a widespread "tendency to view the United States as a country teeming with business activity but having somewhat primitive cultural tastes and accomplishments. A better appreciation of American cultural life would serve to increase our prestige here and thus make for greater sympathy with and support of our leadership."[33]

If this were a goal, the growing American criticism of the Scandinavian version of a good society did little to help achieve it.

SEX, SIN, AND SUICIDE: THE GODLESS WELFARE STATE

"Why, in countries noted for their social services and the almost universal kindness of one man to another, in lands where legislation seemed to have abolished most of the misfortunes of life, should Sweden and Denmark have the two highest suicide rates in the world?" Time's veteran correspondent Negley Farson put this question to Denmark's largest daily newspaper, Berlingske Tidningen, in the fall of 1958. He received a flood of responses published in the newspaper's letters-to-the-editor pages that ranged from "melancholy national character" of the Danish people to "lack of God" in Danish society. One of the factually more accurate responses—that their comparatively high suicide rates were largely due to their more conscientious record-keeping—Farson chose to reject outright. Instead, he identified the culprit as the welfare state, which, with its paternalistic control of people's lives, supposedly killed every instinct of self-preservation and, in due course, resulted in mental problems that often manifested themselves in taking one's own life. By implication, the Scandinavians who did commit suicide were thus resorting to the only way that they could avoid the state's complete control of their destinies.[34]

Farson's piece had been preceded by a series of articles in American journals describing the shortcomings, or outright dangers, of the Middle Way. Most of them focused on Sweden, ranging from the country's extensive social welfare programs to its liberal introduction of sex education in schools and the lack of religion in people's lives. In one of these pieces, entitled seductively "Sin and Sweden," Time's correspondent Joe David Brown reported that "sexual moral standards in Sweden today are jolting to an outsider." He reported that 10 percent of the babies born in modern Sweden were illegitimate. With obvious outrage, Brown added that all one needed to do to get a legal abortion "is to convince a social worker that the birth is 'unsuitable.' " Not only that, but sex education was a normal part of every public school's curriculum. A result of all this, Brown argued, was suggested in a 19-year-old Swedish boy's letter to a Stockholm newspaper that read: "I have no morals. And I would never marry a girl because I had made her pregnant."[35] The article captured nicely the stereotype that still lingers about Sweden, and Scandinavia at large, as a place of uninhibited promiscuity and lax morals. Opponents of government programs used this stereotype as a warning symbol to convince many Americans of the corruptive effects of the welfare state.

The most significant of the pieces written in the late 1950s, however, turned out to be Peter Wyden's article in the *Saturday Evening Post*. Published in December 1959, it was ominously entitled "Sweden: Paradise with Problems" and, in addition to the suicide rates, raised such issues as the rise in divorce rates and number of illegitimate children, the lax notions regarding sexuality, and the rapidly falling interest in religion. The core of the criticism is captured in the following extract: "Is there a cause-and-effect between these difficulties and the security bestowed by the welfare state? In other words, is too much security unhealthy for the human animal? Most Swedes don't think so, but quite a number of thoughtful ones [sic] do. For example, Dr. Sten Martens believes that the Swedish system has freed too many people from too many decisions by its high benefits, high taxes and excessive planning."[36] An abridged version of this effort to discredit the welfare state (an article Marquis Childs, the best-known expert on the Swedish welfare state, had refused to write), appeared in the March 1960 issue of *Reader's Digest*.

The broader significance of Wyden's essay lay not in any new arguments presented, but rather in the fact that one of President Eisenhower's speech writers read it in the midst of the heated Nixon-Kennedy contest for the White House. On 27 July 1960, it became the basis for Ike's speech at a Republican breakfast meeting in Chicago in which he attacked the welfare state by talking about "a fairly friendly country" with "a tremendous record for socialistic operation." The results of such a system, Ike maintained, had been "that their rate of suicide has gone up almost unbelievably. Now, they have more than twice our drunkenness. Lack of moderation is discernable on all sides." The point of all this, he said, was that the United States should "not establish an operative, paternalistic sort of government, where a man's initiative, the individual's initiative is almost taken away from him by force." Ike ended by paraphrasing Lincoln: "Let's do in the Federal Government only those things that people themselves cannot do at all, or cannot so well in their individual capacities."[37]

The Swedes and their fellow Scandinavians were understandably upset. In speeches to a Nordic Council assembly, Tage Erlander and Einar Gerhardsen, the Swedish and Norwegian prime ministers, complained about Eisenhower's speech, saying that it showed the president's complete ignorance of Scandinavian affairs. They were particularly upset not only because the president's shooting from the hip had little foundation in actual fact but also because it was the first time many Americans paid any attention to Sweden at all. The damage inflicted on Sweden's, and by proxy on Scandinavia's, public image could hardly be undone even with such well-meaning articles as Werner Wiskari's piece in the *New York Times* in October 1960. The article's title captured the essence of Swedish thinking: "Rejoinder to Sweden's Critics—the

Country of the 'Middle Way' Is Not Perfect, the Swedes Themselves Admit, but Neither Is It a Land of 'Sin, Suicide, Socialism and Smorgasbord.' "[38] Ike's attack—for which he later publicly apologized as factually (although not ideologically) erroneous while visiting Sweden in 1962—was representative of the growing American scrutiny and criticism in the late 1950s and early 1960s regarding the Scandinavian welfare state model, a topic that seemed to mix well with the type of sensationalism often preferred in American media. Invariably, Sweden was the favorite whipping boy. But why?

There is, of course, no straightforward answer, but the timing of Ike's infamous speech makes one suspect a connection to the ongoing presidential campaign. The implication, of course, was that the opponents—Kennedy, Johnson, and the Democrats—were somehow planning to move the United States toward the same sort of welfare state that was producing such big problems for the Swedes' mental stability. The message was, moreover, adopted most fervently by the extreme right, including such propaganda centers as the Arkansas-based National Education Program (NEP). The NEP distributed a series of leaflets entitled "The Truth about Welfare States." The leaflet focusing on Sweden stated that "measured by any yardstick," Sweden's living standards were "not half as good" as those in the United States. A particular problem, the author noted, was the lack of cars, which made Sweden a nation of cyclists. This absurdity stood in striking contrast to the numerous concurrent pieces that proclaimed the following in 1959–1960: "Sweden is Europe's most motorized," "Cars up fivefold in ten years in Sweden," and "Auto totals zoom in Sweden."[39]

To be sure, the NEP did not represent the dominant views in the United States. Most of the criticism launched against the welfare state model represented a conservative viewpoint, which was fighting a holding battle against advances in civil rights and social legislation but would eventually be overrun by the Democratic Party's domination of the 1960s, the triumph of the Civil Rights movement, and the launching of the Great Society programs. Of course, none of these resembled, except by the longest stretch of imagination, the welfare state models that were being perfected in Scandinavia. Then again, the homogeneity of Nordic societies, their small sizes, and their long traditions of social legislation stood in stark contrast to the racially charged and mixed, vastly populated United States with its stark divisions in incomes and wealth.

Some of the criticism directed toward the welfare state was, however, extremely pertinent. In particular, the expenses incurred to support the social benefits that ranged from free medical care to extensive pension plans required a prosperous economy, which, in case of the Scandinavians, was based largely on foreign trade. At the same time, high wages and a growing tax burden reduced the international competitiveness of Nordic companies, while the fear of losing some of their social programs kept the Scandinavian countries cool to the idea of European economic integration. Nevertheless, when the EEC was formed in the late 1950s, the reluctant Europeans could no longer afford to ignore the clear trend toward integration.

SIXES, SEVENS, AND SCANDINAVIANS

Already in the early 1950s the Scandinavians had indicated that in the matter of trade liberalization and European integration, they preferred functionalism to federalism. They were suspicious of the continent, partly because of tradition and partly as a result of economic concerns, and found themselves to have much more in common with the limited British approach to European integration than the more extensive plans championed by the French and the Germans. The founding of the Nordic Council and its limited economic initiatives (such as the Scandinavian Labor Market of 1954) had been, in part, an expression of the type of cobweb integration the Nordics preferred.

The NC could not, however, offer an acceptable and adequate Scandinavian alternative to the economic effects of European integration in the late 1950s. With the signing of the Treaty of Rome that went into effect on 1 January 1958, the EEC of six nations—France, West Germany, Italy and the Benelux—came to represent a potential economic threat to the Scandinavians. The prospect of tariff walls against outsiders was a particularly menacing development to such countries as Denmark and Sweden, who sent a large proportion of their exports to West Germany. Later in that year, prolonged talks of a Nordic Customs Union broke down, largely because of Norwegian fears that the stronger Swedish and (albeit to a lesser degree) Danish economies would dominate Norway. Something needed to be done to rescue Northern Europe from potential economic isolation.

Fortunately, particularly from the Norwegians' point of view, the Scandinavians were not the only ones suspicious of the Rome Treaty's political implications. The British—who still represented the largest single trading partner for all Scandinavians—could not find a compromise solution with the Sixes. After Charles de Gaulle took over in 1958, the French, clearly in the driver's seat in the EEC, refused to listen to the British arguments in favor of an associate membership. The Anglo-French conflict climaxed when the negotiations between the British and the EEC broke off in November 1958. London was ready to retaliate. But how? After some internal consideration about the potential for unilateral trade retaliation, a possible reinvigorated Atlantic trade partnership (a model the Norwegians viewed favorably), and even a revival of the Commonwealth as a unified free trade area, the British realized that the only effective countergrouping would be one that consisted of the other European countries who had favored a looser integration model: Austria, Denmark, Norway, Portugal, Sweden, and Switzerland.

The Outer Seven, or the European Free Trade Area (EFTA), formed rapidly. After some preliminary talks, the Swiss called a meeting of the Seven at Geneva in December 1958. The eventual founding protocol, the Stockholm Convention, was approved at a ministerial meeting in the Swedish capital in July 1959, signed in January 1960, and became effective on 3 May 1960. Although the Outer Seven, when compared to the Sixes, comprised a much smaller population (90 million as opposed to 170 million) and could not agree on such extensive reductions in duties (agriculture and fishing were not included in the Stockholm Convention), the EFTA countries did create a market area that presented a challenge of sorts to the EEC. Their timetable for reduction of tariffs mirrored that of the EEC—abolition was to be reached within ten years—but when the EEC accelerated its process, EFTA followed suit, and most tariffs on industrial goods were abolished by 1966. It was clear from the beginning that EFTA was formed primarily as a means of pressuring the Rome Treaty countries to modify the conditions for accepting new members to their group. The British, for example, waited only until 1961 to apply for membership in the European Community—although that application was rejected in 1963. Norway and Denmark followed the British example and, when the British were rejected, withdrew their applications.

From the American perspective, the split between the Sixes and Sevens was hardly unexpected, albeit somewhat discomforting. The American attitude toward European integration had grown ambivalent in the latter half of the 1950s because of the potential that such unification might undermine the Atlantic partnership and, indeed, could even lead to creation of a European third force. There was, however, no doubt that the United States was supportive of the EEC. While they tried not to openly discourage the formation of EFTA, American officials tended to display a marked indifference to that organization, a factor that probably had an impact on the British decision to apply for EEC membership already in 1961.

American officials had ambiguous feelings about the three Scandinavian countries' accession to EFTA as well. On the one hand, their membership was viewed as a victory for broader integration schemes and trade liberalization and as a gateway of sorts in bringing the reluctant Europeans closer to the continentals. On the other hand, the United States would not have heralded Denmark, Norway, and Sweden's accession to EFTA as a triumph of European multilateralism over Nordic regionalism. On the contrary, a Nordic common market was still considered a strong possibility in 1960. Indeed, it was considered as the most likely next step, should the broader integration plans—the coming together of the EEC and EFTA—not succeed. The advantage of such an approach, the NSC argued in 1960, "would be that it might include Finland and thus strengthen that country's ties with the West."[40] The Finns had the same concern.

THE EFTA ASSOCIATE

The Finns had significant and varied trade interests in Western Europe that made the Helsinki government look for a way that would guarantee Finland's continued and noncompromised access to the markets in both EEC and EFTA countries. The problem, however, was how to balance this need with the political and economic demands presented by their special relationship with

Moscow. In the second half of the 1950s, the Finno-Soviet economic relationship was relatively stable, with Finns delivering approximately 17–18 percent of their total exports to the USSR. This number paled in comparison to the trade with Western Europe, however, where Great Britain had regained its position as Finland's largest trading partner after a brief interlude in the early 1950s (when the Soviets held that position). This meant that unless the Finns could negotiate some sort of a deal with either, or both, the EEC and EFTA, the country was about to miss the train of European integration and was in danger of being left outside the benefits that could be derived from trade liberalization with the West. If that were to happen, the end result would likely be that the Finns would have to replace lost markets in the West with new markets in the East, a move that was likely to have serious political implications. The Finnish dilemma was obvious: at the same time that they felt cautious about their political relationship with the USSR in the aftermath of the Hungarian events, the Finns had a growing economic need to be, in one way or another, associated with West European integration. Although such a move would be primarily economic in nature, the Kremlin clearly viewed it as a hostile movement.

This dilemma did not escape Western observers. In the late summer and early fall of 1957, both the Americans and the British raised alarm bells about the economic difficulties facing Finland in the coming months and years. For example, Commercial Secretary Albert Horn of the British Embassy in Helsinki wrote to the Foreign Office in London on 7 August 1957:

> there is no evidence that the Russians have given the Finns licence to join any western organizations other than purely Scandinavian ones, i.e., the Nordic Council, the periodic meetings of the Nordic FM's and possibly the Nordic Customs Union. . . . [Finns are] hopeful that through the Nordic Common Market they may be able eventually to link up with the European Free Trade Area without giving Russians any pretext to bring contrary pressure to bear. But it seems highly unlikely that the Russians have already given their blessing to Finnish membership of the Free Trade Area . . . [instead] the Russians may hope that the result will be, not to draw Finland closer to the west, but to draw the Scandinavians away from the West and towards 'Northern neutrality' which is the most obvious Soviet political objective in this part of the world.

Horn closed his assessment by maintaining that "[the Soviets] may think that Finnish membership of Scandinavian organizations can on occasion be turned to their own advantage, but this would hardly apply to Finnish membership of the Free Trade Area."[41]

In late 1958, Finno-Soviet relations experienced a crisis that revealed the relative weakness of Finland's economic position and its vulnerability to pressure from the East. The so-called night frost crisis erupted after the July 1958 elections that gave power to K.-A. Fagerholm's noncommunist coalition government, although the FCP/FPDL had scored a major victory at the polls and were the largest party in the *Eduskunta.* Soviets began with relentless media criticism, then called back their ambassador to Finland without appointing a new one, and finally, froze virtually all economic relations between the two countries in late 1958. By this time, President Kekkonen was growing extremely nervous. In January 1959, the Fagerholm cabinet resigned, Kekkonen appointed a new AP minority cabinet headed by V. J. Sukselainen, and Finno-Soviet economic relations resumed their normal course.

From the American point of view, the night frost crisis illustrated that Finland might be slipping away. The United States sought to take advantage of the sudden freeze in Finno-Soviet trade and strengthen Finland's economic ties with the West. John D. Hickerson, the American ambassador to Finland (and the former chief of the European Division at the State Department) offered $5 million in U.S. aid in the form of an immediate loan and promised additional assistance—"as big as possible"—to counteract Soviet pressure.[42] The Finns, however, remained reserved and the Finno-Soviet conflict was solved without third-party intervention. Nevertheless, the American offers of aid were reminiscent of earlier efforts, as in 1948, to use economic means to guarantee Finland's resistance in the face of Soviet pressure. Finland's failure to accept the American offer of economic aid made it even more urgent to somehow link the Finns to Western Europe's economic integration.

The night frost crisis clearly illustrated that the Soviets had a veto power of sorts not only regarding the conduct of Finnish foreign affairs, but also its internal politics. No matter how hard the Finns denied it, clearly President Kekkonen had decided that it was in his best interests to give in to pressure regarding a matter that, in the end, had little to do with the conduct of Finnish foreign policy. The United States found this particularly disconcerting at a time when Western Europe was otherwise moving closer to economic union. And yet, there was little anyone could do. An NSC policy statement in late 1959 saw "little practical possibility of a major reorientation of trade away from the USSR. It would be politically impossible—and not necessarily advantageous to the West—for the Finns to make such an adjustment in their economy, unless forced by Soviet action permanently cutting off trade." The statement concluded that "the measures which can be taken in support of Finland are restricted . . . because of the necessity of taking into account the danger of Soviet countermeasures and Finland's determination to attempt to avoid that danger."[43]

The Finns were eventually able to establish a separate agreement with EFTA. Soon after the night frost crisis was over, Prime Minister Sukselainen expressed his country's interest in EFTA during a Nordic prime ministerial meeting in July 1959. It took two years of Finnish internal debating and negotiations with the Soviets and the EFTA countries before the seven became seven-and-a-half in July 1961. The major sticking point was, as expected, the Soviet attitude and the unwillingness of President Kekkonen to make moves that might bring upon Finland the wrath of economic and political pressure from Moscow.

The so-called FINEFTA agreement was signed in March 1961. It created, at least on paper, a third free trade area in Europe, comprising the EFTA countries and Finland. The Soviet criticism of EFTA as just another "instrument of imperialist policy," the need to safeguard the continuance of bilateral Finno-Soviet trade, and the demands of the special characteristics of Finnish economy lay behind this outwardly unduly complicated pact. Under the FINEFTA agreement, the Finns were allowed to proceed at a somewhat slower pace in their tariff reductions, which, in the end, led to the removal of trade tariffs by the end of 1967. Only on 1 January 1986 did Finland join EFTA as a full member.

The most interesting, and controversial, part of the FINEFTA agreement, however, was the Soviet connection. A special pact between Moscow and Helsinki was negotiated in 1960 to assuage Soviet economic concerns and appease their antipathy toward European integration in general. The pact had been hammered out during intricate negotiations between Finland's President Kekkonen and Premier Khrushchev in September 1960. The agreement was preceded by a bilateral Finno-Soviet treaty in November 1960 in which—presuming it would be able to join the organization—Finland agreed to reduce duties on Soviet manufactured goods by the same amounts and rates as on EFTA goods.

Such concessions naturally raised eyebrows in the West, including in the United States, where suspicions over Kekkonen's "overtly friendly" attitude toward the Russians had long roots. The antipathy between successive American ambassadors and Kekkonen had been strengthened when he abided by Soviet pressure during the 1958 night frost crisis. Regarding EFTA, Kekkonen had clearly looked for a green light from Moscow. As NSC 6024, "U.S. Policy toward Finland," stated in December 1960, the Finnish president was a man "who believes that Finland's best interests are served by greater accommodation to Soviet pressures than a number of his countrymen consider necessary" and one who "has endeavored to increase Soviet confidence in Finland's posture as an example of peaceful coexistence."[44] Much of this antipathy would later surface in public with the "Finlandization" debates of the 1960s and 1970s.

Despite such antipathy, U.S. support for Finland's association with EFTA was clear. As Secretary of State Christian Herter (who replaced Dulles in 1959) wrote in a directive to Helsinki and the capitals of EFTA countries in March 1960: "the U.S. desires that Finland and Seven be aware that U.S. would view favorably Finnish membership or association EFTA provided parties directly concerned desire it."[45] In the end, the United States was even ready to stomach Finno-Soviet tariff reductions and support the FINEFTA agreement. The reasoning behind such compromising was familiar: Without the ability to associate themselves with the Western European trade liberalization, the Finns would have to tie themselves more closely to the USSR. "The ability of Finland to associate in one way or another with European Free Trade Association is of such far-reaching importance that it may be a major determinant in Finland's fate as an independent country oriented toward the Free World," wrote Herter.[46] At a time when Soviet-American relations were headed for a new crisis about Berlin and the U-2 reconnaissance flights shot down over the USSR, Finland retained its special position with indirect, but unwavering, U.S. support.

Why did the Americans continue supporting Finland's unique relationship with the USSR? Part of the answer lies in the fact that the United States "needed" Finland as a symbol. In the late 1950s and early 1960s, Washington began to shift the terms of the neutrality-coexistence argument to their advantage. That is, some decision makers began to advocate neutrality for Eastern Europe by using the "Finnish example" as a potential solution for all *Soviet* relations with its Western neighbors. In this context, the Soviet actions in Hungary had provided the backdrop against which the United States could start arguing for neutrality for Eastern Europe as a way station to undermining the USSR's Eastern European empire. Yet not until the late 1950s did this kind of "rollback" gain some appeal in the highest administration circles.

During the 1 October 1959 NSC meeting, CIA Director Allen Dulles summarized the argument by maintaining that the United States should be saying to the USSR that "you can live with a Western-oriented democratic Finland, why not with Eastern European countries organized along the same lines?"[47] Thus, the 1959 NSC policy paper on Finland argued that "if Finland is able to preserve its present neutral status it could serve as an example of what the United States might like to see achieved by the Soviet-dominated nations of Eastern Europe."[48] Some time would pass, however, before the idea of using Finland as a tool of American policy, as a lever to change the status quo in Eastern Europe, received its first public pronouncement. Soon after the Kennedy administration had taken office, Zbigniew Brzezinski and William E. Griffith argued in an article in *Foreign Affairs* that U.S. foreign policy should promote: "[T]he creation of a neutral belt of states which, like the Finnish, would enjoy genuine popular freedom of choice in internal policy while not being hostile to the Soviet Union and not belonging to Western military alliances."[49] Neutrality as a potential vehicle of Soviet policy was effectively "neutralized" by turning the tables around and using it as a springboard toward achieving American aims in Eastern Europe. The argument would resurface later (see chapter 5).

FISHMONGERING

In the late 1950s, EFTA represented no solution at all for the economic troubles facing the Icelanders. Almost all (more than 90 percent) of the country's exports consisted of fish products that were specifically excluded from the Stockholm Convention. Thus, EFTA offered little of value for the Icelandic economy. Indeed, coinciding with the negotiations that led to the formation of EFTA, the Icelanders and the British were engaged in a prolonged conflict that kept Iceland outside of any European integration plans until 1970 and could have led to the country's exit from NATO. The issue was fishing limits off the Icelandic coast; the episode was the first of the cod wars between Iceland and Great Britain.

Fishing rights issues had strained Anglo-Icelandic relations throughout the 1950s. The 1952 unilateral extension of Iceland's fishing boundaries (see the discussion earlier in this chapter) and the British boycott that followed it had rapidly opened the door for the Soviets to take advantage of a conflict between two NATO countries. With the de facto closure of the British market (the largest one for Icelandic fish), the Icelanders had turned to Eastern Europe and the USSR as outlets for their cod. This, predictably, irritated the Americans; concern about a Soviet economic offensive in Iceland went hand in hand with the troubled state of U.S. base rights in Keflavík.

In the late 1950s the issue took another, more serious, turn. The Icelanders became irritated when a 1958 U.N. conference failed to produce an acceptable, clear-cut solution to the issue of fishing limits. A Canadian proposal to extend the exclusive rights for fishing from 3 to 12 miles could not muster the necessary support—the United States, for example, did not support it—and in April 1958, the Icelandic Fisheries Minister Ludvik Josefsson demanded an immediate extension of fisheries limits to 12 miles. Foreign Minister Gudmundsson tried to avert unilateral action by discussing the matter at a NATO foreign ministers' meeting in Copenhagen in May. It proved fruitless. On 30 June 1958, the Icelandic government announced that a 12-mile fishery limit off the country's coast would be effective as of 1 September.

Although many countries, including the United States and Norway, protested, only the British refused to abide by the Icelandic action. London sent the navy to protect certain British vessels fishing inside the 12-mile limit in September 1958—something the minuscule Icelandic coast guard (five ships) could not prevent. During the next two years, a constant cat-and-mouse game between the British and the Icelanders took place off the Icelandic coastline. The Icelanders refused to attend the 1959 Atlantic Congress in London, and recalled their ambassador to England for lengthy consultation in the fall of that year. Eventually, prompted in part by outside pressure from Canada, the United States, and the Scandinavian NATO members, the London and Reykjavík governments were able to reach a compromise solution. Early in 1961, the British formally recognized the 12-mile limit while the Icelanders permitted English ships to fish in limited areas inside the parameters for another three years.

The first cod war had a significance that extended beyond the narrow economic interests of fishermen. The disturbance in Anglo-Icelandic relations naturally caused concern over NATO's unity at a time when neutralism was still a potent force in Europe; Iceland's traditional ambivalence about permitting foreign troops and bases was, once again, called into question. Moreover, while the Europeans formed two free trade pacts in the late 1950s, the Icelanders drifted further away from the plans that stressed the need for economic and political integration and continued trading extensively with the Soviet bloc. Indeed, although it would join EFTA in 1970, Reykjavík would remain unimpressed by the unification campaigns that would eventually bring even such traditional neutrals as Finland and Sweden into the EU in the 1990s.

From Washington's perspective, the smallest Scandinavian country continued to be a problem child, if a very different sort than Finland. With its strategic significance still considerable, American presence in Iceland was considered a must. To this effect, the communists' loss in the 1958 *Althing* elections and their subsequent removal from the government had been a welcome shift in Icelandic affairs. In that context, the cod war, of little significance to American interests per se, was an added irritation. It only strengthened the Icelandic need to find new export markets outside of Great Britain. There were ready takers in the East: In the early 1960s the Soviet Bloc received about 35 percent of Icelandic fish. The cod war also strengthened Icelandic nationalism, a source of consternation for the United States, struggling to maintain base rights in Keflavík. In short, the cod war, and Iceland's heavy dependence on fishing that brought it into a conflict with America's most important European ally, was considered "a constant source of concern because of its possible effects on continued Icelandic membership in NATO and on the maintenance of U.S. forces and military installations in Iceland."[50]

The fishmongering between Iceland and Great Britain in the late 1950s was a minor thorn in the troubled alliance. As the 1960s neared, however, NATO's unity was in severe trouble because of Charles de Gaulle's accession to power in 1958 and his obvious desire to reinstate his country's status as a major independent actor in the world arena. One expression of the Fifth Republic's newfound desire for international prominence was the explosion of the first French atomic bomb in February 1960. In Scandinavia, the issue of the weapons of mass destruction had an entirely different spin.

NUCLEAR WEAPONS AND RISING TENSIONS

One of the counterproducts of the doctrines of massive retaliation and New Look was a push to place medium-range nuclear missiles in Europe. In October 1957 when the Soviets launched the Sputnik satellite—thus demonstrating remarkable advances in their long-range missile technology—the United States offered to place medium-range missiles in allied countries in continental Europe. Although the United States never approached Iceland—stationing missiles there would have had little strategic advantage and provoked many new political problems—the Eisenhower administration did approach Norway and Denmark. The response from both Copenhagen and Oslo was strongly negative.

Norwegian Prime Minister Einar Gerhardsen unambiguously announced at the NATO heads of state meeting in December 1957 that his country would not allow the stationing of such weaponry in its territory in peacetime.

Gerhardsen in large part reflected a growing antinuclear movement not only in his ruling Labor party but across the Norwegian political spectrum in the late 1950s and early 1960s. In 1961 the Gerhardsen government and a large majority of the *Storting* also turned down the Norwegian military's recommendation that tactical nuclear weapons should be incorporated into the country's defenses even during peacetime.

The refusal to accept missiles in Norway stemmed from the belief that deterring the Soviets was best achieved through the combination of strength and reassurance that they had practiced since World War II. This meant that the Norwegians needed to keep reassuring the Soviets that their NATO membership presented no threat to Soviet security; unless, of course, the Soviets took military action against Norway. Missiles could too easily be interpreted as offensive in character. In addition, the Norwegians' no-missiles policy could also be seen as a reflection of Gerhardsen's clear desire to play the role of bridge builder between East and West. Toward this end, despite the disheartening events in Hungary in late 1956, the Norwegian prime minister tried to promote a U.S.-Soviet summit meeting in 1957–1958. He received no encouragement from Washington, however. Gerhardsen's hopes of playing a mediatory role in the international arena evaporated further when Khrushchev canceled his planned tour of Scandinavian capitals in 1959, citing "right-wing distortions and attacks" as the basis for such a decision.

Nevertheless, the policy of reassurance vis-à-vis the Soviets continued. It became even more significant in the wake of the U-2 crisis, which catapulted the Gerhardsen government into the midst of a severe international crisis. Francis Gary Powers's spy plane had taken off from Pakistan and was supposed to land at Bødo airport in northern Norway when the USSR shot it down on 1 May 1960 over Sverdlovsk. Soon thereafter the Soviets accused the Americans of criminal activities, and Khrushchev walked out on Eisenhower after lambasting him at the lame-duck summit meeting in Paris. In addition, the Kremlin launched a strong protest to the Norwegian government and even threatened to obliterate bases such as Bødo that were made available for flights that violated Soviet air space. The Gerhardsen cabinet—which had not been briefed about the true nature of Powers's flight—denied being involved in any conspiracy against the USSR and, in turn, launched a protest to Washington.

This did not satisfy the Kremlin. Two months later a similar, if less well known, incident took place. An American RB-47 reconnaissance plane was shot down off the Kola peninsula and the Soviets again claimed that the Norwegians were either willing partners in an American spying scheme or simply did not have the power to stop the United States from exploiting Norwegian territory for its clandestine schemes. "They treat us like a vassal state," complained Prime Minister Gerhardsen about the United States, echoing the Soviet line. When the Soviets launched another protest regarding the activities of an American team of scientists in the demilitarized Spitsbergen island chain north of the Scandinavian peninsula, and the Norwegians discovered that the team had actually been surveying the islands for a possible air base, the Americans were told to leave. This they did. Despite their policy of not admitting nuclear weapons, the Norwegians were deeply affected by the rising tensions in the early 1960s.

In Denmark, the question of stationing missiles that could accommodate nuclear warheads was also met with opposition. At the same NATO meeting in December 1957 at which Gerhardsen reiterated his country's categorical refusal to accept nuclear weapons in peacetime, Danish Prime Minister Hansen had followed suit. As in Norway, the vehemently hostile Soviet reaction was a major issue behind Hansen's announcement. Gerhardsen and Hansen's stand enjoyed widespread popular support among their respective electorates. Reassuring the Soviets was particularly pertinent at a time when the Danes were involved in continued planning of the creation of a unified Baltic Command structure (COMBALTAP) under NATO's auspices. Because the dominant partner in such plans was to be West Germany, the Soviet reaction was predictably negative. Although shrouded in the efforts to propagate the idea of the Baltic as a "sea of peace," the Soviet efforts to prevent NATO's access to the Baltic were mostly manifested in pronouncements against renewed German militarism. This theme, naturally, had some effect on Danish opinion and probably prolonged the conclusion of the COMBALTAP agreement until December 1961. Characteristically, the Danes demanded that no German officer ever be allowed to lead that force.

Despite the gradual rise in East-West tensions in the late 1950s and early 1960s, the thought of stationing nuclear weapons still did not appeal to the United States' Scandinavian allies. In fact, the reverse was the case. Concerned more over reassuring the Kremlin about the defensive nature of their participation in NATO and, sensibly enough, over not making their territories potential targets of a nuclear strike by the Soviets, the Danes and the Norwegians added a no-nuclear-weapons corollary to their no-bases-in-time-of-peace policies. In addition, they began to show increasing interest in the possibilities of nuclear disarmament and/or nonproliferation, ideas that were receiving growing support from pacifist circles and détente proponents from across the political spectrum. Such events as the U-2 affair convinced many Nordics that the Soviet-American confrontation was getting out of hand and, given the advances in nuclear technology on both sides, could lead to nondiscriminatory and widespread destruction. Something needed to done.

THE UNDEN PLAN

In Northern Europe, the question of nuclear weapons was not limited to discussions about whether Denmark and Norway should allow the placement of missiles in their territory. During the late 1950s, a prolonged debate took place in Sweden about the possibility of acquiring nuclear weapons for the nation's military arsenal. The argument in favor of such a move, presented by the military and popular particularly among the air force, was apparently quite compelling. Because of the limited personnel resources of Sweden (with a population of less than eight million), it could never build a conventional force equal to, or anywhere near, the size of its most likely adversary (i.e., the USSR). Thus nuclear weapons might provide "the great equalizer." Accordingly, in 1957 the military high command argued that: "All military considerations speak unanimously and strongly for acquisition of atomic weapons."[51]

In 1959, however, the Swedish government decided to defer a decision on the issue pending further study, since it was dividing the ruling Social Democratic Party. After realizing that the huge cost incurred by building nuclear weapons would have to be covered either by placing an increased tax burden on the already highly taxed citizenry or by severely undercutting the modernization of the conventional Swedish defense forces, the government abandoned its plans. At approximately the same time, a new argument emerged among Swedish strategists that further justified the abandonment of a nuclear weapons program. The bottom line of this thinking, known as the marginality thesis, was, simply, that Sweden's strategic significance was not important enough to justify a major conventional attack, let alone a nuclear offensive, against it. Thus, in the event of an all-out war, any major power would use only marginal forces against Sweden. By the early 1960s, an isolated major assault against Sweden was no longer considered a realistic possibility, and the Swedes needed to ready themselves to counter only a relatively minor attack. Presumably, this could be done effectively with an ultramodern conventional force, something the Swedish army continued to possess.

Not going nuclear and instead placing their trust in the marginality thesis meant an effective end to serious defense debate in Sweden, at least until the Soviet submarine blunders of the 1980s. But it also meant the beginning of another phase in Swedish foreign policy that was to bring the nation—as well as its neighbors—into the international consciousness more clearly than before. Perhaps ironically, one of the men responsible for the rise in Sweden's international prestige was killed at exactly this moment.

Dag Hammarskjöld's years of shuttle diplomacy ended on 18 September 1961 during a peace-mediation mission in the Congo when his plane crashed, under mysterious circumstances, above the war-torn West African nation. In the long run, losing their most internationally visible figure seems to have energized the Swedish government to become more involved in international affairs. During the 1960s, the Swedes became known for their advocacy of development aid to underdeveloped nations—an effort, at some level, to "export" the welfare ideology abroad—and their criticism of the ways in which the United States and the USSR extended their power to the newly independent nations in Asia and Africa. To a large extent, it was a legacy of Hammarskjöld's own efforts during his tenure at the United Nations to try and boost the development aid from the "first" to the "third" world. This criticism would later gain much notoriety in the United States when it was directed against the U.S. involvement in Vietnam. In 1961 the most obvious example of the Swedes' growing interest to play a role in international affairs came in the area of nuclear disarmament.

In October 1961, long-time Swedish Foreign Minister Bo Östen Unden gave a speech to the U.N. General Assembly in which he publicized what soon became known as the Unden plan. The idea was intriguing. Unden argued that countries without nuclear weapons should create a "nuclear-free club" that could then exert moral pressure on the great powers to limit their nuclear arms race. Concurrently Unden also raised the issue of a test ban and actively propagated for the expansion of the U.N. Ten Power Committee on Disarmament. These proposals were partly successful. In 1962, the Committee was enlarged into the Eighteen Nations Disarmament Conference that was stationed in Geneva and headed by a Swede, Alva Myrdal. At the same time, exerting moral influence on the nuclear powers was hardly an immediate success. Although the United States, USSR, and Great Britain signed the first, albeit limited, Test Ban Treaty in 1963, it was not a result of the Unden Plan but rather of the scare that the Cuban missile crisis in October 1962 delivered all over the world. At the same time, however, the countries that were supportive of the Unden Plan—the Scandinavians and the nonaligned nations of the third world—represented an emerging collective challenge to the supposed supremacy, and primacy, of the East-West order that now had a new custodian.

ENTER CAMELOT

John F. Kennedy's grandiose entrance to the White House in January 1961, captured in his inaugural rhetoric of "bearing any burden," signaled a shift not only in the personality and party of the chief executive, but also in the American-Scandinavian relationship. During the Eisenhower presidency, the severest U.S. criticism had focused on the perceived paternalism of the Scandinavian welfare state, while the Nordic countries' foreign policy positions had received little or no public commentary. Even the Swedes, who had felt the Truman administration's scorn when they opted to stay out of NATO, had not been criticized severely for their continued neutrality.

The reverse became true in the 1960s. With the triumphs of the Civil Rights movement and, in particular, with the launching of the Great Society programs, the criticism that climaxed in Eisenhower's 1960 attack against the Scandinavian welfare system subsided. In some ways, the affirmative action programs that began to take shape in the mid-1960s could be seen as part of exactly the same kind of social engineering that had made Northern European countries the models of the Middle Way, countries in which income gaps were low and citizens were provided extensive social benefits by the government. That the Great Society would fall far short of its initial promise was unforeseen in the 1960s when Scandinavians could find much to applaud in the efforts of economic equalization in the United States. They would also find the legislative triumphs of the Civil Rights movement, albeit long overdue, a source of some delight. Lastly, the Scandinavians, like many other Europeans, found Kennedy's youth, good looks, and personality a welcome change from the aging Ike's lack of charisma.

But Kennedy's and the Democrats' ascendancy was not so comforting to Northern Europeans in the areas of foreign policy and international relations. Although the high tide of anti-Vietnam war criticism that would lead to a virtual break in American-Swedish relations in the early 1970s was still a decade away, the tendency of Democratic presidents to portray toughness vis-à-vis the Kremlin in order to undercut domestic criticism from the right was disheartening to Scandinavians. Indeed, eager to prove his anti-Soviet credentials, the young president and his worthy, if erratic, Soviet adversary would embark on a series of crises that has prompted one student of the years 1961–1963 to dub the period, aptly, *The Crisis Years*.[52]

That they would be indeed. The erection of the Berlin Wall, the invasion of the Bay of Pigs, the apocalyptic nature of the Cuban missile crisis, and the gradual increase in American involvement in Vietnam would prompt much criticism and cause great concern in Scandinavia. The hopes of détente were still running high in Northern Europe. Not only that, but the rising Soviet-American and East-West tensions contributed to the commencement of a new crisis in Finno-Soviet relations that threatened to upset the strategic balancing act that had tied the Nordic region together since the late 1940s.

Ironically, it began in Hawaii in the fall of 1961.

chapter 5

FROM HAWAII TO HELSINKI, 1961–1975

"Me and my husband went for a swim . . . when we approached
the beach, we saw Urkki sitting in the water . . . there he sat alone thinking.
And it was just about the first time when he was alone. I think he had been
sitting there for quite some time." In this manner Patricia Seppälä, wife of the
Finnish ambassador to the United States, Rafael Seppälä, described the morning following the sensational news that the Soviet Union had sent a diplomatic note, which called for military consultations in light of "renewed German militarism," to the Finnish government on 30 October 1961.[1] "Urkki"
was the popular nickname of Finland's longtime president, Urho K. Kekkonen; the location was a beach on the island of Kauai in Hawaii, where the
president and his entourage were spending a few days after a tour of Canada
and the United States. Thus far the visit had improved and strengthened Finland's neutral image and negated the popular perception that Finland was a
"semi-satellite" of the USSR. The Soviet note put all such gains in severe
jeopardy.

Fourteen years later, Kekkonen, still in power at the age of 75, would stand
at the center stage of international relations. This time the place was Finlandia Hall in Helsinki and the occasion was the signing of the Helsinki Accords,
the final protocol of the Conference on Security and Cooperation in Europe
(CSCE). Everyone, including Gerald Ford, Henry Kissinger, and Leonid
Brezhnev, was there, everyone praised the Finnish president for providing the
setting in which the CSCE negotiations had been conducted since 1972. The
bridge-building role that Kekkonen had adopted—joining other Scandinavian politicians such as the Swedes Bo Östen Unden, Tage Erlander, and Dag
Hammarskjöld as well as the Norwegians Trygve Lie and Einar Gerhardsen—
had borne fruit.

The period between Kekkonen's diametrically opposed experiences in Hawaii and Helsinki represented a significant change in the role of Scandinavia in international relations. The note crisis set the stage for much of Scandinavian, not just Finnish, diplomacy and security policy for the 1960s and early 1970s. Given that much of the Soviet note was directed at other Scandinavian countries besides Finland, the question many Nordic politicians were asking in the aftermath of the crisis was how to preserve the Nordic Balance, the security framework in Northern Europe? Most answered by trying to reduce the potential that another crisis might occur. They did this in two major ways: first, by continuing their postwar policies that, to a large extent, were a combination of reassurance and deterrence vis-à-vis the USSR. Second, the Scandinavians began to work more deliberately toward détente in East-West relations. In addition, the Soviet note had a long-term impact: it increased the Scandinavian desire for détente that would, in their minds, reduce the potential that their quiet corner of Europe might be upset by a similar crisis in the future. In different ways, they all began to act as midwives to détente.

The Scandinavians did this at a time when the East-West conflict in Europe and American-European relations were undergoing a profound transformation. French President Charles de Gaulle caused more than a few headaches in Washington with his independent stance on world issues, and U.S. prestige in Europe declined as a result of the Vietnam War. The Kennedy administration's vision of a Grand Design—a more effective American-European cooperation that included such components as easing Great Britain into the EEC and involving the Europeans more directly in nuclear planning via the Multilateral Force (MLF)—all but collapsed as Europeans refused to accept American hegemony disguised under the notion of an Atlantic community of equals. Instead, by the late 1960s, as the Johnson administration became increasingly obsessed with Vietnam, the West Europeans were already on their way toward détente with the Soviet Union. Willy Brandt's *Ostpolitik* was succeeding in breaking the stalemate over the key political and strategic issue of postwar Europe: the division of Germany. By the time Richard Nixon and Henry Kissinger took over, European détente was well on its way, and the expansion of Western European economic integration seemed possible with de Gaulle's exit in the late 1960s. With its focus on triangular diplomacy with the USSR and China, and the painstakingly prolonged exit from Vietnam, the Nixon administration could do little to stop the relative decline of the U.S. position vis-à-vis its Western European, including Scandinavian, allies.

In the years 1961–1975, the Scandinavian-American relationship thus underwent a profound transformation that, in large part, mirrored the general development of U.S.-European relations. The Vietnam War became a major strain in the relationship between Washington and all Scandinavian countries, although Sweden was by far the most vocal critic. The concern over the potential domination of American culture and money provoked conflicts in

Iceland, while the Americans became increasingly critical of the notion of a Middle Way between capitalism and socialism so attractive to the ruling social democratic parties in Scandinavia. The Scandinavian (particularly Swedish and Finnish) promotion of nuclear arms limitation annoyed American strategists. All this happened against the backdrop of relaxation in East-West tensions in which the Scandinavians played their own important role.

KEKKONEN'S CRISIS

On the morning of 30 October 1961, Eero A. Wuori, the Finnish ambassador to the USSR, arrived for a prearranged meeting with Soviet Foreign Minister Andrei Gromyko. Gromyko wasted little time in small talk after Wuori entered his office at the Soviet foreign ministry, but handed over a 10-page document that referred to the consultation clause of the 1948 FCMA Treaty and informed the Finnish government that the USSR would like to enter into military consultations with Finland. The purpose of such talks would be to "discuss the appropriate action to guarantee the defense of both countries due to the impending threat of an attack from West Germany and its allies." The time and place for such consultations, the note added, "could be agreed upon via diplomatic channels." Wuori, a man prone to pessimism when it came to Finno-Soviet relations and one who had predicted an upcoming crisis throughout the previous summer, was aghast. He soon got word to President Kekkonen, who was at the time relaxing in Hawaii. Although Kekkonen decided not to take an overtly alarmist view of the situation, he dispatched Foreign Minister Ahti Karjalainen back to Finland while he continued the remainder of his North American tour. Despite his public comments at a press conference in Los Angeles on 1 November that played down the alarmist reaction among Western observers, Kekkonen faced a crisis that tended to undermine much of the work he had done to strengthen the image of Finnish neutrality in the West. Finns were, it seemed, still at the mercy of Soviet "temper tantrums."[2]

Why did the Soviets unleash a crisis with Finland in the fall of 1961? The answer lies partly in developments in Finland's internal affairs that raised some eyebrows in Moscow and partly in the general international situation.

Prior to the note crisis, 1961 was the year of one of the most heated presidential campaigns in postwar Finnish history. Barring the miracle of a communist victor, the Soviets clearly had a preferred candidate; they wished to see Kekkonen continue for a second term. From Moscow's perspective, this was quite natural. After all, Kekkonen, although no ideological sympathizer of communism, was clearly a champion of good Finno-Soviet relations and had a personal bond with Nikita Khrushchev. He was also a strong supporter of the expansive and more active nature of Finnish neutrality policy that seemed to serve general Soviet interests in Northern Europe. In 1961, however, Kekkonen faced a serious domestic challenge. Two of the largest parties, the Social

Democrats and the Conservatives, had allied themselves behind a common presidential candidate, Olavi Honka, the attorney general. The so-called Honka alliance (*Honka-liitto*) posed a dual threat to Moscow's interests: on the one hand, it threatened to remove from power a man whom Moscow had cultivated for years; on the other hand, the forces behind the challenge consisted of the two Finnish parties least liked by the Kremlin: the Social Democrats and the Conservatives. Yet it should be noted that despite his supporters, Honka was by no means running an effective campaign in 1961, and that Kekkonen's handling of foreign policy—in particular his ability to link Finland to EFTA, his trip to England in the spring of 1961, and the visit to Canada and the United States that he was just completing when the Soviet note arrived—was clearly oriented toward improving Finland's relations with the West.

Nevertheless, the note crisis did have an undeniable domestic political impact in Finland that must have satisfied the Soviets. On the one hand, Kekkonen's successful resolution of the conflict strengthened his position in the ongoing presidential race by enhancing his image as someone capable of dealing with the Soviets in a time of crisis. On the other hand, the crisis led to the final breakdown of the Honka alliance, which had already began to crack in the early fall of 1961. Honka himself announced that he was giving up the candidacy on 24 November 1961. As a result, Kekkonen won enough votes to corner the election victory at the first vote by the electoral college in February 1962. By providing a clear margin for victory, the note crisis and the presidential election campaign also represented the last time Kekkonen faced a serious challenge as the undisputed political leader in Finland—he would remain as president for another two decades. Thus, Kekkonen controlled Finnish foreign relations and, in particular, relations with the USSR for a quarter of a century.

There have been many accusations of some duplicity on Kekkonen's part. In particular, a theory that he "ordered" a note from the USSR in order to guarantee his personal ambitions has been somewhat popular among Kekkonen's political opponents and some Finnish historians. Many of the arguments seem to draw their strength from the way the crisis was solved. After Foreign Minister Ahti Karjalainen was unable to get the Soviets to withdraw the call for military consultations during his trip to Moscow on 11–12 November, Kekkonen used his constitutional powers to prematurely dissolve the Finnish *Eduskunta* and order new elections on 14 November. This action did nothing to solve the crisis but instead, quite understandably, resulted in charges that the Soviets were running Finnish domestic politics. The final solution to the crisis came during Kekkonen's visit with Nikita Khrushchev in Novosibirsk on 24–25 November. The result was as dramatic as the commencement of the crisis: Khrushchev withdrew the note and public pronouncements made it clear that the Soviets "trusted" Kekkonen. The next day Kekkonen returned to cheering crowds—many of whom probably felt that he had saved Finland from another Winter War—in Helsinki and rode the wave of popularity to another electoral victory. It all happened, it seemed, with such ease that further charges of duplicity could not be avoided.

But one is hard pressed to believe that a superpower would take such a step simply to ensure an electoral victory for a preferred candidate in a country unlikely to produce any major threat. Indeed, although strengthening Kekkonen's position may have been one of the goals of the Soviet note, its timing also coincided with a significant rise in international tensions in the Baltic and over Berlin. After all, the July 1961 Vienna Summit between Kennedy and Khrushchev had been far from successful; in August the Soviets had erected the Berlin Wall; and that summer the Soviet press was interpreting the COMBALTAP (NATO's United Baltic Command), which integrated Danish and West German forces, as a revival of German militarism that now received willing Scandinavian support. In addition, there is evidence that Khrushchev was under some hard-line criticism at home that may have pushed him to act more decisively. In the fall of 1961, plenty of international and domestic Soviet reasons could explain the timing of the note to Finland.

If Kekkonen indeed had ordered a note from Moscow, as some contemporaries and historians have argued, he certainly would have been doing a severe disservice to his own foreign policy. After all, in 1961 Kekkonen was clearly en route to opening diplomatic links to the West on the heels of Finland's growing economic ties to Western Europe as the country negotiated the FINEFTA agreement. The most public part of the 1961 "Western" campaigns were evident during the high level of diplomatic activity that was geared toward improving Finland's standing in the Western world. In the spring of 1961, Kekkonen made a trip to England and received what he had longed for: an explicit Western endorsement of Finland's neutrality. This visit was followed by the fall excursions to Canada and to the United States. In the meetings between President Kekkonen and Canada's Prime Minister John G. Diefenbaker, and particularly between Kekkonen and President Kennedy, the Finnish president freely commented on his views on the USSR's intentions and, again, received supportive public statements for Finland's neutrality. Indeed, the fact that Kekkonen's trip to Hawaii was rudely interrupted by the Soviet note can be interpreted as a symbolic reminder of the limits that the Soviets wished to put on Finland's "Western leanings."

To be sure, the West never had any great admiration for Kekkonen, who had made it to the "black list" in the United States already in 1952 when he suggested the expansion of neutrality to Denmark and Norway. He seemed far too concerned about pleasing the Soviets and, although his ultimate patriotism was never in doubt, Kekkonen seemed to be seeking power for power's sake and thus be willing to take advantage of Soviet political pressures for his personal gains in domestic politics. At the same time, however, the Americans had continuously tried to strengthen Finland's Western ties. Most recently, they supported Finland's somewhat convoluted road to a special agreement with EFTA (see chapter 4) and viewed Finland as a country with little choice but to try and maintain a neutral position. During Kekkonen's visit to the United States, President Kennedy repeatedly stressed that Finland was a neutral country and asked Americans to support that policy openly. At the same time, however, Kennedy clearly tried to use Kekkonen—who met with Soviet leaders on a regular basis—as an informant of sorts regarding Soviet thinking.

Already during the first months of the Kennedy administration, the NSC had determined that the cautious policy vis-à-vis Finland that had been practiced since the end of World War II should be continued. Because there seemed to be no realistic possibility of overtly "Westernizing" Finland's policies without alarming the Soviets and inviting their adverse reaction, NSC's best option was to encourage Finland's Scandinavian ties. The reasoning was captured in a March 1961 NSC statement that argued that cooperation between Scandinavians and Finns should be supported in order to help "Finland to oppose Soviet pressure and maintain its Western ties."[3]

The note crisis, nevertheless, did call into question the advisability of such an indirect U.S. policy. Although Secretary of State Dean Rusk declined to speculate in public about Finno-Soviet relations, the new American ambassador to Finland, Bernhard Gufler, was directed to verbally (Gufler was specifically directed not to leave "written communication" behind) offer U.S. help to President Kekkonen by conveying to him a message from President Kennedy before Kekkonen's departure to the Soviet Union on 22 November 1961. Kennedy pledged that he wished to "assure you [Kekkonen] of the readiness of my country to give Finland our political and economic support." He maintained that "we stand ready to extend commercial and economic assistance in the event of economic pressure against Finland designed to secure political compliance. We are prepared, when opportune, to speak out firmly in behalf of Finland's security and independence. We would be willing to carry to the United Nations actions seeming to threaten your country's independence, depriving you of the right to follow your chosen path of neutrality."[4]

The message met with a cool response. Kekkonen turned down the offer, saying that the note crisis had been overly dramatized in the Western press. Later, in a letter to Finland's ambassador to the United States, Rafael Seppälä, Kekkonen wondered how anybody could even think that Finland might take such offers seriously; after all, such offers would only call more attention to Finland and thus escalate the crisis into a true East-West confrontation. As in 1948 and 1958–1959, the Finns decided to deal head-to-head with the Soviets rather than risking the possibility that the crisis might turn into a broader Cold War conflict.[5]

Kekkonen's trip to Novosibirsk and the cancellation of the call for military consultation provided only a partial relief for the Americans. In particular, it seemed that although the Finns had averted military consultations, and that the note crisis had probably more to do with developments outside Finno-

Soviet relations, the episode had resulted in placing Finland's neutrality policy even more firmly at the mercy of the USSR. Gufler made this point to Kekkonen during a 2 January 1962 meeting when he said that "it was essential that the nature of neutrality should be defined by a neutral government itself and by no one else." Kekkonen agreed, but added an important caveat: the neutral government "had to satisfy itself that those concerned agreed with its definition."[6] While Gufler was implying that Kekkonen was too eager to get approval for his neutrality from the outside (read: the USSR), Kekkonen maintained that only such approval guaranteed that neutrality was credible.

In a sense, the discussion between Gufler and Kekkonen captured much of the essential problem: that Finns felt they needed outside approval for neutrality and had searched for it in the West in 1961, only to be reprimanded, in a way, by the Soviets; that Kekkonen followed the reprimand by assurances to the East. The discussion also captured another fact. The 1961 note crisis had been, in many ways, a seminal moment for Finland's role in international affairs; Finland had been well on its way to a neutrality position that resembled Sweden's. But the note crisis had crudely reminded the Finns that they could not, without severe complications, rid themselves from the treaty-bound ties with the Soviet Union. To avoid further crises, Finnish neutrality would have to pay lip service to Moscow's interests—in Kekkonen's case it meant that while he became internationally even more active, his moves would follow closely the Kremlin's cues and would be aimed at reducing the possibility of another note crisis. The events of 1961 laid the basis for Finland's role as bridge builder in the 1960s and 1970s.

The Soviet note's potential long-term value was well understood in Washington. As Deputy Under Secretary of State U. Alexis Johnson told Finland's Ambassador Rafael Seppälä during their meeting of 28 November 1961, the U.S. government was certainly pleased that the crisis had passed without military consultations. He added: "We were also of the opinion that the note had certainly not been directed to Finland alone. It was his own reaction that the Soviets had demonstrated that they could crack the whip. Every Finn, politician or citizen, would have this in the back of his mind now."[7] In short, Johnson implied that the Soviets had scared the Finns thoroughly into anticipating and trying to prevent any further crisis through actions that would be more pleasing to the Soviets than would necessarily be expected from a neutral country. Viewed from the State Department, Finland was, clearly, "Moscow's neutral."

SCANDINAVIA'S CRISIS: NORDIC BALANCE TESTED

The note crisis alarmed other Scandinavians. In particular, the Soviet note's references to COMBALTAP and Denmark's participation in it, as well as Moscow's hostile attitude toward Norwegian cooperation with NATO that was clearly evident in the Soviet press, caused speculation regarding the note's actual target. Was it, in fact, directed to Oslo and Copenhagen rather than to Helsinki? That the note itself referred to "West German militarist and revanchist penetration into North[ern] Europe and the Baltic Sea as well as its attempts to use the region as a military base" was clear evidence of the "Scandinavian" connection.[8] Although there was little new in these Soviet accusations (which were, for the most part, pure nonsense), the fact that they were tied to a potential change in Finland's relative position on the East-West axis made the leaders in other Northern capitals treat the note more seriously than if it were simply another part of a continuing barrage of Soviet rhetoric.

The Danes, for example, were clearly alarmed. On his return trip from the United States, Kekkonen made a stopover in Copenhagen on 3 November 1961, where he discussed the situation briefly with Danish Foreign Minister Jens-Otto Krag, who expressed his belief, which concurred with Kekkonen's, that the Soviet note had been directed more toward NATO, Norway, and Denmark than toward Finland. Yet compared to the Norwegians and Swedes, the Danes remained relatively quiet during the note crisis episode.

The Swedish press was particularly concerned. The nation's two major dailies—*Dagens Nyheter* and *Svenska Dagbladet*—even called for a reassessment of Swedish neutrality policy in the light of the note crisis. Some columnists hinted that joining NATO would be reconsidered as a possible alternative for Sweden. The Swedish government, however—in part at the Finns' insistence—maintained a low profile. On 4 November, Erlander made a speech denying rumors of any changes in his country's foreign policy, and a few days later gave an interview stressing the importance of Swedish neutrality to Finland. Foreign Minister Unden, probably the most stringent supporter of neutrality, agreed. After Erlander's visit to Finland in early November, he further argued that Sweden could "trust the Finnish government to take care of this matter successfully."[9] The Swedes also tried to influence the United States not to get involved in public, which probably led to the secretiveness of the Gufler-Kekkonen meeting prior to the Finnish president's Novosibirsk trip.

The Norwegians reacted very differently from the Swedes. They let the Soviets know immediately after the note was made public that it might cause them to reevaluate the limitations placed on their NATO membership. A day before Kekkonen left for Novosibirsk, the Norwegian minister of defense, Gudmund Harlem, gave a speech in Copenhagen stressing that the Soviets were mistaken if they thought that Norway could be scared out of NATO. The eventual result, Harlem argued, was likely to be the opposite. Immediately prior to Kekkonen's trip to Novosibirsk, Norwegian Foreign Minister Halvard Lange began a week-long visit to the USSR during which he provided his hosts with a mixture of reassurance and deterrence. He argued that the Norwegian government had no intention of allowing NATO (or West German) forces—let alone nuclear weapons—to be stationed on its territory; unless, of course, there was a change in the existing strategic balance in Northern Europe. Or, to put it more succinctly, the Norwegian told his hosts that a change in Finno-Soviet relations would mean a more belligerent NATO policy by Norway.

Washington believed that the developments in Finno-Soviet relations stemmed from a Soviet hope to disrupt the broader security arrangements in Scandinavia. As Secretary of State Dean Rusk said in a telegram to the Helsinki Embassy on 21 November 1961, the Soviets were trying to break down the resolve of Scandinavians to "stand up to Soviets," and they wanted "in particular to reinforce neutral and pacifist sentiments and to increase anti-German feeling and acceptance of belief that FRG is becoming threat to status quo in Scandinavia." As a result of such broader Soviet designs, Rusk maintained, "it is no longer realistic to consider [the] Finnish-Soviet problem as bilateral matter," because "If Finland's friends continue [a] hands off policy there is grave risk that Soviets will achieve most of their objectives with serious consequences for entire position of free world." Despite the Finns' pleas that the Western powers stay out of the matter, Rusk concluded that "consequences for West of [the] course which events now seem to be taking would be too serious to justify continuation hands off policy." Rusk, who thought that a direct U.S. involvement would be counterproductive, therefore recommended that Finland's neighbors be encouraged to give the Finns moral and political support in form of public statements and, possibly, economic assistance.[10]

These issues came up during Deputy Under Secretary Johnson's meetings with the Danish, Norwegian, and Swedish ambassadors to the United States on 22 November 1961. The Danish ambassador, Knuth Winterfeldt, thought that one of the Soviet motives was to slow down Denmark's participation in COMBALTAP, but assured Johnson that no such effect was likely. Rather, he stressed Denmark's firm commitment to NATO and the COMBALTAP. Norwegian Ambassador Paul G. Koht argued that the Finns should be left to themselves to handle the matter—yet he also confirmed that Foreign Minister Lange had previously had a long talk with Soviet Foreign Minister Gromyko, in which the Norwegian had put forth a veiled warning about the impact any changes in Finno-Soviet relations might have on Norway's base policies. Lastly, the Swedish ambassador, Gunnar Jarring, maintained that the Finns were already well aware of the strong support from Scandinavia and the United States and that the best course for the moment was to remain silent in order "to avoid prejudicing Finland's position."[11]

The Scandinavians, who all stressed the significance of nonintervention when Kekkonen embarked on his visit to Novosibirsk, judged the situation correctly. A week later the note crisis had virtually withered away without any overt outside intervention. Whatever the Soviet aims regarding Scandinavia had been in provoking the crisis, they had not been successful in changing the basic framework of Scandinavian security. If anything, the note crisis had further confirmed the stability of the Nordic Balance and the correctness of its specific components that stemmed back to the late 1940s: Sweden's armed neutrality, Norway's and Denmark's NATO membership that was balanced with their continued "reassurance" of Soviet security needs, and Finland's "special relationship" with the USSR. Indeed, the Nordic Balance became a virtual liturgy for most Scandinavian governments trying to explain their respective foreign and security policies to the wider world, and was actively propagated as a de facto state of affairs (rather than just a theory) by, in particular, Norwegian political scientists during the mid-1960s.

EEC AND SCANDINAVIA: ACT II

Almost concurrently with the note crisis, some Scandinavian countries considered the possibility of joining the EEC. They were pulled toward the Six by the British announcement in July 1961 that it had decided to apply for membership. Denmark followed suit in August, though making it clear that it would only enter the Common Market if Great Britain did. In contrast, the Norwegians waited until April 1962, when the Oslo government announced that it wished to be considered for membership. Before that, the Finns had, not unexpectedly, made it clear that their foreign policy (read: relations with the USSR) did not permit the Helsinki government to consider membership, while the Swedes had chosen a middle road by applying for associate status in December 1961. Icelanders, still not even members of EFTA, stayed outside these developments, not least because of the bitterness toward Great Britain that still remained as a result of the 1950s fishing boundaries disputes.

These decisions clearly exemplified the different views that each of the Nordic countries took regarding European integration. With their speedy action, the Danes, who had discussed the matter in some detail with the British government in the spring of 1961, showed that they were clearly the most "continental" of the Scandinavians. In addition, the prospect that Denmark's two largest markets—Great Britain and West Germany—would be part of the same economic community naturally appealed to Viggo Kampmann's Social Democratic government. The Norwegians' hesitation, on the other hand, was clear proof not only of the internal divisions—between farmers against and business interests in favor of joining—but also of Oslo's concern over the EEC's political implications and the effect that Norway's membership might have on its continued efforts to reassure the Soviets. Given Norway's common border with the USSR, the Soviet factor naturally played a much larger role in Norwegian than in Danish thinking. Yet if Great Britain were to join, Norway could ill afford to remain outside. The Finnish decision not to apply for even associate membership was, in all likelihood, prompted by the note crisis and the unwelcome prospects of arousing another wave of wrath from the Soviet Union.

The Swedish position, however, was the one that mostly interested, and concerned, the United States. While Sweden's potential EEC membership seemed to offer a way of tying the country more firmly to the West, Washington could not support Stockholm's associate membership. It seemed that the Swedes wanted to acquire "the commercial advantages of the Common Market at no cost to themselves," as Under Secretary of State for Economic Affairs George Ball had put it already in May 1961 to British Ambassador Harold Caccia.[12] Making concessions to such neutrals as Sweden—which had coordinated its policy with Austria and Switzerland, other neutral members of EFTA—was bound to complicate unnecessarily the political nature of the EEC. It would also create problems for the strengthening of the Atlantic community that was linked together through NATO and, it was hoped, that would bring closer economic and political cooperation between the United States and the EEC. The issue was, in short, nothing less than the Grand Design of the Kennedy administration.

In the end, neither the British nor Scandinavian decisions regarding EEC membership applications made it very far. By late 1962, negotiations between France and Great Britain over the latter's entry to the Common Market failed, partly because of the British desire to keep its preferential trade ties with the Commonwealth intact and partly because of Charles de Gaulle's view that, to borrow Frank Costigliola's words, "admitting Britain to the Common Market would be admitting America's Trojan horse."[13] Thus, on 14 January 1963, the French leader announced that he was vetoing Great Britain's admission to the EEC because it was too dependent on the United States and too involved with the Commonwealth. The Danes and the Norwegians quickly pledged loyalty to the British. On 1 February 1963, the new prime minister of Denmark, Jens-Otto Krag (Viggo Kampmann had resigned on 3 September 1962 because of ill health), announced that "an isolated Danish entry is of no interest for us at the present time."[14] The Norwegians, who had not even entered into full negotiations with the EEC by January 1963, took a similar position. Meanwhile, the Swedes' application for associate membership was put on hold until the late 1960s.

In part, the episode proved how tied the Scandinavians still were to Great Britain, collectively their greatest trading partner. In addition, it had shown the reluctance of most Northern Europeans, save the Danes, to get entangled with the continent.

The French veto of January 1963 had also been a hard blow to the economic part of the Kennedy administration's Grand Design. The prospect that the EEC was bound to turn inward and build further walls against American trade interests in Europe at the cost of the Atlantic partnership seemed stronger than ever. Meanwhile, the hope that the Common Market could act as a vehicle of strengthening Western European unity weakened. Moreover, another part of the Grand Design, the MLF, was prompting some Northern Europeans to make disturbing initiatives in the field of nuclear weapons policy.

IN THE ZONE: NUCLEAR NONPROLIFERATION

Sweden's long-time Foreign Minister Bo Östen Unden was the first Northern European politician to seriously and openly approach the subject of nuclear disarmament in 1961. The Unden Plan, unveiled in a speech at the United Nations on 26 October 1961, called for the establishment of "nuclear-free clubs" of countries that would, under U.N. auspices, exert pressure on those countries possessing nuclear weapons to sign a test ban treaty and limit the development of nuclear weapons. The proposal, which came at the heels of the resumption of underground testing by both the United States and the USSR, outlined a number of such zones: the Balkans, a zone around the Baltic, a zone in the Middle East, and a zone in the Far East. Because much of the plan resembled the so-called Rapacki Plan—a Polish-sponsored and Soviet-inspired plan from 1957 that had called for a nuclear-free zone in Central Europe—Unden's proposal met with immediate endorsement from Moscow and Warsaw. Naturally, Washington scorned it.

When Unden's plan to make an inquiry about the establishment of a "nonnuclear club" was tabled as a U.N. resolution, it passed with strong support from Eastern European and most African and Asian countries. NATO nations, with the significant exceptions of Denmark and Norway, objected because such a plan seemed to call into question the existence and deployment of American nuclear weapons in Europe. Indeed, even within Sweden itself there was extensive criticism—accelerated by the note crisis that commenced only four days after the Unden Plan was revealed—about the strategically lopsided (in favor of the Soviets) nature of the scheme. President Kennedy argued further at a press conference in March 1962 that nuclear-free zone proposals were, at best, murky ideas with little practical significance because, he maintained: "If you have a missile that can carry a bomb 5,000 miles, does it really make that much [of a] difference, if you don't have a bomb stationed in this area but you have it 5,000 miles behind, which can cover that area?"[15] Thus, despite the scare provoked by the Cuban missile crisis in October 1962, the Unden Plan could have little chance of making a significant impact as an arms control initiative in the early 1960s.

In May 1963, however, Finland's President Kekkonen presented his plan for a nuclear-free Northern European zone. Concerned over the near-apocalyptic nature of the Cuban crisis, urged on by a desire to improve Finland's relations with the Soviet Union, and further encouraged by U.N. Secretary General U Thant's suggestion in the spring of 1963 that smaller countries should respond to the apparent stalemate in superpower disarmament talks by creating nuclear-free zones, Kekkonen used the prestigious Paasikivi Society as a forum for launching his first Nordic-Nuclear-Weapons-Free-Zone proposal (NNWFZ) on 28 May 1963. In a long speech that touched on the arms race, the world situation, and the general position of Finland and Scandinavia, Kekkonen referred to the Unden Plan and argued that it was time for the

Scandinavians to agree to a formal nuclear-free zone. Kekkonen reasoned that, "I am convinced of the fact that declaring Scandinavia a nuclear-free zone would significantly stabilize the position of all the region's countries. It would remove the northern European countries from the speculations, which the improvements in nuclear weapons strategy has caused and would guarantee that the region would remain outside international tensions."[16]

The Kekkonen plan can be seen largely as a case of preventive diplomacy. It seems to have been aimed in particular at countering the possibility that the Soviets would consider the West German support for the MLF—the American initiative that was meant to provide a measure of collective decision making among NATO countries regarding nuclear weapons—as another incident challenging their security. Kekkonen wrote to Sakari Tuomioja, Finland's ambassador to Sweden, about his motives in making the proposal, saying, "There is no reason to assume that the Soviet Union's reaction to stationing nuclear weapons to new areas close to its territory would be any less determined than the United States' [in the Cuban missile crisis]. It is clear that the Soviets are extremely suspicious over NATO's new nuclear plans (MLF) and concerned that it will somehow allow the West Germans to get their hands on these weapons."[17]

Other Scandinavians did not agree. In Oslo, Copenhagen, and Stockholm, the proposal seemed too similar to the ideas Khrushchev and Bulganin had put forth already in the late 1950s. It appeared to be an effort to shake the established security balance in Northern Europe and preclude the deterrence factor from the Norwegians' and Danes' security policies. If advanced, the Kekkonen Plan might, in the Scandinavian NATO members' view, undermine the Nordic Balance. Halvard Lange, the Norwegian foreign minister, commented in response to Kekkonen's proposal that the different countries' respective security policies had created the Nordic Balance framework, and "It must be in the interest of all countries that nothing is done that would change this situation." Prime Minister Gerhardsen went even further, charging that "the initiative for this has come from the Soviet Union," while the Danish foreign minister stated bluntly that "an agreement that confirms the factual state of affairs [i.e., a de facto nuclear-free Scandinavia] is in the opinion of the government neither necessary, nor desirable [and] can only be envisaged as a link in a general European security system." Similarly Swedish Prime Minister Erlander and Torsten Nilsson, the new foreign minister, immediately made a distinction between the Kekkonen and the Unden plans. The former, they argued, was too limited in space while the Unden Plan had included Central Europe as well. The Swedes further stressed that before any such plans could be implemented, there needed to be "a certain relaxing of tension in Europe."[18]

American opposition to the Kekkonen Plan, as well as Washington's cool attitude toward the Unden Plan, was based on, in addition to its mirroring of previous Soviet proposals, its potential to obstruct the plans for the MLF in

Europe. Originally conceived during the Eisenhower administration, the MLF was meant to satisfy the larger nonnuclear NATO allies' (particularly West Germany's) demands for greater participation in managing the West's nuclear deterrence. The MLF would consist of a number of surface ships with nuclear weapons that were to be administered multilaterally. In addition, the plan was expected to increase Atlantic and Western European unity at a time when Charles de Gaulle challenged it with his consistent opposition to Great Britain's EEC membership and critique of U.S. leadership. As President Kennedy stated, the MLF would "[i]ncrease [U.S.] influence in Europe and provide a way to guide NATO," while at the same time it would "weaken de Gaulle's control of the [EEC]."[19] That the Scandinavian allies consistently opposed the MLF naturally disheartened the Kennedy and Johnson administrations.

The MLF did not die as a result of any nuclear-free zone or club proposals. Indeed, although the NATO Council had approved the MLF a week prior to Kekkonen's speech at the Paasikivi society, the Kennedy administration did not push the idea in the summer of 1963. In large part this was the result of the negotiations that eventually led to the signing of the Limited Test Ban Treaty in July 1963; while involved in the talks with the British and the Soviets, the Americans hardly wanted to be branded as the ones expanding the control of nuclear weapons, no matter how limited that control would be, to the West Germans.

The Test Ban Treaty also undercut any potential Scandinavian support for the Kekkonen Plan. In the Scandinavian foreign ministers meeting in Stockholm on 5–6 September 1963, the Finnish initiative to include even a mention of the zone proposal in the final communique was refused by a strong veto from the new Norwegian foreign minister, Erling Wikborg. After that, the Kekkonen proposal was doomed to remain a particularly Finnish idea; it would linger on infrequently in Kekkonen's speeches, but fail to gather any significant support from Scandinavia. It was, moreover, all but ignored in Washington when a new president took over after those fateful shots in Dallas on 22 November 1963.

LBJ AND SCANDINAVIA

When Lyndon Johnson assumed the awesome duties of the presidency in November 1963, he was no stranger to Scandinavia. Only two months earlier, as vice president, Johnson, accompanied by his wife Lady Bird and older daughter Lynda Bird, included Scandinavia as part of his European trip. To such a larger-than-life figure as the Texan, visiting the barren lands of Northern Europe was hardly the highlight of his political career. The trip did, however, offer an opportunity to get out of Washington, where he had been snubbed by many of the "best and the brightest" of the Kennedy administration. While in Scandinavia, Johnson found a curious, at times even enthusiastic, audience. As historian Paul K. Conkin points out, Johnson's "break-away excursions into the disappointingly small crowds created a bit of [a] bond with the ordinary people [who] seemed to respond to his almost corny approach." The problem was, however, that "journalists ridiculed him, students noted the simplistic nature of his speeches, and sophisticates laughed at such gestures as a Texas barbecue he prepared for three thousand guests in Finland."[20]

Stylistically, it was clearly not the best way to introduce a soon-to-be president. Johnson had little understanding of the more reserved manners of the Scandinavians and acted for the most part as though he were running for office in Texas. Nevertheless, during his stops in Sweden, Finland, Norway, Denmark, and Iceland, Johnson gave a series of addresses designed to strengthen the ties between the United States and Scandinavia. At each stop, his speeches also served to symbolize the slightly different approaches the United States had taken vis-à-vis the five Nordic countries.

In Gothenburg, Sweden, Johnson clearly tried to repair the damage done to Swedish-American relations by the constant U.S. criticism of Sweden as the godless welfare state and the equally stringent Swedish notions that the United States lacked the social safety nets that were the pride of the Swedish welfare state. Johnson's speech, therefore, did not contain any comments on Swedish neutrality, on East-West relations, or on the Soviet threat. Instead, he "reluctantly" spent most of his time discussing the ways in which the Americans took care of their citizens, particularly "the little man." Johnson said, for example: "We believe that the individual without great economic power or great political power must be served by his government. His opportunity must be preserved. His rights, his liberty, his human dignity must be protected against those forces which he is powerless to control alone." And although the vice president included among such forces of evil, "the power of the government itself"—the central point in American criticism of the Middle Way—he went on to argue that the two societies were very much alike in their current hopes and policies: "We recognize that this tradition in America is akin to your traditions and the motivations of your own domestic objectives. In Sweden you would permit no man to starve; you want no family to live in slums, no child to mature without education, no aged citizen to languish without care for his illnesses." Similarly, Johnson maintained, "in America you would find these same values not only in the hearts of the people but in the heart of the public policies as well. We believe government must concern itself with maintaining a floor under the lives and opportunities of the people."[21] The speech embodied, indeed, the goals that were later sought under the rubrics of the Great Society and the War on Poverty. But it also stood in marked contrast to the criticism of the Swedish welfare state embarked on by President Eisenhower in his 1960 speech (see chapter 4), an unrelenting criticism of the Swedish welfare society as the culprit behind high suicide rates and rising crime.

Vice President Lyndon B. Johnson "campaigning" in Bodø, Norway, during his Scandinavian tour in September 1963.
Courtesy of the Lyndon B. Johnson Library.

Johnson's next stop was Finland. The idea for the vice president's tour had actually originated from the new U.S. ambassador to Finland, Carl Rowan, a 40-year-old African-American who had arrived in Finland in late 1962. Johnson's visit was a way for Rowan to further his own career by getting the attention of the White House for future benefit—in this he certainly succeeded because Johnson later appointed him director of the United States Information Agency (USIA). Rowan's career ambitions were also visible in the lavish preparations for the Finnish part of the tour. At every possible opportunity, the vice president would stop to shake hands with curious Finns and give out pens and other mementos—a practice the generally reserved Finns found infuriating. Indeed, his Finnish companion during the trip, the head of the Finnish Foreign Ministry's Political Section, Max Jakobson, felt that Lyndon Johnson "did not care one bit about Finland and would not even try to hide this lack of respect." President Kekkonen considered Johnson "a naive and stupid man, who acts as though he was engaged in his own political campaign."[22] Ironically, Johnson probably considered the visit to Finland, where he was greeted with large enthusiastic crowds, the most enjoyable part of his Scandinavian tour.

In Sweden, Johnson's task had been to praise the common ideas between the Middle Way and the Democratic party's domestic programs (however farfetched that link was). In Finland, his goal was to stress the continuance of Washington's quiet support for Finland's neutrality. This goal was reflected in the different tone that the vice president adopted once in Finland. In Helsinki, Johnson discussed U.S. foreign policy and the Test Ban Treaty, signed the previous month. Yet he did not embark on attacks against the Soviet Union. Instead, Johnson focused in his 7 September 1963 speech to the Finnish-American society on praising Finland's work in the United Nations. It was left for Kekkonen to play the Soviet card during his private talks with the vice president. Clearly, Kekkonen was hoping to rally some support for Finland's efforts to guard its economic interests in Western markets. He latched on to Johnson's comment that the Kennedy administration stressed the need for Finland to "remain strong in order to defend itself." Kekkonen, who clearly understood which strings to pull, replied by pointing out that because Finland had no control over issues of global war and peace, it "concentrated on building economic strength; it must continue to increase living standards in order that [the] Soviets [can]not overtake it and win Finnish workers to Communist ideology."[23]

Johnson continued on to Oslo, Copenhagen, and Reykjavík. Once on NATO territory, his tone changed slightly. Because the Norwegians were only lukewarm allies, Johnson felt it important to stress the reasons that bound Norway and the United States together. He reminded his Norwegian audience on 11 September 1963 "that the age of peril is still with us," and that "the time has not come when free men can drop their guard or cease their vigilance, for eternal vigilance is the price of liberty." He ended on a high note, referring to the important task: "to build and strengthen an Atlantic community to which we both belong—a community of like minded nations, not shackled by an imposed ideology but united by common ideals of democracy and freedom, depending for our strength on the soaring minds of free men."[24]

In Denmark, a country that was firmly involved in NATO's COMBAL-TAP, Johnson saw less of a need to stress the importance of vigilance so he focused on issues of economic and scientific cooperation. At the end of his speech in Copenhagen on 14 September, he did, however, remind his audience of the need to "keep that shield of our NATO alliance aloft, held firmly by our continuing unity and continuing resolve."[25]

In Iceland, Johnson displayed the U.S. government's uncertainty about the island republic's NATO ties. While speaking at the Icelandic-American Society's meeting, he stressed the virtues of the alliance. In particular, Johnson focused on the diversity of the 15 NATO countries and their common democratic heritage, and argued that the alliance was, in some ways, as diverse as the United States was with its 50 states. NATO rejected, he told the traditionally antiforeign (and often anti-American) Icelanders, "the concept of an alliance eroding the integrity of any of our cultures." Thus, aside from its diversity, NATO was "an alliance of equals," Johnson continued, pounding on a theme that was clearly aimed at negating the fears that had long existed in Iceland about the cultural impact of the presence of a large number of American troops that were stationed in the Keflavík base.[26]

They had by no means been a tour de force of American diplomacy, but Johnson's speeches displayed the differences and commonalities in U.S. policy toward the region. This was the first time that American diplomacy linked all five countries together with such a significant gesture as a vice president's tour. Thus, at every stop Johnson referred to the similarities of the northern lands to each other and to America, stressing particularly the values and traditions that could be identified as "Western." On the other hand, Johnson's rhetoric changed subtly as he moved from one country to another. In Sweden his main theme was helping the "little man," in Finland it was the support for neutrality, in Norway and Denmark it was the unity of NATO, and in Iceland it was the diversity of the alliance. Rather neatly, within a two-week period, Lyndon B. Johnson had captured the main outlines of U.S. policy in Scandinavia.

Yet he had not captured the hearts of the Nordics. Only two months after Johnson's visit to Scandinavia, an assassin's bullets killed Jack Kennedy and suddenly catapulted Lyndon Johnson to the White House. For most Scandinavians, Kennedy's murder on 22 November 1963 was a tragedy of immense proportions and the new president, whom they had so recently observed, a potentially unbalancing force for international relations. President Kekkonen probably captured the feelings of his counterparts in most Scandinavian capitals when he worried that "I know Johnson and await his presidency with utmost concern."[27]

Despite his whirlwind tour of Scandinavia, Lyndon Johnson had little interest in Scandinavia or, it seems, in Europe in general. Most of his energy would be spent in fighting two wars: the one he chose to escalate in Vietnam and the one that he hoped would eradicate poverty from the United States. The latter of these wars provided, for a brief period, heightened public interest in the socioeconomic structure of Scandinavia.

THE MIDDLE WAY—A MODEL OR A NIGHTMARE?

The title of an article in *U.S. News and World Report* on 23 November 1964 spelled out the sudden American interest in Scandinavian economic and social structure in a nutshell: "30 Years without Recession—How Sweden Does It." The article began by pointing out that, given Sweden's almost uninterrupted postwar record of economic growth, many American business analysts were looking at it as a possible model. The author attributed Sweden's impressive record to the high level of cooperation between the government, business interests, and labor unions, as well as to the fact that, despite a popular belief to the contrary, there had been no great effort to socialize Swedish industries. The result had been a long period of low unemployment and sustained economic growth throughout the postwar era. Sweden did have some problems, including housing shortages, inadequate number of doctors, lack of room in schools, and, of course, high taxes, which meant the "loss of some personal freedom" to the Swedes. Would the Swedish model work in the United States, the article asked. Not easily; Sweden was much smaller in size, had a far more homogenous population, and was famous for its long tradition of government-business-labor cooperation. One was hard pressed to find that last, rather crucial, legacy in the United States. By implication, however, the Swedish model was a desirable goal.[28]

The growing interest in the Middle Way had been noticeable already during the Kennedy administration. It bore a resemblance to the 1930s, when the New Dealers often searched abroad for alternative models to the American economic and social structure that was suffering from a severe depression. The 1960s, of course, had no similar depression, but after eight years under a Republican administration and a continued struggle to equalize the racially divided American society, the Democrats were certainly ready to try some form of social experimentation. A growing American interest in the Middle Way was evident in 1962–1963 when several articles—most of which were drafted with the help of the Swedish embassy in Washington—that were complimentary to the Swedish model appeared in such prominent journals as *Fortune* and *Business Week*. Titles such as: "How Swedish Free Enterprise Coexists with Socialism," "Sweden—a Free-Enterprise Welfare State," and "How Sweden Keeps the Labor Peace" were characteristic of a whole genre of articles that, rather clearly, praised certain features of the cooperative relationship between business, labor, and government in Sweden. Indeed, on 7 March

1963, the *Philadelphia Inquirer* reported that "President Kennedy's Advisory Committee on Labor-Management is studying closely the economy of Sweden, which has almost full employment [Sweden had less than 2 percent unemployment at the time], maintains a competitive position in the world market and has relatively few strikes and lockouts." The article also did a great service to Sweden's image by pointing out that, "Although it is widely believed in this country that Sweden is a socialist state, 90 percent of its industry is in private hands. The government interferes less in labor-management problems than in the United States and subsidies to industries with inadequate productivity are unknown." A few weeks later, the *Washington Post* continued the theme by maintaining that Sweden "is fast becoming an economic model for the world's most prosperous nation and its 185 million population."[29] This time around, Sweden's publicity contained little or no talk of high suicide rates or lax morals, which had been the main themes of articles on Scandinavia in the late 1950s and early 1960s.

In part such positive publicity—much of which occurred during the last months of Kennedy's and the first months of Johnson's presidencies—was due to a large-scale Swedish public relations campaign (dubbed "Meet Modern Sweden") aimed at improving the country's image and stimulating American public interest in Sweden in order to boost exports. It is hardly an accident, however, that the rush of positive publicity came just before Johnson launched his ambitious, albeit unsuccessful, domestic programs.

Such positive publicity naturally gave great delight to the Swedes and to the Scandinavians in general. Their socioeconomic experiment had paid off; the wealthiest and most powerful nation on earth was turning its eye on a region that had one of the smallest population bases and was often discarded as an insignificant actor in international politics. It was no wonder, then, that some heads were swelling in Northern Europe. Had the Scandinavian Social Democrats perhaps founded a peaceful utopia? A Danish writer, Henrik Stangerup, certainly thought so. In 1965 he wrote: "We are experiencing today in Scandinavia one of the most important experiments in world history. That may sound pretentious, yet it isn't. Scandinavia of today is the world's avant-garde society. What is taking place among us will happen in other countries tomorrow, as soon as they have reached a comparable level of freedom and welfare." Stangerup concluded that: "We simply have every imaginable opportunity to lead our lives in free development of our human and creative possibilities. If we only know to use our freedom and realize it in our lives, our experience . . . will be of profit [to] the entire world around us."[30]

It was bold talk, in part self-serving and without a doubt overly laudatory. Yet Stangerup's assessment contained a grain of truth: the Scandinavians had reached one of the highest living standards in the world by the mid-1960s, their populations were, for better or worse, provided for from cradle to grave, and the great majority of Scandinavians supported the governmental policies that had led them there. The Scandinavians, moreover, seemed to have thought that all this was exportable; that they had a mission to take the "blessings" of social democracy to the outside world—if not to the Western countries, at least to the undeveloped nations. Thus, it was no accident that in the 1960s, the Nordics became increasingly active in U.N. organizations designed to help third world countries. Sweden, which argued that such policies represented an international "mirror" of the country's domestic welfare programs, was the first to establish an official development aid program in 1962, with the other Scandinavian countries following suit. And although the Scandinavians rarely realized their ambitious goal of devoting 1 percent of GNP to development aid, they were among the top contributing members of the Organization for Economic Cooperation and Development (OECD); in contrast, the United States was, almost without exception, at the bottom of the list. The Scandinavians, with the Swedes at the helm, were clearly trying to "export," with limited results, the welfare model in the 1960s, the same time that Americans were coming under increased scrutiny because of their policies in Southeast Asia.

Perhaps ironically, however, the Scandinavian welfare state was running into some serious domestic trouble in the mid- and late 1960s. In Norway, the Gerhardsen Labor government was defeated in the 1965 *Storting* elections and replaced by a coalition of conservatives, centrists, and liberals. New Prime Minister Per Borten, although he did not cancel any of the social programs instituted since World War II, clearly stressed the importance of individual responsibility. In Denmark, the 1968 *Landsting* election resulted in the removal from power of the Danish Social Democrats, who were replaced by a center-right coalition. Prime Minister Hilmar Baunsgaard's cabinet quickly moved to cut the national budget. Only in Sweden did the Social Democrats remain in power, despite a strong protest vote in the 1968 elections. Although reports that Norway and Denmark were "turning away from socialism" were slightly overblown, there is no question that the Middle Way was, in a sense, on trial in the late 1960s.[31]

Because of these changes—as well as the fact that LBJ's Great Society was turning out to be less great than he had promised—the Scandinavian model, by the end of the Johnson administration, no longer held the appeal in the United States that it had in the early 1960s. Already in 1965–1966, several journals criticized the "spiritual poverty" and lack of "higher values" that seemed to have permeated Swedish society. In a manner that was reminiscent of President Eisenhower's statements in 1960, A. Zanker of *U.S. News and World Report* captured this revival of criticism. He wrote in February 1966: "If you wonder about the rewards of a 'Great Society' in which poverty and social troubles are absent, Sweden can provide an understanding . . . [it] is faced with a rising wave of crime and juvenile delinquency, as well as alcoholism, drug addiction, suicides and moral recklessness among teenagers."[32]

That last point, "moral recklessness," seems to have aroused some of the strongest conservative condemnations of where Sweden, and by proxy Scandinavia, was heading. In the September 1966 issue of *Christian Century*, for example, Deane W. Ferm wrote a damaging appraisal of the lack of religious interest and the resulting moral decay in Sweden. Only 5 percent of Swedes go to church regularly, Ferm complained, adding that official "Sweden today is definitely antichurch." Why was this the case? Ferm thought that it was partly the church's own fault: "One reason for this antagonism is that the church fiercely resisted social legislation and the rise of the common man. The Social Democratic Party, which has been dominant for over 30 years now, was forced to become anticlerical." The church's conservatism notwithstanding, Ferm found "unparalleled permissiveness in matters of sex." He gave examples: "Stark-naked women are shown on TV and in store window displays; bare bosoms are boorishly boring; Sweden's sex-slanted literature and pornographic publications make *Confidential* magazine look like the *Wall Street Journal*. In fact, the Swedes are having a tough time coming up with something that the public will consider shocking or even vulgar." Not only that, but sex education had been compulsory in lower grades since 1956, "everything" was discussed in these classes where "Audio visual aids do wonders!" As a result, 80 percent of Swedish boys and 65 percent of girls had sex by the age of 18, and almost half of all children were born out of wedlock. Ferm offered a practical explanation for this state of affairs by stressing one of the shortcomings of the Middle Way: "Undoubtedly this statistic is due in part to Sweden's critical housing shortage. In fact, couples who desire municipal housing can expect a place to live a full year earlier if the woman is pregnant." Indeed, even those Swedes who took the traditional route and got engaged were acting differently from the old moral codes, taking it for granted that such commitment implies sleeping together. The theory among young Swedes was clearly, Ferm added, that "the couple that sleeps together keeps together." The list of moral criticism went on. Abortion laws were constantly relaxed, and Ferm predicted that in a few years all one would need to do was to ask for one. Indeed, gender rights issues in general seemed to have gone way too far in Ferm's opinion, as "an unmarried woman and her baby are considered a family; school books actually refer to one-parent families [sic]." It was, indeed, high time to make the Swedish Lutheran church understand, Ferm ended his article, that its duty was to go out and bring salvation to these godless Swedes.[33]

By 1968, with the American presidential campaign under way, the tone regarding the Middle Way had dramatically changed from the positive appraisals of the early 1960s. The praise lavished on Scandinavia's very real economic success gave way to criticism over the Nordic countries' moral weaknesses. Many of the arguments were reminiscent of the publicity that Sweden had received during the Nixon-Kennedy campaign in 1960. Even mostly positive books like Frederic Fleisher's *The New Sweden: The Challenge of a Disciplined Democracy* (1967) and David Jenkins's *Sweden and the Price of Progress* (1968) reflected the trials of the Great Society at home by cautioning readers not to assume that the Swedish model could be replicated in the United States. It would have been foolhardy indeed to try and apply the methods and policies used in Sweden's homogeneous nation of 8 million to restructure a heterogeneous society of almost 200 million. In the early 1970s, the criticism increased further when Roland Huntford charged that the Swedes were new totalitarians who ignored severe societal stress and basic values of Western democracy in the name of building their social democratic utopia, in which "personality has been suppressed [and] the collective worshipped at the expense of the individual."[34]

But what of the Scandinavian views of America? They were, as always, bifurcated. On the one hand, the Scandinavians still held the United States in high regard; they were envious of the material well-being in North America and generally receptive to American popular culture. But an undercurrent of criticism was growing. An example of latent anti-Americanism in Scandinavia in the 1960s was the cultural clash in Iceland that centered around the supposed "invasion" of U.S. popular culture via the TV station that operated at the Keflavík base.

A TV WAR

During the Democratic administrations of the 1960s, there was relatively little Icelandic opposition, save from the local communist party, to the existence of the Keflavík base itself. NATO membership was not challenged as it had been periodically in the 1950s. However, the fears about the effects of Americanism on Icelandic culture still disturbed many nationalists of this young republic. In the 1960s, such xenophobia tended to focus on the corrupting effects that U.S. popular culture might have on the country's youth—a concern naturally felt in most European countries as American movies, music, consumer goods, and TV shows became the most visible U.S. export item.

In 1955 the Icelandic government had granted permission for the Keflavík base to operate its own TV station. Named TFK, the station was originally allowed to have a 50-watt transmitter, which limited its reach to the base and its immediate proximity. In 1961, however, Iceland allowed TFK to have a 250-watt transmitter, which meant that the TV station could reach most homes in Reykjavík and, therefore, most of Iceland's population. At the same time, the growing prosperity in Iceland, due in part to the existence of the U.S. base, made it possible for Icelanders to buy TVs at a high rate. The end result was that by the mid-1960s, American programming was suddenly reaching large numbers of Icelandic homes, a fact that alarmed many nativists. In March 1964, 60 prominent Icelandic intellectuals presented the *Althing* with an appeal that called for limiting American television transmission to the confines of the U.S. base in Keflavík. The appeal maintained that, "We believe that in many ways it is dangerous, as well as dishonorable for the Icelanders as a civilized, independent nation, to permit a foreign state to operate a television station in this country, reaching more than half the population."[35]

The critics of TFK employed a "cultural" argument in their campaign; they argued that television was such an influential medium that it had the potential to destroy Icelandic culture by forcing American "trash" down people's throats. This argument against an abundance of foreign programming and its corrupting effects on national culture was not unique to the Icelanders. The Icelanders, however, made an added point, arguing that an abundance of foreign programming, in a foreign language and by a foreign operator, was against the principle of national sovereignty, especially because the Keflavík operators dominated the waves. The protesters referred to Icelandic laws that stipulated that the media must be "impartial." TFK did not, they maintained, comply with this requirement.

Like most other instances, such nativist appeals against American culture had only limited popular support. The substance of the argument was most important for the intellectuals. Soon after the plea was publicized, the *Althing* was presented with a contrary appeal signed by almost 15,000 Icelanders. They expressed the concern that if the state were to place limits on TFK's programming rights, their TV sets would be rendered useless—there was virtually no Icelandic TV programming at the time. Although the cultural and political arguments against widespread American programming may have reflected some deep-rooted concerns about foreign influence in a country that had been independent for only two decades, the economic argument was clearly on the side of TFK. The majority of the Icelandic population wanted to enjoy the benefits of prosperity in their homes just as much as their counterparts in other Western countries.

The Icelandic TV war of the 1960s ended with a compromise of sorts: to avoid an anti-American backlash, the Americans themselves imposed limits on their programming, while the *Althing* granted the Icelandic State Radio adequate funds to begin six-day TV programming in 1967. The TV debate in Iceland, an expression not so much of anti-Americanism but of nativism directed against any kind of foreign presence and influence, thus withered away. It did, however, exemplify the continued difficulty that the Americans had in trying to find common ground with the small island republic, a difficulty that had existed already in the 1940s and would linger on well into the 1970s. Despite Johnson's attempts to assure the Icelanders during his trip to Reykjavík in September 1963 that NATO was a partnership of equals and that each country's culture was not to be jeopardized by its membership in the alliance, the Icelanders continued to guard their national heritage with a jealousness that brought the country of 200,000 into conflicts with its large ally, a nation of 200 million.

In their resistance to American cultural penetration, the Icelanders displayed clear traces of isolationism that, in addition to the nation's small size, removed the Icelanders further from the center stage of international relations. Although they were members of NATO, they had little interest in the alliance's external relations or, indeed, in the shifting pendulum of East-West relations. The other four Scandinavian governments, however, played a more active role in the gradual shift from high tension to détente in the 1960s. In part, this activism reflected their limited interest in, or even rejection of, the Cold War as a normal state of international relations. They could not, of course, dictate to the superpowers how to conduct foreign policy. They could, however, encourage and, at times, mediate.

MIDWIVES TO DÉTENTE

In addition to their efforts toward nuclear arms limitations in the 1960s, the Scandinavians—both neutrals and allied ones—showed a clear desire to promote détente. In the years following the erection of the Berlin Wall and the note crisis, the Scandinavians, always uneasy about belonging to a bloc, latched on to different initiatives that were, or seemed to be, designed to promote an easing of East-West tensions in Europe. The reasoning was simple enough: An atmosphere of reduced tensions improved the sense of security for small countries such as the Scandinavian ones.

In part the work toward détente was linked to President Kekkonen's efforts to embark on some more preventive diplomacy and relax the potential that the northernmost part of Scandinavia would become a focus of international tension in the future. In the 1960s, the so-called Northern Cap—an area that included the Svalbard and Bear Islands, the Kola peninsula, and the parts of Norway, Sweden, and Finland located north of the arctic circle—began to gain increased significance in U.S. and NATO strategy. This increase was due largely to increased Soviet buildup in the Kola peninsula, which, although it would reach its most significant proportions in the late 1970s and early 1980s, was threatening to disturb the Nordic Balance. Thus Kekkonen proposed in the early 1960s—with little success—a treaty arrangement that would neutralize the border area between Finland and Norway. The Soviet-Norwegian frontier was left outside of Kekkonen's proposal, but it certainly would have been influenced by such a pact.

The Norwegians would have none of it. At the time they were more influenced by the ideas of such Norwegian experts on defense and diplomacy as Nils Örvik, who had written a study on the issue for Harvard University's Center for International Affairs in September 1963. Unlike Kekkonen, Örvik argued that Finnish, and Scandinavian, security would be strengthened if Norway and Denmark firmed up their ties to NATO and accepted the stationing of nuclear weapons in their territory. Although successive Norwegian and Danish governments had refused such ideas since the 1950s, their representatives did work within NATO to promote a more fruitful dialogue between the East and West. Both governments also renewed high-level contacts with Moscow in the mid-1960s. In February 1964 Danish Prime Minister Krag met Khrushchev in Moscow, and the Soviet leader came for a return visit to Copenhagen in June. A month later, Khrushchev visited Prime Minister Gerhardsen in Oslo, and the Norwegian returned the visit, after Khrushchev's fall, in June 1965 to talk with the new Soviet leadership in Moscow.

Perhaps more significant than these bilateral meetings, however, was the role that Denmark and Norway played as some of the earliest and strongest NATO proponents of a European security conference. During a NATO meeting in June 1966, the Danes suggested that a European security conference that would include the United States and Canada could be a useful tool for improving the international atmosphere in the continent. Although this proposal met with a rather cool reception, the Scandinavians did play a key part in drafting the so-called Harmel Report (named after Belgian Foreign Minister Pierre Harmel). Approved by all members of the alliance in 1967, the Harmel Report stressed the need to redefine NATO's political role. It maintained that the alliance should proceed on a double track: while continuing its role as a defensive organization aiming to preserve the military balance, NATO should encourage its member countries to individually and collectively take on the task of improving relations with the Soviet bloc. Or, as the declaration put it, NATO should "pursue the search for progress toward a more stable relationship in which the underlying political issues can be solved."[36] To the Scandinavians, the most appealing phrase of the Harmel Report was the one that insisted that "military security and a policy of détente are not contradictory but complementary."[37]

The Harmel Report was a result of the changing dynamics within NATO and of the growing resentment toward U.S. leadership, exemplified throughout the 1960s by French President Charles de Gaulle's policies. In June 1966, the founder of the Fifth Republic visited Moscow and stressed, as he did during his follow-up visits to Poland and Rumania, the view that the division of Europe was a "European" issue, implying that the United States and Great Britain did not need to be involved. To make his independent stand more substantive, the French president withdrew his country from NATO's integrated military structure during the same year. De Gaulle's bold talk and shows of independence were probably major reasons behind the Warsaw Pact's Bucharest Declaration of July 1966, which renewed the call for a European conference on security and cooperation. While the Scandinavian NATO members saw de Gaulle's actions largely as a futile effort to recreate some of France's lost grandeur, his strong rhetoric and some of his actions did help in reawakening the continued uneasiness felt in Denmark and Norway about belonging to a bloc. Indeed, in Denmark a debate ensued in 1966–1967 about ending Scandinavian participation in NATO when the alliance's initial 20-year term ended in 1969. Most feelings, however, were directed toward promoting policies along the lines of the Harmel Report.

The key factor that allowed for a European détente to take hold in the late 1960s was the changing policies of the Federal Republic of Germany (FRG). In the mid-1960s, the Hallstein Doctrine—which meant that West Germany would refuse to have diplomatic relations with any state (other than the USSR) that recognized East Germany—came under growing criticism within West Germany and would by the end of the decade give way to Willy Brandt's *Ostpolitik*. The Scandinavians, particularly the Swedes, were able to claim some of the credit for the eventual successes of the Soviet-West German rapprochement that ensued.

The Scandinavians' role as midwives to *Ostpolitik* was due to a twist of fate that had forced the principal architect of that policy, Willy Brandt, to spend a large portion of his life in exile in Northern Europe. In 1933 he had fled the Nazis to Norway, where he was active as a journalist, attended the University of Oslo, worked against Hitler's regime, and was stripped of his German citizenship in 1938. He became a Norwegian citizen. The Nazis, although they imprisoned Brandt briefly during the occupation of Denmark and Norway in 1940, did not recognize him; Brandt was able to escape to Sweden. Between 1940 and 1945, he was active in the neutral country, crossed the border to Norway several times, and returned to Oslo after V-E Day. Only in 1948 did Brandt become a German citizen again and enter into politics as a member of the Social Democrats (SPD), the major opposition party. The SPD provided Brandt, by then a legendary figure, a medium for a rapid rise to power: in 1949, he was elected to the *Bundestag*; in 1957, he became the governing mayor of Berlin; in 1966, the foreign minister; and in 1969, the chancellor of the Federal Republic of Germany (FRG).

The West German leader thus owed much to the Scandinavians who had adopted him during World War II. Brandt spoke fluent Norwegian and Swedish. Both his first wife, Carlota, and his second wife, Rut, were Norwegians. He knew most of the leading Social Democratic politicians of Scandinavia—Erlander, Unden, Palme, Lange, Gerhardsen, and so on—and kept in touch with them throughout the rest of his life. In Norway and Sweden, Brandt had found, as he put it, "what it means for state and society to be involved in a constant process of shedding outworn concepts, and that material want can be banished, and the democratic idea carried beyond the civic and state framework into wide areas of society."[38] Clearly, it had an impact on the framing of the SPD's domestic programs once Brandt returned to Germany. Most significantly for the purposes of this work, however, Brandt found the Scandinavians—particularly the Swedes—eager to assist in laying down the foundation of *Ostpolitik* in the 1960s.

In May 1966, after months of behind-the-scenes activity, the Soviets and West Germans agreed that Sven Backlund, the Swedish consul-general in Berlin, would arrange a meeting between Brandt and Pyotr Abrassimov, the Soviet ambassador to the GDR. Over drinks at the Swede's residence in Pucklerstrasse, Dahlem, on Sunday 8 May, in a "semi-private" setting (as Brandt put it), he and Abrassimov began down the long road that eventually resulted in a series of treaties in the early 1970s. A month later, they met again at Backlund's residence during Sweden's National Day reception. Brandt also took Backlund and his wife to a meeting at the Soviet embassy in East Berlin on 12 October 1966. After the dinner, Abrassimov, Backlund, and Brandt conversed past midnight and reached an understanding that in order to successfully work toward a Soviet-FRG rapprochement, the various contentious issues could be "bracketed," i.e., the negotiators could set aside more difficult ones and begin dealing with less controversial topics such as trade and culture. A similar meeting took place in November. Because the SPD had yet to consolidate its hold on power in the FRG, these meetings, which Backlund thought "might well acquire 'historic' significance,"[39] did not yield immediate results. However, they were significant in building up the contacts necessary for Brandt's policies once he gained a position of power. In other words, while encouraging détente within NATO, Brandt's Scandinavian friends also played a role in paving the way for the eventual successful implementation of *Ostpolitik*. They acted, in short, as midwives to European détente.

CRITICIZING THE SUPERPOWERS I: VIETNAM

In the late 1960s, the Vietnam War produced the most serious rift in the Scandinavian-American relationship since the end of World War II. In particular, the war gave the Swedes a chance to return some of the verbal abuse that the Middle Way had endured in the United States. The fact that, aside from Canada, Sweden played host to the largest number of American draft evaders naturally infuriated both the Johnson and, later on, the Nixon administrations. Although the criticism never occupied a center stage in the international arena, it did lead to a virtual break in Swedish-American diplomatic relations in the aftermath of the Christmas bombings of 1972. The roots of such a severe conflict lay, however, in the 1960s.

In part, the Swedish concern over Vietnam was linked to the country's increased interest in the developing world. Since the days of Dag Hammarskjöld, the Swedes had been pioneers of U.N. efforts to bridge the economic gap between the first and the third worlds (like most "firsters," the Swedes had less interest in bridging the gap with the second world) as the decolonizing process unraveled. Alva and Gunnar Myrdal, probably Sweden's best known intellectuals, became particularly active in this field during the 1960s, and saw the American war effort in Southeast Asia as a serious disservice for the type of global social engineering the Swedes were interested in. The element of racism that was part of the Vietnam War and the American atrocities in Vietnam—which were always more prominently featured in the Swedish press than in those of their adversaries—were, to many Swedes, only further proof of the arguments that Gunnar Myrdal had presented in his *American Dilemma* already in the 1940s. To the Swedes, involved in a quest to enhance their profile as a type of a moral voice in the world, the Vietnam War offered an opportunity to criticize more than the actual war effort; it enabled them to focus attention on the many evils that the Middle Way had suppos-

An October 1967 demonstration in Stockholm against American policy in Vietnam. American involvement in Southeast Asia became one of the sore points in U.S. relations with Scandinavian countries, particularly with Sweden. ("Stöd FNL" means "Support the NLF.")
Courtesy of the National Archives.

edly eradicated. Among the most important of these were racism and economic inequality, both notably absent from the homogeneous and wealthy Sweden of the 1960s.

In retrospect, the best known Swedish critic of U.S. policy in Vietnam was Olof Palme, who in 1969 became the prime minister of Sweden at the age of 41. Palme's rise had been meteoric, helped immeasurably by his political mentor, Tage Erlander. Before becoming the Social Democratic Party's grand old man's prize student (and private secretary) in 1954, however, Palme had enjoyed his own American experience: he spent his senior year at Kenyon College in Ohio in 1947–1948. Prior to returning to Sweden to obtain a law degree from the University of Stockholm in 1951, Palme toured the United

Finland's President Urho Kekkonen greets American and Soviet SALT
negotiators in July 1971. The talks that lay the basis for the 1972 SALT
I Treaty were mostly conducted in Helsinki, highlighting the significance
of neutral countries as bridge builders between East and West. The
leader of the U.S. delegation, Gerard Smith, is shaking hands with
Kekkonen.
Courtesy of the National Archives.

States extensively, visiting more than thirty states. He had also become a
Social Democratic political activist and served as the president of the
National Swedish Union of Students, a post that brought him into contact
with Erlander. It also gave Palme his first touch with Vietnam: in 1953, the
26-year-old student activist spent three months in Southeast Asia and became
a critic of French policy there. The criticism resurfaced in July 1965 when
Palme, by then the minister of communications in Erlander's cabinet, gave a
speech in which he criticized the U.S. policy in Vietnam and expressed sympathy for the suffering of the Vietnamese people. Despite the protests of the
U.S. ambassador to Sweden, Graham Parsons, Swedish Foreign Minister
Torsten Nilsson—who had earlier publicly expressed his hopes that the conflict would not escalate—refused either to reprimand Palme or to issue an official apology to the U.S. government. The Swedish-American brawl over
Vietnam had begun.

To some extent, the mounting Swedish concern over American policy in
Vietnam was in line with the country's desire to serve as a mediating force in

international conflicts. In 1966, Erlander and Nilsson decided to establish a secret channel of communication, code-named ASPEN, that nurtured contacts to Hanoi and the National Liberation Front (NLF). The initiative, which lasted from 1966 to 1968, proved of little practical use except that it curbed official Swedish criticism of the war. On the other hand, the Swedes did invite the Johnson government's wrath when they allowed the Bertrand Russell International War Crimes Tribunal to hold its session—essentially a forum in which prominent intellectuals condemned U.S. policy in Vietnam— in Stockholm in May 1967. The Swedish government encountered further criticism from Washington when the Swedish Vietnam Committee organized a mass demonstration against U.S. policy in Stockholm the next year and invited Nguyen The Can, Hanoi's ambassador to Moscow, to lead the protesters. Palme, by now the minister of education, walked alongside Can and gave a critical speech that ended with the following denouncement: "If one is to speak of democracy in Vietnam it is obviously represented to a much higher degree by the NLF than by the United States and its juntas."[40] Again, despite strong protests from Ambassador William Heath, Erlander and Nilsson denied that Palme had been out of line. In response, Johnson called Heath back to the United States and did not nominate a new ambassador.

Such an obvious conflict in American-Swedish diplomatic relations did not go unnoticed by the American media. The *U.S. News and World Report*, for example, reported in March 1968 about Sweden's open "hate America" campaign. "[B]aiting the U.S. is almost a national pastime in Sweden," the magazine reported, comparing, rather unconvincingly, the anti-Vietnam rallies held in Sweden to the Nazi rallies of the 1930s in Germany. Later the magazine took issue with Sweden's generous policies toward allowing draft dodgers into the country. While in Sweden, these young American males— approximately 100 were granted asylum on "humanitarian grounds" by the fall of 1968—were, according to *U.S. News and World Report*, in for a "rude awakening." They were, if nonwhite, subjected to racism; all of them found it hard to find a job; many ran into social problems; and some resorted to alcohol abuse. Sweden turned out to be no paradise for the young American men evading the war, although most of the problems can be explained by pointing out the difficulties encountered in trying to adjust to a different society, a different climate, and a different culture. Such difficulties were made no easier by the fact that few of the draft dodgers thought of their stay in Sweden as permanent, and thus had less of an incentive to try and adjust to the Swedish lifestyle.[41]

The 28 October 1968 issue of *U.S. News and World Report* also noted another important point about official Swedish attitude toward the United States by stressing the Stockholm government's apparent lessening of criticism. Why was this the case? In part, the recall of William Heath in the spring of 1968 must have concerned Swedes. There was also talk on Capitol Hill about the possibility of imposing economic sanctions on Sweden. Peace talks had begun in Paris. Yet the most likely explanation for the lessening of anti-American activity had little to do with the United States. Rather, it can be explained by the refocusing of Swedish and Scandinavian criticism toward the actions of the Soviet Union in August 1968.

CRITICIZING THE SUPERPOWERS II: CZECHOSLOVAKIA

The criticism of America and things American was hardly a symptom of all-out anti-Americanism in Scandinavia. The Swedes along with other Scandinavians (with the notable exception of the Finns) were equally eager to criticize the Soviet Union. It was as if Scandinavia—most often Sweden—wished to play the role of a moral voice in international affairs by criticizing any and all actions that violated international norms.

The Warsaw Pact invasion of Czechoslovakia in August 1968 certainly was one such incident. After coming into power in January 1968, moderate Czech party leader Alexander Dubcek announced that his aim was to "give communism a human face." In March, the Soviets called a Warsaw Pact meeting and warned the Czechs not to go too far with their plans of "liberalization." In April, however, the Dubcek government published a new Czech party program. It sought to extend parliamentary rights, to permit free movement abroad, and to end censorship. The program created hopes of further reform within Czechoslovakia but raised fears among the communist elites in other East European countries about a possible spillover effect of reformist sentiments that might follow if the Czechs were allowed more reforms. Indeed, in mid-July, a meeting of the so-called group of five (Soviets, East Germans, Poles, Hungarians, and Bulgarians), which Dubcek refused to attend, ordered the Czech leader to end the "Prague Spring." He did not abide, and the group of five eventually launched its invasion on the morning of 21 August. Faced with little resistance, the invaders restored totalitarian control and expelled reformers from party ranks. Dubcek was eventually appointed the Czechoslovakian ambassador to Turkey. A few months later, in Poland, Brezhnev made the Czechoslovakian invasion the basis of a doctrine that would carry his name when he announced that the Warsaw Pact countries had the right and duty to intervene in a socialist country if its socialist system was being threatened. The message was clear: not only was there to be no "liberation," but even evolutionary development away from totalitarian socialism in Eastern Europe would be prevented by the Soviets, if necessary with military force.

The crushing of the Prague Spring and the announcement of the Brezhnev Doctrine caused some serious soul-searching among Scandinavians regarding the roles they had played in promoting détente with the USSR or in critiquing the United States. For the NATO members of Scandinavia, the Warsaw Pact invasion was instrumental in ending any serious debate about leaving the alliance at the end of their original 20-year term (1949–1969). Much like the Hungarian events of 1956, the crushing of the Prague Spring highlighted the continued significance of the East-West division in Europe and certainly served to undermine the arguments of Charles de Gaulle regarding the potential of solving Europe's problems without the United States. Anti-American nativism in Iceland declined and criticism of the Vietnam War abated in Denmark and Norway. Similarly, pressure toward détente experienced a momentary lapse within NATO.

The official Swedish reaction to the Soviet invasion was harsh. "My thoughts go back to 1948," Prime Minister Tage Erlander told a mass meeting in the old university town of Upsala on the night of the invasion. He added, "The Soviet Union and the other countries participating in this morning's invasion have gravely violated the principle of nonintervention," and joined in with his fellow Scandinavians in protesting the events in Prague.[42] To Erlander, however, the Czech events also provided an opportunity to redeem himself in the eyes of those critics who, in referring to the anti-Vietnam War policies of Sweden, charged that the Stockholm government had somehow abandoned the principles of neutrality. Indeed, only six months prior to the crackdown in Prague, the *Riksdagen* had been involved in a serious debate on the balance or imbalance of Swedish neutrality. Thus, the Warsaw Pact invasion allowed Erlander and Foreign Minister Nilsson to show that they were by no means "tilting" toward either side in the Cold War, as their critics had charged.

For the Finns the issue was more difficult. Tradition offered only very dubious guidance about how to react. During the Hungarian crisis in 1956, President Kekkonen anxiously debated what to do when the United Nations voted on resolutions condemning the Soviet invasion, and instructed his envoy to refrain from taking a stand against the USSR. It had caused an uproar in Finland, where charges of immorality had been launched against the newly elected president. This time he had, to be sure, a much firmer domestic base, having been reelected by a wide margin in January 1968. This time Kekkonen's foreign policy goals and his hopes of playing midwife in both the Strategic Arms Limitation Talks (SALT) and the potential Conference on Security and Cooperation in Europe (CSCE) meetings could easily be dashed if Finland openly criticized the USSR. Thus, he showed restraint or, as his critics would argue, cowardice. The Finnish government, through its foreign minister Ahti Karjalainen, simply expressed its "hope" in the United Nations "that foreign forces will be withdrawn from the country and that all external restraints will be removed as soon as possible in accordance with the wishes of the people of Czechoslovakia."[43]

The invasion of Czechoslovakia had another significant consequence in Finland. It deepened the rift between two rival factions of the FCP. While the Stalinist minority remained loyal to the Kremlin, the majority faction, led by Aarne Saarinen, joined the "Eurocommunists" of Italy and France in openly criticizing the Soviet Union's policies. No longer, it seemed, could the Soviets count on the Finnish communists to act as their unequivocal supporters in Finland.

In the end, the Warsaw Pact invasion that so brutally ended the Prague Spring did not permanently crush hopes of East-West détente. To be sure, President Johnson did cancel a summit meeting that had been planned between him and Brezhnev. Perhaps because the invasion was relatively bloodless, perhaps because it seemed to change very little in the general political dynamics in Europe, the Czechoslovakian invasion slowed down the implementation of *Ostpolitik* and the momentum toward European détente only momentarily. Meanwhile, the Scandinavians contemplated their economic role in a gradually uniting Europe.

SCANDINAVIANISM'S LAST STAND? THE NORDEK DEBACLE

For the Scandinavians, Richard M. Nixon was hardly a welcome choice as the new American president. Since his role in the anticommunist crusades of the early 1950s, the Californian had come to symbolize the "reactionary" tendencies in his country that often disturbed not only the left-wing politicians in Scandinavia, but many moderates around Europe. His choice of vice president was unfortunate—Spiro Agnew appeared an even more conservative, if not outright racist, politician than the number one man on the Republican ticket in 1968. Domestically, observers expected the Republican ascendancy to end the Democratic Great Society programs that Scandinavians had generally viewed as a positive step toward building a society somewhat akin to the Middle Way. In foreign policy, Nixon appeared—although he had ducked the difficult questions about Vietnam during the election campaign—ready to take a hard line in Southeast Asia. That he promised to end the war "with honor" gave little comfort to the Scandinavians. That he would also bring with him an era of Soviet-American détente and an opening of Sino-American relations was hardly evident in late 1968.

What was evident was the fact that by 1968 the Scandinavians faced important decisions regarding their place in the European state and economic systems. In 1967, another French veto of a British application blocked Scandinavia's possibility of joining the EEC, but the continent's growing economic interdependence was placing increasing demands on all the Nordic countries to get more involved in economic integration. Yet political problems prevailed. The Swedes and the Finns were not ready to compromise their neutrality by joining a community that had a clear political function. The note crisis of 1961 loomed large in the minds of Finland's political leaders, and the events in Czechoslovakia in 1968 could not but help strengthen Finland's need to adhere to a strict policy of neutrality. The Swedes had gone to great lengths to display their neutrality in open criticism of both the United States and the Soviet Union. Moreover, even the NATO countries of Scandinavia were—perhaps with the exception of Denmark—far from devoted to the cause of joining the EEC. Indeed, Iceland was not even a member of the EFTA. In the sphere of economic integration, the challenges were daunting for the reluctant Europeans.

Since they had joined the EFTA in the early 1960s, the Scandinavians had sporadic conversations regarding further economic cooperation among themselves and/or with the rest of Western Europe. Indeed, during the Kennedy round of GATT, the five countries coordinated their policies relatively successfully. At the same time the potential for true Northern European economic integration—as opposed to the traditional model of cobweb integration—was never higher than in the years 1968–1970. The Nordic Economic Union, or NORDEK, was first suggested by the Danes after the French (and de Gaulle) rebuffed the British in their effort to join the EEC in 1967–1968. Particularly to Denmark, which was dependent on selling much of its agricultural produce to the continent, EEC seemed like an inward looking institution unable to come to grips with the common economic interests that the Danes had expected would lead to the fusion of EEC and EFTA.

Because of the stalemate in EEC-EFTA discussions that resulted from de Gaulle's extremely negative stand vis-à-vis British membership, the Danes suggested that Northern Europeans should increase their cooperation in order to safeguard their economic interests. During the 1968 meetings of the Nordic Council and during gatherings among Northern European prime and foreign ministers, the Scandinavians—with the exception of Iceland—hammered out proposals for the creation of NORDEK. It was clear from the outset that the most enthusiastic proponents were the Danes, who viewed NORDEK as a way of improving their bargaining position and eventually joining the EEC; accordingly, for example, external tariffs were to be set at the same level as those of the EEC. NORDEK was also limited to economic questions—the Finns and Swedes were afraid of the implications any political clauses might have on their neutrality, while the Norwegians (and to some extent the Danes) worried about what effect association with the two neutrals might have on their relationship with NATO countries. The Scandinavians did, however, agree on a number of issues that had previously seemed intractable. For example, they reached agreement on coordinating fishery policies and reducing raw material and agricultural tariffs. Eventually, in early November 1969, the NORDEK plan was approved by Nordic prime ministers and the presidium of the NC. In April 1970, the plan was to be backed up by the full Nordic Council and then be submitted to the national parliaments for final ratification. All seemed to be going smoothly. Yet, external developments did not allow the planned union to go ahead.

In April 1969, Charles de Gaulle resigned. His successor, Georges Pompidou, made it clear that he had no objections to Britain's joining the EEC. Six months later, the Social Democrat Willy Brandt, a long-time supporter of Britain's EEC membership, came to power in West Germany. The two leaders agreed in December 1969 that negotiations with Britain and other applicants to the EEC should continue rapidly. This decision, and the prospect that a deal might be struck in the near future between EFTA and EEC, reduced the Danes', as well as the Norwegians' and Swedes', enthusiasm for NORDEK. On the other hand, the Finns, always wary of a hostile Soviet reaction, grew concerned over the type of Western move that now seemed to be in the cards. In late December, the Finnish government advised its Scandinavian counterparts that if any of them entered into direct talks with the EEC, Finland was unlikely to continue with the plans for NORDEK. The Norwegians and Danes assured Finland that, if they ever were to join the EEC, NORDEK could be revised to meet the needs of Finnish neutrality and its special relationship with the Soviet Union; nonetheless, Finland eventually refused to sign the Northern European pact in the spring of 1970. Clearly under pressure from the USSR, particularly after a strong swing to the right in the March 1970 parliamentary elections, President Kekkonen and Prime Minister Karjalainen chose not to challenge Moscow.

Why were the Soviets so opposed to Finland's joining NORDEK? The answer lies largely in Finland's foreign trade patterns since the signing of the FINEFTA agreement in 1961. Despite the concurrent most-favored nation pact, Finno-Soviet trade had gradually declined during the 1960s. NORDEK might have led to a continuation of this trend, which caused some concern in Moscow. Yet this was hardly the only explanation. Aside from being pressured by the Soviets, the Finns also had their own plans of working out a deal with the EEC that freed them from the political burden of having a NATO country, like Denmark, do their bidding.

NORDEK, which turned out to be the last full-blown effort to create a Nordic common market and move Scandinavia from cobweb integration to economic union, failed largely because economic issues could simply not be divorced from political ones in the Cold War world. The Danes, and to a lesser degree the Norwegians and Swedes, viewed NORDEK primarily as a means to a larger end: joining the EEC from an enhanced position. The Finns, meanwhile, although eager to enter into an agreement with the Six, could not act without taking into account the political pressures from the East.

Thus, in the early 1970s, the Scandinavians redefined their relationships to European economic cooperation. The end result was a myriad of arrangements that diminished the prospects of Scandinavian integration: Iceland joined EFTA in 1970; Finland concluded free trade agreements simultaneously with the EEC and the Council for Mutual Economic Aid (COMECON) in 1972; after a successful referendum, Denmark joined the EEC in 1973; the same year Sweden, while rejecting full membership, signed a free trade agreement with the EEC. Perhaps the most perplexing case was Norway, which applied for EEC membership in 1972. Although the EEC accepted their application, Norwegian voters rejected the proposal in a referendum the following year. With the failure of NORDEK, Scandinavian economic integration had become a distant dream.

From the U.S. perspective, the struggles of the various Scandinavian countries to redefine their positions in the economic reshaping of Europe—that would be the gradual undoing of the Nordic bonds so carefully created throughout prior decades—must have looked like an act bordering the tragic and the comic. Because of the Nixon administration's relative disinterest in economic foreign policy and the equally diminishing concern over Europe in general, little heed was given to such configurations. The United States could not, however, completely ignore the Scandinavians.

FISHMONGERS AND VIETNAM REVISITED

Few things annoyed Henry Kissinger and Richard Nixon more than when a small and presumably insignificant player disturbed their grand geopolitical schemes. Indeed, Nixon himself had made it very clear after his first year as president that he had no interest in spending time on "little" things. In March 1970, he sent a memo to Kissinger and his two other major aides, H. R. Haldeman and John D. Erlichman, demanding that, "The only minor countries in Europe which I want to pay attention to in the foreseeable future will be Spain, Italy, and Greece. I do not want to see any papers of the other countries unless their problems are directly related to NATO."[44]

It was harsh talk and, if known to them, would probably have caused a bit of a stir among some Scandinavian politicians. But the message was clear: Nixon, like Kissinger, had little interest in small countries unless they had a direct bearing on the Soviet-American confrontation. Iceland and Sweden were unlikely to do this, yet in the early 1970s they managed to disturb the smooth operation of the Nixon-Kissinger foreign policy.

In the early 1970s, the main issue that concerned most observers of Iceland was still the country's almost total dependence on fishing. In 1964 and 1972, the Reykjavík government extended its territorial waters to 12 and 50 nautical miles respectively, moves that aroused protest from the British, whose fishermen frequented the same waters. On both occasions the extensions and the British reluctance to comply with them resulted in a series of cod wars, similar to the one in the late 1950s (see chapter 4). Nixon, Kissinger, and Secretary of State William Rogers's visit to Reykjavík in the spring of 1973 was almost thrown off course because of the Anglo-Icelandic conflict that had intensified after the 1972 extension.

The main purpose of the Americans' trip was to attend a Franco-American summit billed as one of the highlights of "The Year of Europe," but the Icelanders captured the moment in order to push their own agenda. Kissinger, the penultimate balance-of-power practitioner, was astonished to see how his superiors (although Rogers was hardly Kissinger's "superior" in any way other than according to protocol) simply could not dictate anything to the leaders of this small island nation. He recalled the 30 May 1973 meeting with President Kristan Eidjarn: "I sat there in wonderment. Here was an island with a population of 200,000 threatening to go to war with a world power of 50 million over codfish, and here was a superpower that considered it necessary (a) to express a view and (b) to restrain not the stronger but the weaker. Nixon and Rogers made soothing noises while the Icelandic ministers implacably insisted on what in any previous period would have seemed suicide." Kissinger

President Richard Nixon talks with President Kristjan Eldjarn of Iceland in Reykjavík in May 1973 while National Security Advisor Henry Kissinger and Secretary of State William Rogers listen in. The Americans were in Iceland for a summit with France's President Pompidou, but Icelanders seized the moment to discuss their ongoing "cod war" with Great Britain.
Courtesy of the National Archives.

continued: "That little tableau in the town hall in Reykjavík—the beseeching superpower, the turbulent tiny country threatening to make war against a nation 250 times its size and to leave NATO (without which it would be defenseless)—said volumes about the contemporary world and the tyranny that the weak can impose on it."[45]

It took more than three years from that meeting in Reykjavík until an effective solution to the Anglo-Icelandic cod controversy could be reached. In October 1975, Iceland again extended its fishing limits, this time to 200 nautical miles, and yet another cod war erupted. This time there were casualties and armed clashes at sea, and in February 1976 Iceland broke off diplomatic relations with Great Britain. It was the first time that such a severe diplomatic crisis had occurred between two NATO members. Eventually, with mediation aid from NATO members and skillful diplomatic exploitation of the Keflavík base, the Icelanders won their case: the Oslo Agreement of June 1976 confirmed the 200-mile zone they had unilaterally imposed.

If it was a disheartening prospect to Kissinger that such a tiny country as Iceland could disturb the operation of American foreign policy, it must have been equally disturbing to Nixon to be wasting time on such a minor matter as Iceland. He and Kissinger were after much bigger game; their administration did not wish to get bogged down and be distracted from its grand design of building a new "structure of peace" by practicing triangular détente with the USSR and China.

Sweden's issue with the United States was one of the central concerns of and, at times, obstacles to détente: the Vietnam War. In early 1969, Stockholm had become the first Western government to grant North Vietnam full diplomatic recognition, an act that had brought Swedish-American relations to a boiling point as Nixon entered the White House. Although little happened during the first nine months of 1969, a severe crisis loomed on the horizon when the most visible and vocal critic of American involvement in Vietnam, Olof Palme, became Sweden's prime minister in September of that year. Palme did not make matters any easier: the Swedish government pledged to give Hanoi $40 million in humanitarian aid during the first month of his premiership.

By then, Swedish policies had begun to attract increasing interest from domestic U.S. audiences as well. Americans called for boycotts of Swedish-made goods (one shipment of SAAB automobiles was actually prevented from being unloaded), and the Export-Import Bank considered withholding credits for the Scandinavian Airlines System (SAS). Congressional criticism increased toward the end of the year, with such influential figures as Senator Strom Thurmond leading the charge. "There is no reason why Sweden cannot cooperate with our foreign policy when it is for the common good," Thurmond fumed during one session.[46] In the U.S. press, articles on "hate-America campaigns" in Sweden began to appear and the New York Times' C. L. Sulzberger complained about the Swedes' ungratefulness for the U.S. defense effort in Europe that, in his mind, made Swedish neutrality possible.

For the moment, however, Swedish criticism subsided after Olof Palme took office, partly because the Nixon administration promised to negotiate a peace settlement and begin a gradual withdrawal of American troops from Vietnam. Palme was also burdened by domestic problems, including labor unrest, that left him little time to focus on international issues. Moreover, the flow of American draft evaders to Sweden slowed down noticeably in 1970— the total number would never reach more than six hundred. In addition, the new U.S. ambassador to Sweden, the former president of the Hampton Institute in Virginia, Jerome Holland, turned out to be a wise choice: as an African-American, his appointment undermined some of the Swedish cries of racism often linked to U.S. policies in Vietnam. Yet the Nixon administration unwisely insulted the new prime minister during Palme's unofficial visit to the United States in June 1970 by not arranging a meeting with the president. In return, Palme—who met protesters at most of his stops—criticized U.S. policy in Vietnam in a speech to a Foreign Policy Association meeting in New York. But the critique was still relatively mild. Palme simply pointed out that great powers (in this case the United States) have an unfortunate tendency to "use the smaller nations" (in this case Vietnam) for their own purposes, which often are very different from the real interests of the countries being manipulated. Palme denied charges of anti-Americanism and argued that the Swedes had great admiration for the United States. He maintained, however, that his government could not sit idly by when injustices occurred, no matter who the perpetrator was.

That was mild compared to what Palme said two years later in the midst of the so-called Christmas bombings. On 22 December 1972, four days after the massive bombing raids on North Vietnam commenced, he voiced the following denouncement:

> What is happening today in Vietnam is a form of torture. There can be no military justification for the bombing. The fact is that people are being tormented, that a nation is being tormented in order to humiliate it, to compel it into submission by force. That is why the bombing is an outrage. There have been many such outrages—Guernica, Oradour, Katyn, Lidice, Sharpeville, Treblinka. Now there is another name to add to the list— Hanoi, Christmas 1972.[47]

Kissinger and Nixon were livid, particularly over the comparison made with Treblinka. How could the Swedes, asked Kissinger, who had remained neutral during World War II and the Nazi atrocities against European Jewry, make such judgments? Given that he had left Germany in 1938 and had lost thirteen relatives in the Holocaust, Kissinger naturally had a good rationale for asking such a question. After some consideration, however, the newly reelected president and his celebrated national security advisor (and soon to be secretary of state) decided not to take any overt action, such as imposing economic sanctions on Sweden, because that would only have drawn more attention to Palme's comments. Instead, the White House froze diplomatic relations by retaining the vacationing chargé d'affaires, John D. Guthrie, in the United States and advising the Swedes that their new ambassador-designee, Yngve Möller, was not welcome in Washington. Although Palme toned down his rhetoric, he did not back down. Indeed, it took more than a year before relations between the two countries returned to normal. Finally, in May 1974, Robert Strausz-Hupé landed in Stockholm as the new U.S. ambassador and his Swedish counterpart, Wilhelm Wachtmeister, arrived in Washington. There was, however, no agreement on who had been right or wrong, no apologies for what had been said or done. But with the American involvement in Vietnam over, the basis of the conflict had disappeared.

What was the conflict all about? At one level, it was part of a pattern in Swedish policy of playing an active role in world affairs and being particularly involved in issues that transcended the East-West and North-South conflicts. In part, it could also be viewed as "payback" of sorts for American criticism of the Middle Way. No matter what the origins, however, the criticism of the Vietnam War was by no means an aberration or a sign of strong anti-Americanism in Sweden or in Scandinavia in general. Rather, it displayed the utter resentment felt toward the bipolar order and its tragic side effects. In this sense, the Swedish criticism of Vietnam fit the pattern evident in the critique following the Czechoslovakian events of 1968. In both cases, albeit in very different contexts, the main adversaries in the Cold War had severely violated certain basic principles of human rights and national self-determination, and had subjected the inhabitants of small countries to their own perceived needs of security, prestige, and power.

This interpretation seems even more valid given that the Palme government did not limit its criticism of the United States to that country's conduct of the war in Vietnam. During the 1973 events in Chile that led to Salvador Allende's downfall, the Swedish prime minister again criticized Washington for its clandestine involvement in the overthrow of a democratically elected leader. While the public criticism was hardly as harsh or poignant as in the case of Vietnam and the Christmas bombings, Palme did have a strong feeling that the Nixon administration was acting as a "reactionary" force in South America. As he wrote to West German Chancellor Willy Brandt upon learning the speculations about U.S. involvement in Chile: "The United States seems unable to understand and face in a constructive way the process of liberation which is already underway in the Latin American subcontinent. The position taken by the Americans in relation to the struggle of the Latin American peoples for freedom is as narrow-minded and myopic as the one they took in the cases of China and Vietnam with people like Mao Tse Tung and Ho Chi Minh."[48] In Palme's view, clearly, the United States had become too concerned over its spheres of influence to pay attention to moral considerations in its foreign policy.

The Erlander and Palme governments' criticisms had, however, done a disservice to the Swedish hopes of playing a significant mediatory role in the gradual relaxation of East-West tensions that took place despite the violence in Prague and the butchering in Southeast Asia. It fell to their eastern neighbors to play the largely symbolic role of host to some of the more momentous negotiations and agreements over arms reductions and security in Europe during the first half of the 1970s and to pick up the eventual public relations coup that came with playing host to what many were soon to call the ending point of the postwar era. Nixon, forced to resign in the fall of 1974 because of Watergate, saw none of it.

TO THE HELSINKI STATION

Throughout the 1960s, the Scandinavians had encouraged the reduction of Cold War tensions and the curbing of the nuclear arms race. The Swedes and the Finns had advocated nuclear-free zones and clubs, while the Norwegians and Danes had continued to take a negative stand regarding the stationing of nuclear weapons on their territory. The Swedes provided a mediatory service to Willy Brandt as he gradually edged his way toward *Ostpolitik*, while the Scandinavian NATO members were active in drafting the Harmel Report that provided for a de facto policy statement in favor of détente between East and West. Perhaps with the exception of the Icelanders, all Scandinavians played the roles of midwives in the gradual process that eventually led to the ushering in of an era of détente.

Of the Nordic countries, it was Finland that played the most visible role in the détente process as host to both the strategic arms limitation negotiations and to the negotiation and signing of the CSCE agreements. While the Finns clearly offered little of substance in terms of the SALT agreements, the choice of Helsinki as the setting for these talks clearly symbolized the usefulness of Finland's bridge-building policies in an era of superpower accommodation. The negotiations commenced between the Soviets and the Americans in 1969 and eventually led to the signing of SALT I in 1972.

The usefulness of bridge building was further highlighted during the CSCE process that reached its climax with the signing of the Helsinki Accords in August 1975. Given Finland's special relationship with the Soviets, the country was in an ideal position to offer its mediating services. On 5 April 1969, Finland opened talks with European and North American countries on a possible conference on European security. Thus began the process that first coincided with the SALT negotiations in Helsinki and the progress of *Ostpolitik*, then led to the opening of exploratory talks in Helsinki in November 1972, and after years of deliberation, finally culminated in the signing of the Helsinki Final Act in 1975. These negotiations would naturally not have amounted to much had there not been a preexisting disposition among the greater powers toward some sort of conciliation. Indeed, the CSCE would not have succeeded without West Germany's *Ostpolitik*, the Soviet desire for a formal recognition of the postwar division of Europe, and the Nixon-Kissinger détente doctrine. However, there was no question that a small Northern European neutral had made a significant contribution to the relaxation of East-West tensions.

The final meeting in August 1975 was, therefore, doubly exciting for Urho Kekkonen. It was the first time since the Helsinki Olympics of 1952 that the Finns could make a substantive claim on their position as a "neutral meeting place." While such claims were naturally overshadowed by the ongoing Finlandization debate, the final outcome of the three-day meeting that brought together all the major leaders of Europe (East and West) and North America was, arguably, one of the seminal documents of the era of détente. The signatories agreed to respect the inviolability of borders; they promised to work hard to avoid conflicts; they pledged to increase economic cooperation and cultural cooperation across the East-West divide. The Helsinki Final Act seemed like the perfect symbol of a new era in international relations. Some even believed that the Cold War in Europe had come to an end.

President Gerald R. Ford speaking upon his arrival at Seutula airport for the signing of the Helsinki Accords in August 1975. Behind him are Mrs. Ford, Secretary of State Henry Kissinger, and Finnish President Urho Kekkonen.
Courtesy of the Gerald R. Ford Library.

Of course, it had not. After the signing of the Helsinki Accords in the fall of 1975, questions were soon raised regarding the meaning of CSCE. Divided as the Final Act was into four Baskets, it ended up meaning different things to different sides. For example, the Soviets stressed the significance of Basket I that focused on security, territorial integrity, and the inviolability of borders. Moscow interpreted this as an international recognition of Europe's postwar borders and the legitimacy of the Soviet empire in Eastern Europe. The West, on the other hand, focused on the parts in Basket I that were related to "freedom of thought, conscience, religion, or belief." The other Baskets also provided the basis for two diametrically opposed interpretations: while the Soviets wished to focus on Basket II, which called for cooperation in economic, scientific, and technological issues, the West, and the United States in particular, stressed Basket III, which laid the basis for cooperation in humanitarian efforts. The most important questions behind the different interpretations were very basic for the East-West division in general: Did the CSCE legitimize and recognize Soviet rule in Eastern Europe? Or did it open Eastern Europe to Western ideas and trade, thus providing the contractual bridge to undermine Soviet hegemony in that area?

The political détente in Europe that climaxed with the signing of the Helsinki Accords was, of course, not Kekkonen's or the Scandinavians' doing. They did not have the necessary leverage to pressure and thus merely played the roles of midwives, providing the services and the medium needed for the conclusion of the agreements. In the short term, as the Finnish historian and member of the *Eduskunta*, Jukka Tarkka, put it, the Helsinki Accords were perhaps most important for Finland and President Kekkonen. "In Finland," he wrote, "it felt as though the CSCE was almost purely Kekkonen's doing, that Finland had donated the CSCE to the world and done a historic service to mankind." In reality, Tarkka added: "Kekkonen had simply understood earlier than most that this kind of a meeting could be arranged. Otherwise it would have taken place somewhere else and perhaps at a slightly later date."[49]

The pride that the Finns took from their role as the successful organizers of the Helsinki meeting was not diminished even by the fact that already at the time of the signing of the Helsinki Accords, some of détente's basic foundations were being severely challenged in the United States, where critics from the right and the left charged that détente had been a thorough sellout: the Soviets had, according to these critics, won significant concessions in SALT, and the Kremlin and its East European satellites had been given a green light to continue abusing their citizens' human rights. In contrast, in the USSR, the CSCE process and the Helsinki Human Rights Watch Groups that grew out of it quickly made it seem that the West had "tricked" the Soviets into allowing outsiders to meddle in their international affairs by outrageously claiming that denying citizens some of their basic political rights went against the spirit of Helsinki. Although in the long term, the human rights aspect of the Helsinki Accords clearly worked to undermine the repressive authority of the totalitarian states in the East—it is no accident that such figures as Vaclav Havel belong to this generation of "Helsinki watchers"—the short term results in this area were limited. If anything, they may have provoked further repressive measures against, for example, Soviet dissidents and would-be Jewish emigrants.

Thus, despite its initial promise, the Helsinki Final Act—the culmination of European détente and the first stage of the CSCE process—was only a limited success. A new Cold War was already on the horizon as Jimmy Carter prepared to enter the White House in the fall of 1976. During his and Ronald Reagan's terms, the American-Scandinavian relationship was, once again, subjected to the changing fluctuations of the Cold War.

chapter 6

OFF BALANCE, 1976–1989

It was a cool February night in Stockholm. At 11:20 P.M. Olof Palme and his wife Lisbet were walking toward an underground station on the corner of Sveavägen and Tunnelgatan in central Stockholm, after seeing *The Mozart Brothers*, a little-known movie by the Swedish left-wing director Suzanne Östen. The Palmes enjoyed taking the underground and did not think much of the potential dangers involved; after all they were in Sweden, in the land of social equality, peace, and harmony, a country that had not been at war since the early nineteenth century. Suddenly a man appeared from the shadows, produced a Smith & Wesson .357 Magnum revolver from his pocket, and fired at the Swedish prime minister in the back at close range. Olof Palme fell on the ground, while Lisbet, who was walking a few steps ahead of her husband, turned around. The assassin fired at her, slightly scraping her back. Soon the murderer, wearing a dark coat and covering his face with a cap, disappeared up a flight of stairs at the end of Tunnelgatan. Olof Palme was declared dead in a hospital soon after midnight and Ingvar Carlsson, the deputy prime minister, took over the premiership.[1]

Prime Minister Olof Palme's assassination on 28 February 1986 stands out as the most blatant case of political violence in post-1945 Scandinavia. Although the assassin was not to be caught and convicted, there was no shortage of theories regarding the murderer's identity. The CIA, the KGB, the Chilean government, the Iraqi secret service, the followers of Ayatollah Khomeini, and the South African secret police were all identified as likely suspects at various points. In the end, the most plausible explanation, however, was that the deed had been committed by a deranged lone individual. Christer Petterson, a Swedish man with a long record of violent crime and drug abuse, was actually tried for the murder but was later released, despite Lisbet

Palme's positive identification. In the end, the speculations of the Palme murder with its "grassy knoll"–style theories have made it almost what the assassination of John F. Kennedy in 1963 has been to millions of Americans. More importantly, the killing in central Stockholm was a symbol that a new era, characterized by collective insecurity, fear of terrorism, and the ever-present prospect of random violence, was dawning in the quiet corner of Europe.

Palme was the last of the Scandinavian Cold War–era "bridge builders" to pass from the scene; his mentor Tage Erlander had died in 1985, Finland's Urho Kekkonen had retired in the fall of 1981 (he died in the fall of 1986). In the 1980s, a new style of leadership took over in the two Scandinavian neutrals, at once more moderate and less flamboyant, but at the same time more European-oriented, more pragmatic, and, apparently, less interested in playing the roles of mediators in the Cold War. It was symbolic of the dawn of a new era that the only major superpower summit of the Reagan-Gorbachev years that was held in Scandinavia took place in Iceland (Reykjavík, October 1986) rather than on neutral territory.

The American-Scandinavian relationship during these last years of the Cold War was one of continuous ups and downs. In the late 1970s and early 1980s, the strategic significance of the High North, particularly of the Arctic Seas, increased rapidly as the Soviet naval buildup in the Kola peninsula continued. At the same time, the Scandinavians, along with most West Europeans, reacted negatively to the breakdown of détente, holding the Soviets responsible. They were, however, no fans of Ronald Reagan; they saw the U.S. president and his defense initiatives as far more dangerous and potentially disruptive to peace than anything the Soviet leaders did. These feelings were particularly strong after Mikhail Gorbachev's ascendancy and the rise of "Gorbymania," which played its part in the Scandinavian NATO allies' decisions to hold firm to (and even strengthen) their nonnuclear stands.

Olof Palme's violent death was symbolic of the rapid changes taking place in Scandinavia during the late 1970s and 1980s. Internationally, their position proved more vulnerable to changes in Soviet-American relations than perhaps during any other period since the late 1940s. With the advent of continuous superpower summitry by the mid-1980s, the Scandinavians' position as bridge builders lost much of its significance. Domestically, Scandinavia took a clear swing to the right as the Social Democrats lost support and right-wing splinter groups began to emerge. Economically, their reluctant stand toward the EEC was bound to bring trouble as the continentals increased the pace of integration. With the Cold War winding down, the Scandinavians, to varying degrees, faced a new world order that they were ill-equipped to handle.

NORDIC UNITY IN CRISIS

During the second half of the 1970s, Scandinavians, with the notable exception of the Norwegians, suffered their worst postwar recession. After decades of almost uninterrupted growth, the malaise that spread to the Western world as a result of the OPEC oil embargo of 1973, the failed efforts at Nordic economic integration in the early 1970s, and the failure to establish a common front vis-à-vis European economic integration were taking their toll. The economic downturn, however, had no uniform pattern in Scandinavia. During the second half of the 1970s, the Norwegians in fact prospered, while the Finns and the Icelanders agonized, the Swedes were troubled over the "over-socialization" of their society, and the Danes, the lone Scandinavian members of the EEC, were most severely influenced by the spillover effects of the oil crisis. As *Business Week* put it, a glance at Scandinavian economic conditions in the late 1970s "dispels any notion that the Nordic nations can be considered a single economic entity."[2] With economic heterogeneity increasing, Scandinavians suddenly found themselves victims of their own inability, less than a decade earlier, to take the logical steps toward regional integration. At the same time, the widely heralded successes of the Middle Way were brought into question.

The April 1976 issue of *Current History* included a unique special section on the Scandinavian countries that described these economic difficulties in some detail. For example, Eric S. Einhorn reflected on Denmark's declining economic fortunes that were brought on by the OPEC oil price hikes. The new EEC member was in a situation in which, "After nearly 15 years of economic prosperity and expansion in the public service sector, the current period of recession and cutbacks in popular public programs is a test of Danish sense and tolerance."[3] In his article on Iceland, Richard F. Tomasson pointed out that the economic crisis was compounded by the ongoing need to diversify the country's economy. Because approximately 85 percent of the economy was reliant on fishing (Norway was the European runner-up with 10–11 percent) and 45–50 percent of the country's GNP was dependent on foreign trade, Iceland was extremely sensitive to price fluctuations and had the "most inflationary economy" in Europe in the mid-1970s. Even with the extension of Iceland's fishing boundaries in the 1970s, moreover, overfishing had become a serious economic and ecological problem. As Tomasson wrote, Iceland was in a situation in which "increase in world prices, combined with a relative deterioration of the price of fish because of competition from Japan and Korea, an enormous trade deficit and a pressing need to reduce fishing efforts" were putting a major squeeze on the Icelandic economy.[4]

In Sweden, the effects of the economic downturn were felt, for the most part, in politics. After the 1976 election, a new Swedish government was formed, for the first time in the postwar era, without the Social Democrats. In order to fight back the potential rise in unemployment, however, Thomas Fälldin's three-party nonsocialist coalition actually expanded the government's expenditures by spending more on such schemes as worker training and employing new people in the public sector. Thus, even with Olof Palme and the Social Democrats in opposition, Sweden retained its character as a welfare state intact. While Sweden suffered from a social and economic malaise, Martin Schiff maintained that "the symptoms of social stress in Sweden are generally less pronounced" than elsewhere in Western Europe.[5]

Unlike its Scandinavian and Western European neighbors, Norway experienced a period of astonishing prosperity in the 1970s, when the discovery of oil in the North Sea between Great Britain and Norway made the thinly populated Scandinavian country into one of the richest nations in the world. Statoil, Norway's state-owned company that began to exploit the oil resources, invested much of the money back in the Norwegian economy. The new oil sheiks of Scandinavia were, however, of two minds over the discoveries: on the one hand, they were naturally jubilant, but, on the other hand, a Gallup poll in the mid-1970s disclosed that "76 percent of the population believe that their national standard of living is already too high."[6] It was one of the curiosities of Scandinavia, something that Americans could hardly understand, that the majority of people were bold enough to think that more was not necessarily better. In the long run, however, a structural problem would complicate Norway's traditionally independent stand vis-à-vis European integration: by 1985, oil amounted to half of Norway's exports while employing only 2 percent of the population.

If Norwegians were doing too well, Finland's economic situation was by far the most alarming of the Nordic countries. The 1973 oil crisis preempted the expected growth in exports to the EEC that were thought to result from the conclusion of an industrial agreement in the same year. At the same time, trade with the USSR and other COMECON countries grew as a result of a cooperation agreement signed in May 1973. The end result was a sudden Easternization of Finnish foreign trade. For example, in 1975 Finnish trade with Great Britain declined by 28 percent while trade with the Soviet Union went up by 62 percent. Political scientist Peter Krosby described the panic resulting from Finland's economic emergency as follows: "There was talk of an eventual national bankruptcy; the government at times found itself without ready cash to meet its obligations; and major industrial concerns with growing stockpiles of unsold commodities began to lay off workers by the thousands."[7] Foreign investors began to shy away from Finland and thousands of Finns began to move to Sweden in search of work.

Largely because of these sudden shifts in Finland's trade patterns, which did not turn out to be permanent, the Finnish situation attracted increasing attention from a number of commentators in the West, particularly in the United States. The crux of the commentary had, however, little to do with the Finnish economy or, in the end, with Finland itself.

FINLANDIZATION: A DÉTENTE COUNTERCULTURE

In his memoirs, Henry Kissinger made a rather flattering comment about the Finnish leadership regarding their handling of relations with the Soviet

Union. In *The White House Years,* he wrote: "Finland should be dancing to the tune of its powerful Russian neighbor. It isn't. Finland is not only free but has firm ties with the West that are becoming stronger." Why was this the case? "The answer is 'trust'—and creation of a 'special relationship' with the Soviets," Kissinger maintained.[8] Although it could be argued that Kissinger made some use of that "special relationship" as a helpful channel in the SALT talks, his comments would not have been favorably received among the opponents of détente, particularly those from the right of the political spectrum. In the mid-1970s, as a part of a general pattern of attack against the redefined East-West relationship, several journalists and scholars began to present the Finno-Soviet relationship as a nightmare scenario, a symbol of Soviet foreign policy toward Western Europe at large. Although it was discussed already during the Nixon administration, the Finlandization controversy reached its golden age in the late 1970s.

Finlandization has been defined as "[b]ehavior of a country whose foreign policy and domestic policies are strongly conditioned by a conscious desire to mollify and maintain friendly relations with Moscow, at the expense if need be of close ties with formal allies and traditional friends or of its own sovereignty."[9] The roots of the theory go back to the 1950s, when many Austrians were concerned that they might have to pay a heavy political price for removal of Soviet forces from eastern Austria; Karl Gruber termed potential political concessions as *Finnische Politik.* The term implied submission to Soviet political control, first in foreign but later, possibly, in domestic politics as well.

With Kekkonen's tenure and his role as an active bridge builder, the Finlandization controversy gradually took shape. When Kekkonen, for example, promoted the establishment of a nuclear weapons-free zone in Scandinavia, he was seen as acting on Moscow's orders. Numerous Finnish decisions in the 1960s and early 1970s—such as rejecting NORDEK, making special arrangements with the COMECON, and actively proposing and supporting the CSCE process—were all, and to a large degree rightly so, seen as Finnish attempts to appease the Soviets. At the same time, Kekkonen's unchallenged role as the political leader of his country began to arouse increasing interest in the West, especially when Kekkonen used his influence to curb—without actually censoring—anti-Soviet media coverage. By the late 1970s, his position had become so firm that none of the four major political parties—the conservative *Kokoomus,* the centrist *Keskustapuolue* (the AP had been renamed in the early 1960s to reflect the declining agrarian population in Finland), the Social Democratic Party, and the socialist-communist coalition FDPL—could, or dared to, find a suitable candidate to oppose Kekkonen in the upcoming 1978 presidential campaign. With such authority vested in one man, who seemingly accommodated the Soviets at every possible twist and turn, the notion of Finlandization seemed to be a fairly accurate description.

Those observers in the West who were interested in discussing the notion of Finlandization were not, however, primarily interested in Finland or in the

Finno-Soviet relationship. Rather, they addressed a broader concern about the future of Western Europe and U.S. leadership role in NATO that many thought was being undermined as a result of détente. As Walter Laqueur, one of the champion voices of Finlandization, argued in 1977: "Finland is something of a model and the Soviet leaders regard it as such. If Poland and Hungary constitute one example of a close relationship between the Soviet Union and its smaller neighbors, Finland provide[s] another. Under certain conditions, this kind of relationship might spread to other parts of the globe. Those 'certain conditions' are to some extent already visible in Europe." Laqueur's real worry was not Finland itself, a country apparently already under a Soviet stronghold, but that "[i]f the economic crisis deepens, if nationalism and communism continue to prevent closer European cooperation, if NATO, shrunk and weakened, no longer offers effective protection, and if the paralysis of political will is not overcome, accommodation seems bound to turn into appeasement, and appeasement lead to a diminution of sovereignty." In other words, unless Western Europeans remained uncompromising and united in their dealings with the USSR, they would go down a slippery path that would eventually result in a significant expansion of Soviet influence.[10]

This détente-era domino theory had its influential American critics as well. The most prominent of these was George F. Kennan. The father of containment countered the Finlandizers by reminding them that such generalizations were often based on shortsighted partisan views rather than on careful reflection. As Kennan argued in 1979: "The comparison that has been drawn between Finland's position vis-à-vis the Soviet Union and that of Western Europe is neither fair to the Finns—whose position is not at all that weak or humiliating (they have materially increased their freedom of action in the last 25 years)—nor is it fair to Western Europe, because the latter's relationship to Moscow rests on wholly different geopolitical, demographic, and economic realities than that of Finland."[11]

Although Kennan was probably correct in his criticism, the Finlandization theory did offer an attractive weapon in the arsenal of the critics of détente. The theory was a simple way of explaining why accommodation with the Soviet Union, albeit masterminded by such a conservative duo as Richard Nixon and Henry Kissinger, was a dangerous path. With the upsurge in Soviet-American tensions in the late 1970s and the ushering in of the "new Cold War" in the early 1980s, the notion of Finlandization helped the opponents of détente explain why accommodation with the Soviets was not only undesirable, but downright dangerous.

THE UPS AND DOWNS OF DÉTENTE

In the United States, the Nixon-Kissinger-Ford détente policies had been questioned from both extremes of the political spectrum all along, but during the Carter administration, which placed strong emphasis on the issue of human rights in Eastern Europe, the CSCE bogged down. In the first 1977 CSCE Review Conference in Belgrade, the differences between the American and Soviet delegations prevented any significant results. Three years later the Madrid follow-up conference suffered severely from increased East-West tensions brought on by the Soviet invasion of Afghanistan and the nonratification of the SALT II Treaty. The Madrid conference was interrupted when the Polish government declared martial law in late 1981 in order to quell the rise of domestic protest (the Solidarity movement) and did not reconvene until the end of 1982. Although East-West tensions were still running high, the Madrid conference was able to reach a concluding agreement by late 1983. Instrumental in providing assistance and mediation was the European neutral and nonaligned (NNAs) grouping that included, among others, Finland and Sweden. The CSCE process was kept from falling apart only because of a number of compromise solutions—ranging from human rights to struggles against international terrorism and freer flow of information—introduced by the NNAs and supported, in particular, by the other Scandinavian countries and West Germany. Of particular significance was the Finno-Soviet connection and Kekkonen's clear role as a link providing information to all sides. As Viktor Vladimirov, a senior official in the Soviet Embassy in Helsinki, wrote in his memoirs: "We informed Kekkonen regarding our opinion on certain concessions we were willing to make, on what we expected in return, etc. On his part Kekkonen would let us know what the Western countries, as well as the neutral and nonaligned ones, regarded as their terms before a compromise could be met."[12] As a result, while Soviet-American détente vanished, European détente—albeit hampered—was kept alive in the early 1980s.

Viewed from the United States, however, the Scandinavians (the Finns in particular) had reached a dangerous juncture. They seemed too eager to pursue détente in the early 1980s despite the—at least from the American perspective—arrogant and offensive behavior of the Soviets. After the Reagan administration took over in early 1981, the reinvigoration, both rhetorical and substantive, of U.S. foreign and national security policies played a major part in the resurrection of Cold War tensions. In the context of the new Cold War, the Scandinavian attitude seemed far too relaxed, far too compromising. Although, by a twist of fate that resulted from a significant shift in the Kremlin, Reagan the cold warrior eventually turned into Reagan the negotiator, there were no compromising proposals in 1981. Rather, the new administration proposed, apparently with public approval, a return to global containment and the restrengthening of the American defense posture. With the Strategic Defense Initiative (SDI), much more "buck" would create much more "bang." It was a prospect many Scandinavians, as well as other West Europeans, abhorred.

NUCLEAR-FREE ZONE AGAIN

The limited success of the CSCE stood in stark contrast to the almost complete breakdown of Soviet-American détente. It was partly a result of the reheating of the arms race. In the 1970s the Soviets had armed their forces in Eastern Europe with new types of mobile missiles, SS-20s, which were almost impossible for the West to track down. Because SALT I had not covered these types of weapons and the SALT II negotiations were breaking down in the late 1970s, the SS-20s became a particularly disconcerting prospect for NATO. Such leaders as West German Chancellor Helmut Schmidt were quick to point out that the SS-20s, if left unchecked, would mean a dramatic rise in relative Soviet military might in Europe. In December 1979, prompted in part by the Soviet invasion of Afghanistan, NATO decided to deploy a new grouping of American intermediate missiles to Europe. At the same time, however, NATO made a decision to use a double track approach: seek limitation via strength by pursuing arms limitations talks while modernizing the alliance's nuclear forces.

All this raised eyebrows in Scandinavia, where the attitude toward nuclear weapons had remained consistently negative. Concerned over the breakdown of détente, the problems of the CSCE, and the prospect of a reinvigorated arms race, Finland's President Kekkonen had already, prior to the double-track decision, resurrected the idea of a NNWFZ (see chapter 5). In a speech in Stockholm in May 1978, Kekkonen lamented that, "New weapons technology is likely to introduce new uncertainties into the Nordic situation." Therefore, he suggested that "[t]he Nordic countries should in their own interest enter into negotiations among themselves and together with the great powers concerned about arms control. The objective would be a separate arrangement covering the Nordic countries which would isolate them as completely as possible from the effects of nuclear strategy in general and new weapons technology in particular."[13]

Kekkonen's proposal was, once again, rejected in Scandinavia and branded in the United States as another example of Finlandization. The Soviet buildup in Kola, for example, made the Norwegians reluctant to embrace any proposal that might expose their country even more and close the door on any further deterrence efforts in the High North. Oslo simply reiterated its earlier stand: a month after Kekkonen's speech, Norwegian Foreign Minister Knut Frydenlund stressed to the U.N. General Assembly Session on Disarmament that the concept of a NNWFZ had very little meaning because the Nordic region contained no nuclear weapons. The idea should, however, be considered in a broader European context, Frydenlund added. Prime Minister Anker Jørgensen of Denmark went further by asking whether there were any similar nonnuclear areas in the East. The Swedes, meanwhile, agreed with Kekkonen's concern over nuclear weapons, but offered little substantive support—the Fälldin government was too overburdened with domestic economic problems and rather eager to rid itself of the activist legacy of the Social Democratic Palme cabinet to get bogged down in a potentially controversial issue.

It was the Soviets, however, who undermined any chance of success for Kekkonen's renewed call for a NNWFZ by publicly refusing to allow the zone to be extended to any part of Soviet territory. Although the Soviets would guarantee that they would not use nuclear weapons against any nonnuclear country, their arguments did little to arouse enthusiasm in Scandinavia. As Yuri Komissarov (a pseudonym of an unknown senior Soviet foreign ministry official) wrote in a Finnish magazine in late 1978: "The Soviet Union is a nuclear power and therefore neither can its territory nor any part thereof be included in a nuclear-weapons-free zone or in a so-called 'security belt' adjacent to the nuclear-weapons-free zone; nor can the stipulations of the nuclear-weapons-free zone be an obstacle to navigation by Soviet naval vessels in the straits of the Baltic Sea, regardless of the type of weapons they carry."[14]

It was this sort of argument, along with the Soviet buildup in the Kola peninsula and the general rise of East-West tensions in the early 1980s, that prevented any success for the NNWFZ. Isolated attempts were made in the Norwegian and Swedish parliaments to try and reintroduce the Kekkonen Plan in the early 1980s. In both countries, however, the possibility of a NNWFZ was linked to broader developments in international politics. As Ronald Reagan defeated Jimmy Carter in the U.S. presidential election in November 1980, no reinvigoration of détente was in sight. Indeed, a Swedish joke following Reagan's election maintained that the new president, with his ambitious defense initiatives, had clearly misunderstood the Scandinavian calls for a nuclear-*free* zone as a proposal to create a nuclear *free fire* zone. Notwithstanding Reagan's rhetoric, however, the evidence of an unprecedented Soviet buildup in the High North prevented any significant progress regarding the NNWFZ.

THE FORGOTTEN FLANK REDISCOVERED

In the spring of 1978, the Norwegian *Storting* experienced one of its fiercest debates over foreign policy. At issue was a fishing rights agreement with the USSR in the so-called Grey Zone—the waters in the Barents Sea that lie 200 miles north of the Soviet-Norwegian border. The supporters argued that the Grey Zone agreement was an economic necessity: it would guarantee fishing rights for Norwegians in an area that had been disputed since the interwar period. The opposition, however, charged that Olav Nordli's Labor government was giving in to Soviet pressure and, in effect, giving a green light to Soviet nuclear submarines to operate within Norwegian waters. In the United States, *Business Week* writer Sol W. Sanders agreed with the opposition and characterized the Grey Zone agreement as a sign of Norway's Finlandization. He further warned that the Norwegian left's argument about the need to accommodate Soviet demands was bound to be strengthened with the recent "publication of American naval strategy options that include abandoning the sea-lanes to Norway in the event of a war." Such news was bound to strengthen "the argument by Norway's political left that reliance on NATO is outdated and that an accommodation with Moscow is not only possible but necessary."[15]

These arguments were in large part responsible for the continued firm Norwegian and Danish stand against allowing nuclear weapons in their territory, despite NATO's dual track decision in late 1979. Although the North Atlantic Council unanimously approved on 12 December 1979, after three years of controversial negotiations, a decision to go ahead with deploying and modernizing the Long Range Theatre Nuclear Forces in Western Europe, the Jørgensen Social Democratic government in Copenhagen and Olav Nordli's Labor cabinet in Oslo held firm. They would not allow deterrence to take precedence over reassurance. This stand did not change the fact that by the latter part of the 1970s, the North Sea had acquired new strategic significance. In large part this significance was because of the rapid Soviet buildup in the Kola peninsula, which coincided with the gradual decline of détente in the late 1970s and early 1980s. It reflected the increasing reliance on submarine-launched ballistic missiles (SLBMs), which made the Kola peninsula, located just east of Finnish Lapland, a lucrative base for the Soviet Northern Fleet. By the mid-1980s, 60 percent of the USSR's SLBMs were based on the Kola peninsula. As NATO strategists responded to the challenge, a previously overlooked area was gaining in importance. What had become the forgotten flank in the 1960s was quickly rediscovered when American defense experts such as Robert Weinland argued in 1979 that "World War III may not be won on the northern flank, but it could definitely be lost there."[16]

In the late 1960s and early 1970s, the gradual Soviet buildup and occasional Norwegian pleas to increase NATO presence in the Northern Flank had gone unnoticed, partly because of détente and partly because of Scandinavian criticism directed against the Vietnam War and against American policy in general. In the early 1970s, the debates over Norway's potential EEC membership meant that Norwegian internal politics underwent an especially turbulent time, which directed attention away from defense and security issues. Moreover, with the discovery of oil in the Norwegian Sea, the country was suddenly marching toward a new era of economic prosperity that focused attention away from the changing strategic situation in the North. Norwegian Defense Minister A. J. Fostervoll, for example, had warned as early as 1971 that if Soviet buildup continued, "Norway would have to creep further under the NATO umbrella." In the mid-1970s, the growing strategic imbalance between NATO and the Warsaw Pact in the High North still remained primarily a concern for defense analysts.[17]

During the second half of the 1970s, however, things began to change.

Several critical studies, such as Marian K. Leighton's *The Soviet Threat to NATO's Northern Flank* (1979) and Robert G. Weinland's *War and Peace in the North* (1979), helped focus attention on the growing strategic disparity. In the 1970s, the Soviets also presented the Norwegian government with numerous proposals regarding the island of Svalbard. These included such ideas as the building of a joint Soviet-Norwegian airport and a joint declaration that Norwegians take no unilateral action regarding the demilitarized status of the island. During the Ford administration, Norwegian pleas for increasing U.S./NATO presence were largely neglected, although a defense dialogue started in December 1976 with the establishment of a bilateral U.S.-Norwegian Northern Flank Study Group (NFSG). It eventually led to a shift in NATO's strategy in the Arctic.

NFSG's first phase ended in the summer of 1979 with a detailed report that called for deployment of additional ground troops and aircraft to northern Norway, as well as for increasing the number of NATO exercises in the region. Norway had also been included in NATO's Airborne Early Warning System in 1979. From the Norwegian perspective, these measures greatly enhanced their sense of security by improving the credibility of deterrence in the High North. From the American perspective, establishing a firmer foothold in northern Norway had become important for safeguarding the North Atlantic as a result of the rapid Soviet buildup in the Kola peninsula. Thus, after the signing of an American-Norwegian agreement on 16 January 1981, a number of air defense and air support squadrons, various air support aircraft and helicopters, and a Marine Corps unit of 5,000 were stationed in Trondelag, Norway. In addition, other NATO units began to assign North Norway as their major deployment base.

Strengthening air defenses and adding more conventional troops did not, however, solve the problem of Soviet naval buildup in the High North, particularly because it was combined with the continued reduction in the overall size of the American navy. For example, although the United States had between 800 and 1,000 vessels in the 1960s, the number was down to 459 units by 1978. The United States still had a technological edge over the Soviets, but for the Norwegians, concerned about the Soviet buildup, that edge seemed to be a minor consolation, especially because the reduction in sheer numbers was combined with President Carter's 1978 directive that placed more emphasis on the use of the American navy outside of Europe. In short, American naval presence in the High North suffered from the simultaneous impact of reductions in numbers and shifts in geographical priorities away from the NATO area in general. This meant that NATO maritime activity in the Norwegian Sea was at its low point in 1975–1985, when NATO carrier battle groups were present on the Norwegian sea for only 33 days of the year. The combined effect was that the specter of a *Mare Sovieticum* in the High North remained a threatening prospect in the early 1980s.

At that point, the shift from the Carter to the Reagan administration, the advent of the new Cold War, and the growing tensions between Sweden and the USSR raised East-West tensions in Scandinavia to new heights. The possibility of another *Mare Sovieticum*, the Baltic Sea, appeared to be a serious prospect.

WHISKEY ON THE ROCKS

Several submarine incidents occurred in Swedish waters throughout the 1960s and 1970s. From 1980 onward, however, Soviet submarine incursions along Sweden's Baltic coast became more frequent and increasingly visible. Although the Soviet submarines had previously never come close to the Swedish coastline and retreated immediately after being detected, in the early 1980s they could be found in close proximity to Swedish military installations and would try to evade Swedish radar once they had been spotted. One of the more prominent examples of this activity took place in the fall of 1981 outside Karlskrona, a naval base in southern Sweden.

The incident was in many ways a great embarrassment to the Soviets. In early November 1981, a Soviet Whiskey-class submarine containing atomic weapons ran aground outside Karlskrona after having negotiated its way through a complex archipelago. What made matters worse was that the Soviets, denying any sinister motives and expressing regret over such an "accident," tried to pressure the Swedes into releasing the submarine by placing a group of battleships close to Swedish territorial waters. To calm down the international public uproar that focused attention on the bungled mission, the Soviets allowed Swedish inspection of the submarine's records and interrogation of crew members. Nine days after running aground, the submarine and its crew were released on 11 November 1981.

It was not an isolated incident. In the fall of 1982, for example, the Swedes detected a group of Soviet submarines in relatively close proximity to Stockholm. Despite extensive efforts no vessel was captured, but the Swedes and the Soviets exchanged angry protest notes. The Soviets denied any accusations as false and disruptive to "good neighborly relations" while the Swedes referred to mountains of data that clearly indicated Soviet complicity. Although Stockholm's vigilance hardly scared the Soviets away from conducting submarine missions in Swedish waters, it did make them more careful about the way in which such missions were managed. The strain in Soviet-Swedish relations, however, remained severe and increased again in 1984 when the Swedes accused Moscow of a flagrant intrusion of their air space. The Soviets, once again, denied any wrongdoing.

Together with the Soviet buildup in the Kola peninsula, the submarine incidents served to shake the Nordic Balance in a fundamental way. During the early 1980s, it seemed hard to argue in military-strategic terms that the balance based on the special Finno-Soviet relationship, the long tradition of Swedish neutrality, and the conditional (i.e., no nuclear weapons) NATO membership of Norway and Denmark could remain unaltered by the "unbalancing" actions of the USSR. After all, where was the counterbalance to the

Kola military machine? Norway's Minister of Defense Johan J. Holst, for example, argued in 1983 that the Soviet Union had shown little interest in maintaining the balance of military-political alignments and nonalignments that its small Nordic neighbors seemed to think was part of an existing, and essentially static, reality. To the Soviets, Holst argued, Scandinavia represented a group of capitalist countries showing "a decreasing degree of inclusion into the connecting tissue of the Western system."[18]

In the end, this assumption proved to be false. The 1980s were, by and large, a "Western" decade in Scandinavia. To be sure, the official Scandinavian response to the fall of détente was rather cautious and the Scandinavian NATO members were not about to change their limited partnership by accepting nuclear weapons in their territory. Similarly, the Swedes and Finns continued to play the role of "neutral mediators." Despite all this, however, the 1980s were a decade during which Scandinavian public opinion, notwithstanding the official criticism of many of the Reagan administration's actions and of the president's doomsday-like rhetoric, shifted to the right.

DESPITE REAGAN, A SWING TO THE RIGHT

It is hardly surprising that during the late 1970s and early 1980s, Scandinavian opinion polls reported a marked shift in the Nordic peoples' attitudes toward the Soviet Union and the United States. Although the United States had in the 1960s and early 1970s become an unpopular country—due in large part to the Vietnam War—the Soviet Union's buildup in the Kola peninsula, the submarine incidents off the coast of Sweden, the Soviet invasion of Afghanistan, and the declaration of martial law in Poland resulted in a marked increase in anti-Soviet sentiments. At the same time, public opinion regarding the United States experienced a renaissance of sorts.

The most dramatic example of this shift took place in Sweden. The United States had become the "evil empire" for many Swedes because of their bungling of Vietnam in the 1960s and early 1970s, but the pollsters found that by the early 1980s the majority (approximately 65 percent) of Swedes held a favorable opinion about the United States. Yet at the same time, official government opinion appeared as critical of the United States as before. Foreign Minister Lennart Bodström expressed Swedish criticism of the U.S. role in Latin America when, in a speech to the United Nations in 1982, he said: "In Central America centuries of oppression have set off a revolutionary situation ... it is obvious that a foreign power, the United States, plays a crucial role when it comes to keeping tottering dictatorships on their feet."[19]

Perhaps in part because of the continued U.S. intervention in the affairs of its small Central American neighbors, but mainly due to their unwavering interest in détente, the official Swedish response to continued Soviet submarine incursions was not as harsh as it might have been. While Prime Minister Olof Palme lambasted Soviet behavior repeatedly in the early 1980s, he concurrently restated his support for seeking ways to advance some form of nuclear arms reduction in Europe. Palme was particularly, and given Sweden's geographic location quite naturally, intrigued by the possibility of a nuclear-free Baltic Sea. For example, in June 1983 Palme, in a speech at the high-profile Paasikivi Society in Finland, argued that it was "essential that we in Scandinavia develop the dialogue and attempt to build a common basis for continued efforts."[20] In January 1984 Sweden began to host the conference on Confidence and Security Building Measures and Disarmament in Europe (CDE), which at the time was one of the few forums in which Soviet and American leaders were talking to each other. Its most significant result, after three years of intermittent discussion, was an agreement in which the Soviets for the first time conceded to the principle of onsite inspections. Thus, despite the rise in East-West tensions and the growing military tensions in Scandinavia, bridge building was still an important part of the Swedish premier's foreign policy.

The problem was that nobody in Washington was interested in Palme's efforts. From the American perspective, Palme was still the stubborn troublemaker he had been during the Vietnam War. During the four years (1982–1986) that preceded his assassination, Palme vehemently criticized the Reagan administration's policy in Central America. He was the first European leader to visit Nicaragua after the Sandinistas seized power, an act that on its own was enough to earn Washington's wrath. But Palme did not stop there. He then delivered a speech at the 1985 Young Socialist conference that resembled his previous attacks on U.S. policy in Vietnam. Palme said that American aid to the Contras was basically equivalent to the Soviet invasion of Afghanistan and attacked "the so-called crusade against communism in Nicaragua" as "nothing more than a plundering expedition against poor peasants."[21]

Indicative of the trend away from the left-wing radicalism that had been so evident in Sweden during the Vietnam War and had resulted in an added domestic bonus for Palme's vehement criticism of the United States was that that fewer and fewer Swedes were interested in what Palme had to say about Central America and disapproved of his lame stand vis-à-vis the Soviets. In posters that appeared in Stockholm, Palme was denounced as a traitor following reports that he had instructed his government to tone down criticism of the Soviet Union. His inability to solve Sweden's persistent economic problems added to the unpopularity of the Social Democrats in the mid-1980s. The Swedish electorate was, clearly, swinging to the right prior to the Palme assassination in February 1986.

During the same period, Swedish attitudes toward the Soviet Union changed even more: in the early 1970s more than 50 percent of Swedes had a positive opinion about the USSR's handling of its foreign policy (with the rest expressing mostly a neutral stand); by 1983 the result was exactly the opposite. Similar trends were found in the other Scandinavian countries as well, although the Finnish pollsters, with characteristic deference to the USSR, did not ask questions about which superpower was the greater security problem; in Norway, Denmark, and Iceland, support for NATO membership remained strong.

This change in general attitudes did not mean that the Finns had become open supporters of Ronald Reagan's policies. In fact, the Finns often found themselves annoyed at what they considered "clumsy" American politicians, who seemed unaware of Finland's delicate position next to the USSR. In early 1983, for example, the Finns became upset over comments made by General Bernard Rogers, the supreme commander of NATO, who suggested that Finland had made some sort of a secret agreement to fight against the Soviets if necessary, but at the same time he doubted whether the Finns would show "the determination we would hope for." Some Finns were outraged at the less than diplomatic statement that caused some expected and unpleasant queries from the Kremlin. However, as T. M. Pasca pointed out, most Finns did what they always did in situations like these: "shrug[ged] their shoulders in frustration."[22]

At the same time, some American observers noticed a slight change in the Finno-Soviet relationship that was, apparently, the result of a much-awaited change of leadership. Urho Kekkonen's sudden resignation on 27 October 1981 and the ascendancy of the SDP'S Mauno Koivisto, the former prime minister, began a gradual shift away from the use of foreign policy as a weapon in domestic policies. This shift was due in part to the fact that Koivisto, a carpenter's son and a former dockworker, had never, despite his widely acknowledged leadership position in the SDP, served in elected office. His shy appearance and nonbelligerent style were also far different from that of the autocratic and often combative Kekkonen. As historian Peter Krosby wrote, Koivisto "is a man one likes immediately, instinctively. He appears to care about the people he is with, and he knows how to talk with them, be they manual laborers, white-collar workers, or erudite academics." Most importantly, in marked contrast to Kekkonen, whose style had at times been compared to that of Charles de Gaulle, Koivisto seemed "to have no particular craving or use for the perquisites of power that most Finnish politicians are conspicuously addicted to." As a result, unlike his predecessor, who had embarrassed and destroyed his political opponents by publishing critical letters or chastising them in public view, Koivisto—although unlikely to change the country's central foreign policy positions—was bound to have "a more vigorous and freewheeling debate on issues of importance to Finland."[23]

Despite Koivisto's low-key approach to foreign policy, Finlandization was bound to have less relevance in the Finland of the 1980s than it had during Kekkonen's heavy-handed presidency. In the aftermath of the KAL 700 incident—the shooting down, by Soviet air defense forces, of a Korean airliner that had strayed over the Sakhalin peninsula on 1 September 1983—and the Finnish decision to boycott commercial flights to Moscow, Joyce Lasky Shub

Finnish President Mauno Koivisto with President Ronald Reagan at the White House in September 1983. After Kekkonen's sudden retirement in late 1981, the Social Democratic Koivisto, although concerned with Reagan's Star Wars plans, gradually moved Finland closer to the West. *Courtesy of the Ronald Reagan Library.*

wrote in the October 1983 issue of the *New Republic:* "For the first time since World War II, Finland was putting moral distance between itself and the Soviet Union." Shub interpreted Koivisto's visit to the United States earlier in 1983 as a way of "balancing" the public image of Finnish neutrality—it had been preceded by the Finnish president's trip to Moscow in June 1983. Unlike Kekkonen, who had clearly leaned to the East, Koivisto was gradually molding Finland's image "from a silent victim of Soviet power to an active international player."[24] That is, the image (and reality) of Kekkonen's close relationship—at times a "messenger status"—with Soviet leaders was bound to be replaced by a more Western-oriented approach championed by Koivisto, who did not have and would not endeavor to develop the close personal relationship with Soviet leaders that his predecessor did. Ironically, this did not mean that Finland's international significance was bound to rise; if the Kremlin could no longer "use" the Finnish president as a medium, they would have to find another venue. With Kekkonen's retirement, "the Finnish channel's" usefulness in East-West relations was greatly reduced.

Koivisto's Finland was internally very different from Kekkonen's and the Swedes were disturbed by the activism of the Soviet military, but the NATO members of Scandinavia remained committed to their "semi-aligned" position. Yet even in Norway, Denmark, and Iceland, a moderate swing to the right was in evidence. Norway's (and Scandinavia's) first female prime minister, the Labor Party's Gro Harlem Brundtland, was forced to become opposition leader in 1981 and would not regain office until 1986. Voters in Denmark ousted Prime Minister Anker Jørgensen and the Social Democrats in 1982 when Poul Schluter's multiparty nonsocialist coalition took over, while in Iceland a nonsocialist combination of Independence and Progressive party members had replaced Benedikt Gröndal's Social Democratic minority cabinet in 1980 (Gunnar Thoroddsen of the Independence Party and Steingimur Hermansson of the Progressives headed the nonsocialist cabinets that followed). Indeed, in addition to Palme's Sweden, only in Finland, where Koivisto appointed the Social Democrat Kalevi Sorsa as prime minister in 1982, did the Social Democrats remain in office during the early 1980s.

The swing to the right was not a swing to an extreme. Social Democratic parties remained the largest single political units in all of Scandinavia. Nevertheless, by the 1980s the Middle Way itself appeared to have come to a dead end.

A PARADISE IN TROUBLE

The Scandinavian public opinion shifts in the 1980s were in large part a result of the crisis facing the Middle Way. Decades of increased public spending on various welfare state initiatives had created welfare societies that were, in terms of income distribution, the most egalitarian societies in the world. Indeed, as Professor Gunnar Hecksher of the University of Stockholm argued in 1979, the Swedish welfare state was "a virtually classless society." A new kind of problem had emerged, however. With the expansion of the social welfare system had come higher and higher taxes which, by the late 1970s, meant that "the traditional economic system no longer works. Economic incentives lose most of their importance, because this kind of welfare state is achieved through a system of taxation and transfers which takes, in taxes—even for the industrial workers—at least seventy per cent of any increase they might receive in their wages." Sweden was, another author pointed out, "a paradise in trouble."[25]

At the same time, in a world suffering from high inflation and continued recessions, the Swedes' (and other Scandinavians') ability to sustain a welfare system that required more than half the country's GNP appeared slim indeed.

Not unlike many other industrial countries, the Nordic countries (with the exception of Norway) faced an apparently endless stream of budget deficits. And yet, the welfare state appeared too well entrenched to be significantly revamped. In Sweden, for example, even the conservative/centrist governments that were in power in 1976–1982 felt unable to tamper with the basic structure of the Middle Way. In 1986 Eric Willenz (a former State Department official who was a senior associate at the Carnegie Foundation in 1985–1986) pointed out that the nonsocialist government "actually broadened a policy started by its Labor predecessor of offering wage subsidies to firms to pay workers who might otherwise have been laid off." Why were the nonsocialists so ready to follow the Social Democrats' lead? The answer appears to be that by the late 1970s and early 1980s, the welfare state had become a major part of Scandinavian, and particularly Swedish, national identity. Politicians found it impossible to forge any significant changes by curbing public spending, unless they wished to commit political suicide. The result was an internal political malaise into which successive governments—regardless of their political leanings—were unable to introduce changes in public policy. As a result, the Swedish (and to a large degree other Scandinavian) cabinets of the 1980s were no longer builders of a new society; their role had been reduced to "stabilizing the adverse impact of the halt in growth and of high unemployment."[26]

In the 1980s the Middle Way was, indeed, declared all but dead. The idea that the government should play a paternalistic role was being challenged by several, albeit still small, political splinter groups all over Scandinavia. What had previously been presented as an avant-garde society and as a social laboratory for the rest of the world appeared to have lost its position on the "cutting edge." Or, to put it another way, the Social Democrats and their societal model had been too successful; by the 1980s they could only promise more of the same. In Scandinavia, previously radical politicians like Olof Palme had become, in effect, "social conservatives." What sustained them in power was the lack of a plausible and forcefully argued alternative. But there was no question that, as Kurt Samuelsson put it, the model that "helped Sweden prosper both by building a very wealthy economy and creating a solid welfare state" was becoming a thing of the past. The Swedes, along with their Nordic neighbors, needed to "search for and endeavor to build something new, a model more suitable for the very fast-changing environment [of the late 1980s]."[27]

In the end, the crisis of the Middle Way was as much cultural as economic. "The mythology of modern Sweden"—the notion that the nation had built a society as close to perfection, as egalitarian, as democratic as possible—was approaching, if not already suffering from, a deep crisis, commented Arne Ruth in 1984. Since the 1930s, Swedes had, first gradually but never with hesitation, accepted the role as an internationally recognized model society that combined the best parts of capitalism and socialism. Because they had championed the "exportation" of social democracy, because the Swedes considered their country a prototype of a modern society, because of all these reasons a serious identity crisis was bound to hit home hard once the "model" ceased to function. Indeed, as Ruth pointed out, "the age of Swedish exceptionalness appears to be drawing to a close."[28]

It was a tough statement, but one that would resonate loudly as events in the Soviet Union forged a major change in the nature of international relations. It was a change that discredited the Middle Way even further.

NEW THINKING

Ironically, just as the specter of a *Mare Sovieticum* in the High North, the Soviet submarine incursions to Swedish waters, and the general fear of Finlandization were in the headlines, a chain of events in the Soviet Union signaled the beginning of the end to the USSR. After Brezhnev's death in 1983, Yuri Andropov indicated that Moscow wished to shift away from the arms race and devote more attention to domestic problems. Although Andropov's 13-month long administration was followed by the conservative backlash of Konstantin Chernenko, the latter's death in 1985 finally opened the way for a new type of Soviet leader, Mikhail Gorbachev. A generation younger than his predecessor, energetic, deeply concerned about the domestic problems of the Soviet Union, Gorbachev was determined to reform Soviet society. He certainly did, although the price of those reforms was, eventually, the dissolution of the empire and the nation itself.

Gorbachev's American counterpart was no easy negotiating partner. Ronald Reagan has richly deserved the reputation, whether negative or positive, as the man whose flamboyant rhetoric and efforts to build up the American defense forces—the Strategic Defense Initiative (SDI) in particular—helped reinvigorate the extremely anti-Soviet strand of U.S. policy. During his first term, the Reagan Doctrine had meant, in essence, the globalization of containment: the resumption of aid to the Contras in Nicaragua, the invasion of Grenada, and the giving of financial support to Cambodian and Afghan rebels. In 1986 the Reagan administration provided help for the National

Union for the Total Independence of Angola. In stark contrast to the previous Republican administration, which had avoided equating ideology with security, the Reagan Doctrine in many ways represented a flashback to the early days of the Cold War, when the administration represented the Soviet-American conflict as a clash between two civilizations. Most significantly, as Robert E. Osgood pointed out in 1981, the Reagan administration's goal was "to make American and Western power commensurate to the support of greatly extended global security interests and commitments. There was no disposition to define interests more selectively and no expectation of anything but an intensified Soviet threat to those interests. Hence, the emphasis on closing the gap between interests and power would be placed on augmenting countervailing military strength."[29]

In this context, it was no wonder that when Gorbachev came to power, the military buildup in the High North had made Northern Europe one of the principal concerns of U.S. and NATO defense planners. As J. J. Holst wrote in the 1985 book *Deterrence and Defense*: "Northern Flank is a front line region in the context of the global confrontation between the two major powers, the Soviet Union and the United States."[30]

Perhaps so in 1985. But military strategists had little constructive advice to offer while the most dramatic chain of events in Europe since World War II unfolded. Upon taking office in 1985, Gorbachev moved quickly. He introduced glasnost and perestroika and pressed for the renewal of serious arms limitation talks between the United States and the Soviet Union. The 1985 Geneva Reagan-Gorbachev Summit produced relatively few tangible results, but in early 1986 Gorbachev delivered a message that called for the elimination of nuclear weapons by the year 2000. In June 1986 he followed with a Warsaw Pact Appeal to NATO. In October he traveled to Iceland.

THE ARCTIC "ZONE OF PEACE"

"For a day and a half, Gorbachev and I made progress on arms reduction that even now seems breathtaking. George [Schultz] and I couldn't believe what was happening. We were getting amazing agreements. As the day went on, I felt something momentous was occurring." In this manner Ronald Reagan later recalled the Reykjavík summit between himself and Gorbachev in October 1986. Gorbachev concurred: "Reykjavík marked a turning point in world history. It tangibly demonstrated that the world could be improved. A qualitatively new situation had emerged. The East-West dialogue has now broken free of the confusion of technicalities, of data comparisons and political arithmetic."[31]

They were both right. Something truly momentous was occurring. Yet it was probably more significant than what the former film star or the charismatic Soviet leader could ever have imagined. After all, the Reykjavík summit did not produce any significant treaties, but ended with mutual accusa-

President Ronald Reagan with Iceland's President Vigdis Finnbogadottir during the October 1986 Reykjavík Summit between Reagan and Gorbachev. The summit was a major turning point on the road to the end of the Cold War.
Courtesy of the Ronald Reagan Library.

tions; Reagan refused to make restrictions on the SDI while Gorbachev demanded such limitations as the necessary concession before he would sign an Intermediate Nuclear Force (INF) treaty. However, by providing the first instance when Gorbachev's eagerness was on open display and a forum in which he renewed the call for a "zero option" in Europe, the Reykjavík summit represented a significant point on the path that, a few years later, would lead to the end of the Cold War. Although the response in the United States and Western Europe was initially skeptical, although there was continued concern that the zero option for Europe was simply another Soviet tactical move aimed at undermining Western resolve and unity, it is clear in retrospect that Gorbachev meant business. In 1987 he separated the INF from the SDI and the superpower leaders signed the much coveted INF Treaty in Washington on 8 December 1987.

One of Gorbachev's favorite slogans during this period was "Our Common European Home," a phrase reminiscent of Charles de Gaulle's earlier call for a "Europe from the Atlantic to the Urals." In Scandinavia Gorbachev's slogan translated into a campaign aimed at reversing people's fears of a resurgent and aggressive USSR that had resulted from the buildup in the Kola peninsula and the submarine incidents in Swedish waters during the previous decade. It was officially launched in a speech Gorbachev gave in Murmansk—the choice of the setting having obvious symbolic significance—on 1 October 1987. While Gorbachev was critical of NATO's buildup in the High North, the Soviet leader called for an "Arctic Zone of Peace" that would result from reductions in military activity in the Baltic and Arctic Oceans. He suggested a limit to the number of military exercises held in the High North and, once again, reiterated the Soviet desire for a nuclear-free zone. Although this part of the speech was directed, in large part, to the United States and its NATO partners, Gorbachev went even further. He proposed economic and environmental cooperation, called for a joint energy plan among the countries of Northern Europe, and even offered to use Soviet icebreakers to open up the Arctic sea routes from Northern Europe to the Far East.

The Murmansk speech was one of the high points of Gorbachev's attempt to advance his foreign policy goals in Northern Europe. It was preceded and followed by increased Soviet diplomatic activity throughout Northern Europe in 1986–1989. In late 1986, soon after the Reykjavík Summit, Gorbachev had assured the new prime minister of Norway, Gro Harlem Brundtland, that the USSR "had no malicious intentions with regard to Norway."[32] In 1988 Prime Minister Nikolai Ryzhkov traveled to Oslo, trying to enlist support for Soviet initiatives in the Arctic. The Norwegians did not get excited about a proposal to make the Barents Sea into a joint partnership zone, however, but adopted a wait-and-see attitude. In Sweden Ryzhkov was more successful as he agreed to solve a long-standing dispute over the location of the border line between the coasts of Lithuania and Sweden. In April 1988 the Carlsson government signed an agreement that gave the Swedes control over three-fourths of the disputed area.

What were Gorbachev's motives? The first observers of the Arctic Zone of Peace initiative criticized its vagueness and considered it another move by the Soviets to decrease NATO influence in the High North by offering an elaborate set of carrots—environmental plans, economic initiatives—to the Nordic countries. In retrospect, however, the plan seems to have reflected the larger goals of the Soviet Union's, and Gorbachev's, policy, that is, to reform the USSR from within while improving its relations, economic and political, with the West. The approaches to Scandinavia fit clearly into the latter category. Perhaps the most significant result prior to the dramatic events of 1989 was the dividend in the Western public's perception of the Soviet threat. Gorbachev's new thinking seemed to allay many of the fears that the previous decade's arms race had produced while placing the blame for any lack of improvements in East-West relations on the Reagan administration.

The changes were evident in the public opinions of many Scandinavian countries. Finland provides a good example. As was explained in a report that cited recent opinion surveys in early 1987, the Finns tended to "see Russia as an Orwellian society with no freedom and miserable living standards." However, Ronald Reagan's rhetoric, years of official "friendship" policy with the Soviets, and Mikhail Gorbachev's ascendancy had their impact on the Finns as well: in the same report, two-thirds of the population saw the USSR as "no threat to peace." Indeed, the majority of Finns thought that Soviet foreign policy was "more responsible than President Reagan's."[33] At the same time, a quiet but significant revolution in Finnish internal politics took place: in the March 1987 parliamentary elections, the Conservatives received 53 of the 200 seats in the *Eduskunta* and their former party leader and governor of the Bank of Finland, Harri Holkeri, formed a coalition cabinet with the Social Democrats. Kekkonen's former party (the Center Party) was forced into opposition. Perhaps most significantly, the Soviets, who in decades past had often criticized both the Finnish Social Democrats and Conservatives as threats to Finno-Soviet "friendship," remained silent as these two parties joined forces for the first time since the 1950s.

Meanwhile, prompted by the new Soviet leader's apparent sincerity in efforts to diffuse the military tensions in Northern Europe, the Danes took their own steps toward advancing the idea of a nuclear-free zone. On 14 April 1988 the *Folketing* passed a resolution that specifically stipulated that no vessels carrying nuclear weapons, regardless of their nationality, would be allowed to enter Danish ports. Despite Prime Minister Poul Schluter's efforts to convince outside observers that this action was by no means incompatible with the country's NATO membership, Secretary of State George Shultz was furious. He warned the Danes about "extremely serious consequences" that would accrue from a policy that implied the right to search any foreign vessels.[34]

In short, while the Arctic Zone of Peace may not have produced many tangible results in the overall balance of military forces in Northern Europe, it certainly helped usher in a new climate of opinion that was at the same time more willing to take Soviet suggestions seriously and increasingly critical of what appeared to be a slow American response. The changes were enough to make one observer caution the Scandinavians against lulling themselves into a false sense of security. In the wake of Gorbachev's December 1988 announcement of unilateral Warsaw Pact troop cuts (25 percent reduction in overall strength and 50 percent in Soviet tank strength in Eastern Europe), Kirsten Amundsen admitted that the Soviet leader may have appeared sincere in his desire to transform the adversarial East-West relationship. She warned, however, that "whether it is Norway, Sweden, Denmark, or Finland to which we direct our attention, it seems clear that these states could be very much living in the 'shadow of the bear' in the new and 'secure' Europe Mikhail Gorbachev is promoting."[35]

Then, however, came the year of miracles that made all such warnings seem unwarranted.

THE YEAR OF MIRACLES

For George Bush, that first year in the White House could not have been more eventful. Prior to his victory in the November 1988 presidential elections, Bush had been, among other things, the American ambassador to the United Nations and the director of the CIA. He had just served as the vice president for eight years. He was a man of the Cold War, one whose attitudes about international relations had been shaped—irrevocably, many would argue—by the persistence of the Soviet-American confrontation. Although not as eager to embark on apocalyptic rhetoric as was his predecessor, George Bush was, clearly, a cold warrior, a firm believer that the United States had pursued the correct policies vis-à-vis the Soviet Union. He also believed that these policies were finally bearing fruit. As Bush said in his inaugural address on 20 January 1989: "The totalitarian era is passing, its old ideas blown away like leaves from an ancient lifeless tree." During the months that followed, Bush may have ruminated over these words as he did his best to cope with the events that fundamentally transformed the nature of international relations: the USSR's East European empire collapsed and the Berlin Wall came down. By the time Bush entered his second year in office, the United States appeared to have a good claim for victory in the Cold War.

In terms of Soviet-American relations, however, 1989 did not get off to a good start. After a 12 February meeting with his foreign policy experts in Kennebunkport, Maine, Bush ordered a pause in diplomatic activity with Moscow. He had decided to adopt a hard line as a way of ensuring further Soviet concessions. In the end, the strategy seems to have worked, perhaps better than Bush and his advisors could have expected: by the end of the year, Eastern Europe was no longer living under communist rule and the Baltic states were moving toward independence. The big question now was: What sort of relationship would evolve between the former satellites and the USSR? Ironically, Finlandization suddenly appeared to provide an answer of sorts.

During his visit to the United States in September 1989, Soviet Foreign Minister Eduard Shevardnadze and Secretary of State James A. Baker discussed the problem of secessionism in the USSR. The two paid particular attention to the Baltic republics. On a flight from Andrews Air Force Base outside of

Washington, D.C., to Baker's ranch in Wyoming, the secretary of state suggested that the Kremlin should simply allow the republics to hold a referendum on whether or not they wished to stay with the Soviet Union. Baker said: "Even if you were wrong about the majority view there, and the referendum passed, you'd end up with a lot of Finlands around you. Cut the Baltics loose! You'd be better off with three little Finlands."[36] The Baltics were, however, a sore point for the Soviets. While they would eventually gain their independence, it was in Eastern Europe that the great drama of 1989 unfolded.

In early October, a few weeks after the Baker-Shevardnadze talks, Gorbachev went to East Germany, urging Erich Honecker to initiate a program of reform that would embrace the ideas of glasnost and perestroika. The old hardliner resisted. He was deposed less than two weeks later. A week after that, on 25 October 1989, Gorbachev, who had little time in 1989 to worry about Scandinavia, came to Helsinki and made one of his most pivotal comments, announcing that the USSR had no right to interfere in the events of Eastern Europe. In a speech at Finlandia Hall, the site of the 1975 signing of the Helsinki Accords, he also pointed to Finland as a model for Eastern Europe, thus turning the Finlandization argument on its head. Gorbachev's press aide Gennadi Gerasimov soon declared the remarks as a public repudiation of the Brezhnev Doctrine. In its place, Gerasimov told anxious reporters, had come the "Frank Sinatra Doctrine." The satellites could do it their own way.

They did. Within two weeks' time, the Berlin Wall came down and Germany's unification process began in earnest. At the same time, the processes that led to the democratization of Poland, Hungary, Bulgaria, and Czechoslovakia were completed peacefully. In Rumania, where Nicolae Ceauşescu refused to budge, the end of communist control took a violent form; Ceauşescu himself was executed on Christmas Day. The Soviets did not intervene, perhaps hoping, in Baker's words, that they would end up with "a group of Finlands." In the end they did not, nor could they hold back the rising tide of independence. For all intents and purposes, the Cold War had ended.

THE MIDDLE WAY, THE NORDIC BALANCE, AND A NEW ERA

Finland was not the only Scandinavian country to figure prominently as a symbol in the talks between Soviet and American leaders during the year of miracles. In December 1989 at the Bush-Gorbachev meeting at Malta, the two leaders discussed, among other topics, the future economic system of the USSR. While Gorbachev clearly acknowledged that the Soviet system needed serious reforming, he was still hesitant to acknowledge that the answer to the ineffective state-controlled economy of the Soviet Union was unbound privatization. Instead, he told Bush that his plan was to move away from state ownership to what he called "collective ownership." Gorbachev added that what he had in mind was "the Swedish model," because "Swedish socialism was fairer and more public-spirited than American capitalism." Bush's response was simple, belligerent, and to the point: "But it's still the private sector in Sweden that makes the money, not the public."[37]

This brief exchange is indicative of the warped, but partially correct, view that each world leader had about the Swedish (or Scandinavian) "model." Gorbachev, looking for a systematic alternative for the bankrupt state-controlled economy of the USSR, could see the welfare state in Sweden as an ideal option, a combination of private and public ownership. Adopting something similar to the Middle Way would not have meant an outright capitulation to the old nemesis, capitalism. But Bush was also correct in implying that the Middle Way was possible only because it was supported by a successful private sector. They seemed to have agreed on one thing, however: there was a Middle Way, a Swedish-Scandinavian model, that had been economically successful and stood in stark contrast to the Soviet–East European model and appeared far more appealing to many than the rigid conservative models championed by, say, Margaret Thatcher in Great Britain. As one observer put it: "Sweden is an economic paradox. It has the largest public sector of any industrial economy, the highest taxes, the most generous welfare state, the narrowest wage differentials, and powerful trade unions. According to prevailing economic wisdom, it ought to be suffering from an acute bout of 'eurosclerosis,' with rigid labour markets and arthritic industry. Instead, Sweden has many large and vigorous companies, and one of the lowest unemployment rates in Europe."[38]

And sure enough, in the late 1980s, some Scandinavians appeared extremely successful. The Finns, for example, had experienced an unexpected boom. There was "satisfaction in saunaland," an observer commented, noting that the Finns, whose GNP had risen by an average of 2.8 percent during the 1980s (compared to a West European average of 1.6 percent), were "the nouveaux riches of Europe."[39] In Norway, the main problem was *too much* success in one area of the economy: the oil boom was still undermining everything else. In stark contrast to the relatively successful economies of Finland, Sweden, and Norway, however, was Denmark, the lone Scandinavian EC member that had, under Conservative Prime Minister Poul Schluter, implemented wage freezes and price controls. Since 1982, Denmark's growth rates (1.5 percent annual growth in the GNP) had fallen below the West European average. In the late 1980s the Danish misfortunes, which contrasted with Finnish and Norwegian successes, were enough to calm down, for the time being, Europhoria in most Scandinavian countries.

At the same time it was clear that by the end of the 1980s, Scandinavian-American relations were bound to undergo significant changes as the Berlin Wall crumbled and Eastern Europe underwent a profound transformation. For one thing, during the decade and a half prior to the year of miracles, Soviet-American relations had profoundly altered the strategic significance of Scandinavia. The buildup in Kola and the increased Soviet submarine activities in the Baltic had turned the quiet corner of Europe into a major focus of great strategic planning. With Gorbachev's ascendancy and his call for an Arctic Zone of Peace, however, this newfound strategic significance quickly became a mere footnote in the rapid chain of events that eventually produced the undoing of the Soviet Union itself. At the same time, the Scandinavians' role as bridge builders appeared no longer necessary in the changed international context while the concept of Finlandization suddenly seemed to be more appropriate for Eastern, rather than Western, Europe. In addition, the Nordic Balance, a cherished but relatively untested security concept that was an integral part of pan-Scandinavian identity, appeared to have lost its meaning when one of its integral ingredients, the Soviet threat, diminished radically. There simply was little balancing left to do.

For the Bush administration, Scandinavia meant relatively little in the whirlwind of the most dramatic shift in international politics since World War II. Having grown in strategic significance since the late 1970s, Scandinavia was suddenly but firmly reduced once again to the position of the forgotten flank. There were too many other issues and challenges—the reunification of Germany, the future of Eastern Europe, the breakup of the Soviet Union, the future of NATO, the brewing crisis in the Persian Gulf—that consumed the attention of the last Cold War (and the first post–Cold War) president and his advisers. And so it was that as the Scandinavians embarked on a new search for security in a world filled with disorder and uncertainty after the largely self-perpetuated fall of the Soviet empire, their only choice appeared to be the one they had been so reluctant to pursue in past decades. With the Cold War and the Nordic Balance gone, they would have to turn to Europe.

chapter 7

A SEARCH FOR IDENTITY, 1990–1996

Just before midnight on 11 March 1990, the Lithuanian parliament declared independence. The Lithuanians, headed by Vytautas Landsbergis, had to face months of harassment, including a Soviet economic embargo. In early 1991 Soviet troops seized a number of buildings in Vilnius and on the so-called Bloody Sunday on 13 January 1991—three days prior to the beginning of the Persian Gulf War—15 Lithuanians were killed. But they stood firm. The Latvians and Estonians also declared their independence, and during 1991 it became clear that they were not going to back down. U.S. support for Baltic independence, however, was complicated because of America's need for the Kremlin's support on other issues. In 1990 the United States needed Soviet acceptance for the reunited Germany's inclusion in NATO, and in early 1991 Bush had to secure Gorbachev's acquiescence to keep intact the Gulf War coalition against Iraq.

Some of the strongest external support for the Baltic states' campaign for independence came from Scandinavia. In February 1991 the Nordic Council invited the presidents of the three Baltic republics to attend a meeting in Copenhagen. Later during the same month, Iceland's *Althing* voted to recognize the independence of Estonia, Latvia, and Lithuania and offered to "act as a mediator in negotiations between the Soviet Union and the Baltic states."[1] Such an offer meant little in practice, however, as the last dramatic events that relegated the USSR into history books unfolded. On 21 August 1991, following the failed hard-line coup, Boris Yeltsin seized the day. A few days later, Russia and the Scandinavian countries recognized the Baltics, while the United States waited until early September before it followed suit.

The differences in the American and Scandinavian attitudes toward the independence struggles of the Baltic states spoke volumes about the confusion and eventual reconfiguration of policies and attitudes that resulted from the end of the Cold War. If the Scandinavian countries had previously defined their international role as somewhere in between East and West, they were now taking their first steps toward a position "Between the Balts and Brussels," as Ole Waever put in a November 1994 article in *Current History*.[2] At the same time, however, the idea of a united Norden was challenged, mostly by the fact that by 1995 three of the five had become members of the EU, while Norway and Iceland—traditionally the most Atlantic-oriented—still refused to embrace the lure of Europe. In the 1990s the common Nordic identity was further challenged by the apparent irrelevance of the Middle Way in a new era where the welfare state was under constant attack from the champions of privatization.

Across the Atlantic, the Americans were wondering about their role in a world that was no longer conveniently divided. It was a world in which George Bush led the United States into the Gulf War, a world that saw both reunification (Germany) and disintegration (Yugoslavia), a world without (after December 1991) the Soviet Union. Bush, like many other postwar presidents, spoke of a "new world order," but appeared unable to deliver. If anything, the post–Cold War world was more crisis-prone than the era preceding it: there were crises in Somalia; continued and escalating bloodshed in former Yugoslavia; dangers of an outright civil war in Russia; trade disputes between the United States, the European Union, and Japan; specters of Islamic fundamentalism; internal and external terrorism. Amidst all this, Bush could not even hold on to the presidency. Bill Clinton—the youngish Arkansas governor with little experience in foreign affairs—seized the day in November 1992. While trying to focus on America's domestic problems, he soon faced external crises that were both more limited in scope and more numerous than those with which his predecessors had contended. In the fall of 1994, voters rejected Clinton's more conservative brand of liberalism as the Republicans gained control of the Congress and Newt Gingrich's "Contract with America" apparently ushered in a new era of conservatism.

The common link between the Americans and the Scandinavians in the cacophonous post–Cold War world was that they were both seeking to redefine their international roles and domestic priorities. The Scandinavians found that the world had not been made in their image, that the Middle Way and the welfare state had been, for the most part, discredited. At the same time, the Americans faced their own identity crisis. With the Soviet threat gone, the world had become a chaotic place in which American military power had become less meaningful and the U.S. economy appeared stagnant. While the military justification for continued U.S. presence in Europe had decreased, Washington searched for a role in the restructuring of post–Cold War European security.

At the same time, however, the Scandinavians still held a potentially significant role in American foreign policy as mediators and bridge builders. One

prime example was the Oslo Channel, a secret negotiating structure established in January 1993 to nurture an agreement between Israel and the PLO;
it eventually climaxed in the joint appearance of Yasser Arafat and Yitzhak
Rabin on the White House lawn in September 1993. In a different context,
the Scandinavians could play a potentially major role in building a bridge
between the EU and the former Soviet bloc. By the mid-1990s, they proved
particularly important as partners in a Baltic Growth Zone, an economic sub-
region that consisted of the Baltic States, Denmark, Sweden, Finland, Russia,
Poland, and Germany.

With the acceleration of European integration, the significance of the
bilateral and multilateral relations between the United States and the five
Scandinavian countries was bound to diminish. The Baltic region and Brussels
rapidly replaced Moscow and Washington as the central concerns of Scandinavian foreign and security policy. By the mid-1990s, the end result was
that—notwithstanding the complications of Icelandic and Norwegian decisions to remain outside the EU—relations between Scandinavia and the
United States were becoming an increasingly minor part of a much broader
transatlantic relationship.

THE UNITED STATES AND THE EUROPEAN SECURITY CONUNDRUM

The end of the Cold War had opened a true Pandora's box in terms of European security. With the ascendancy of Mikhail Gorbachev in 1985, glasnost
and perestroika had clearly exposed the intractable problems within the Eastern bloc that led to the rapid dissolution of the Eastern European communist
dictatorships in 1989. Eventually, after a series of ups and downs, they would
lead to the collapse of the Soviet Union in December 1991. At the same time,
Germany, the country that had symbolized the division of postwar Europe,
unified. The collapse of the postwar international and European security systems freed an underlying current of nationalism and ethnic rivalries that the
Cold War had overshadowed for almost half a century. The effects of this lack
of restraint soon erupted in the Balkans as the Yugoslav federation came apart
and descended to an orgy of violence. Americans and West Europeans, meanwhile, had to contend with another unsettling conflict of the post–Cold War
world as the Iraqis invaded Kuwait. President Bush, between discussions about
the new world order, mustered together an impressive coalition that eventually had little trouble in pushing the Iraqis back to Baghdad. In short, the 1989
"Year of Miracles" was followed by years of unanswered problems, tough challenges, and a need to rethink common principles and institutional arrangements regarding security and foreign policy.

As the Soviet threat faded away, Western Europe, including Scandinavia,
faced exciting new opportunities and unsure prospects. For all its unpleasant-
ness and wasteful spending on the nuclear arms race, the Cold War had made
security and foreign policy decisions relatively straightforward. While living in

the shadow of a nuclear holocaust, most West Europeans had at least agreed on their "vital" security interests. But with the threat that produced such relative unanimity gone, the search for a new common denominator proved difficult. In the years 1989–1992, trying to find agreement was further hampered by the institutional rivalries between the CSCE, NATO, and the WEU—all creations of the Cold War. An added problem was that the major decision makers involved in the process were all children of the Cold War, with little vision about how to adjust to a chaotic new world. While George Bush may have spoken of a new world order, the reality consisted mostly of disorder, competition, distrust, and, inevitably, incoherent policies and institutional readjustments.

At the same time, however, the collapse of the Soviet Union and the dissolution of the Warsaw Pact spelled the need to redefine NATO's role and the notion of security in general. With the relative stability and predictability of the Cold War gone, with nationalism and ethnic conflict increasingly rampant, with the strategic significance of the North Atlantic area diminishing as the need to control northern waters no longer appeared to be an important strategic objective, and as traditional military notions of security appeared to be losing their significance, the focus shifted elsewhere.

Initially, the end of the Cold War seemed to enhance the role of the CSCE. After all, it was the only European-based security organization that included the members of NATO, the neutrals, and the former Soviet Bloc. Thus, it was the only Cold War security structure to which the five Scandinavian countries and the United States belonged. In the early 1990s the CSCE was viewed, momentarily, as an institution that offered a chance to resolve the many security issues—political, economic, and military—that were rapidly coming to the fore. Its stated aims of promoting human rights and economic cooperation between East and West appeared particularly appealing to the emerging democracies in Eastern Europe. Also, in November 1990, hopes were high when the CSCE member countries signed the Paris Charter that emphasized cooperation in a broad field of issues ranging from human rights and democracy to economic liberty and environmental responsibility. Notable was the downplaying of military security, a reflection, perhaps, of the optimism of the times.

In the summer of 1991, however, military security became a major European issue as the turmoil in Yugoslavia erupted after Slovenia and Croatia announced that they were leaving the Yugoslav federation. The CSCE was quickly paralyzed as the Yugoslav vote (and, given the unanimity rule, veto right) in the CSCE was controlled by the Serbs. In addition, during the early 1992 meeting of CSCE foreign ministers, the German proposal for the creation of a CSCE peacekeeping force was rejected and the CSCE was relegated to a minor, all but insignificant, role. At best, it could provide only a moral voice as the atrocities grew and the frustration mounted.

In the meantime, a limited rivalry between NATO and the WEU developed. At issue was the redefinition of the relationship between the United

States and Western Europe in the post–Cold War era. In the spirit of Europhoria, the French in particular hoped that the WEU would overtake NATO as the preeminent institutional framework for European security and defense matters. During the Gulf War the WEU, in fact, coordinated the military contributions of its member countries, albeit within the general framework of NATO.

The apparent enhancement of the WEU's role in 1989–1991 was partly a result of the concern by NATO, and particularly by the United States, with the major issues unfolding at the time. While NATO's initial reaction to the fall of the Soviet empire was rather muted, its main focus was on the impact of German unification and the still-outstanding arms control negotiations. Throughout the 1990s NATO, in fact, seemed to be relinquishing the major role for post–Cold War European security to CSCE. In 1990–1991, NATO's main concerns were the Gulf War and the relationship with the former Soviet bloc, particularly the future control over the vast nuclear arsenal stationed in the various former Soviet republics.

From the Scandinavian perspective, the continuance of NATO as the preeminent security organization in post–Cold War Europe and the emergence of the WEU as a potential challenger that, after the Maastricht Treaty of 1992, was earmarked to become the EU's security policy apparatus, complicated their position. By the mid-1990s, none of the Scandinavian countries were members of the WEU (although Iceland became an associate member and the rest became observers) and Denmark, Iceland, and Norway were clearly reluctant to support a movement toward a Western European, rather than a transatlantic, security structure. In the uncertain post–Cold War Era, Scandinavia placed a high value on continued American presence in Europe. At the same time, Sweden and Finland remained unwilling to join NATO, but appeared to be more positive about American initiatives than during the Cold War.

In January 1994, the Clinton administration's "Partnership for Peace" (PfP) formula could be seen as a U.S. effort to seize control over establishing a future pan-European security framework. For the Scandinavian neutrals, however, PfP appeared to offer a meaningful alternative in the midst of the continued insecurities of the post–Cold War world, especially after Russia also signed the PfP agreement in May 1994. Sweden's Foreign Minister Margaretha af Ugglas could hardly contain her enthusiasm, labeling the PfP initiative as one that embraced "a security concept that is broader than the Cold War concept of military security alone." In a bold statement that appeared to throw Swedish neutrality into the dustbin of history, the conservative foreign minister added that "as the pace of history accelerates and our involvement with the rest of Europe deepens, the policy we pursue could no longer be labelled neutrality." Finally, in a statement that clearly recognized Swedish appreciation for the presence of American troops in Europe, af Ugglas maintained that Sweden "continues to see an American presence in Europe at its currently planned level as a precondition for a viable and effective NATO."[3] The nation that had been one of the foremost West European critics of the United States had apparently turned into one of its supporters.

The implications of the new European security policy conundrum to Scandinavian neutrality had been recognized by the Finns as well. Already before the formal dissolution of the USSR, the Finnish foreign minister (until the spring of 1995), Pertti Paasio, maintained in a speech in Oslo on 3 January 1991: "Neutrality has served Finland well. But neutrality is not enough. Participation in the development of European cooperation is vital for the small countries. We have to maintain a viable and satisfactory relationship with the EC."[4] It was a statement unimaginable only a few years earlier.

BEYOND FINLANDIZATION

Of the five Scandinavian countries, Finland's position underwent the most profound change during the early 1990s. It was linked, to a large extent, to developments in the Baltics. The delicate role that Finland had acquired during the Cold War had been largely based on its ability to maintain a cordial relationship with the Soviet Union, a relationship that was not based on equality, but on a tacit understanding that Finland would pay lip service to the USSR's foreign and security policy needs. The clearest example of this was the FCMA Treaty that had been signed in April 1948 (see chapter 2). It had made Finland part of the Soviet security system—the Finns had, among other things, agreed to counter any attacks against the Soviet Union through Finnish territory. While accommodating the Soviets and accepting a somewhat limited sovereignty, the Finns had tried to make a credible claim to neutrality and countered charges of "Finlandization." After Gorbachev's ascendancy in 1985, the Finno-Soviet relationship had gradually changed. *Finlandization* had become a term used to express the type of relationship that might have developed between the USSR and its former satellites; indeed, Secretary of State James Baker even suggested to Gorbachev that he not obstruct the Baltic states' claims for independence but let them leave the USSR and become "three little Finlands" (see chapter 6).

When the Soviet Union dissolved at the end of 1991, the last remnants of the postwar restrictions imposed on Finnish independence were removed. On 20 January 1992, Finland and Russia exchanged notes canceling the FCMA Treaty. The two countries signed a treaty that based itself on the U.N. Charter and the CSCE Final Act. The 1992 treaty contained no military or security clauses, no talk of potential military assistance or consultations, but simply a mention that in case international peace and security appeared to be endangered, Finland and Russia should "contact each other, as necessary, with the purpose of using the means offered by the United Nations and the CSCE in the settlement of the conflict." Other parts of the treaty concerned mostly commercial and financial issues. Article 6, for example, called for the "promotion of cooperation between Finland and the adjacent neighboring regions of Murmansk, Karelia, and St. Petersburg."[5]

As John Lukacs wrote in a 1992 article in *Foreign Affairs*, the cancellation of the 1948 FCMA Treaty removed "the last remnant of restrictions on an independent Finnish foreign policy."[6] Finns themselves clearly enjoyed the new freedom. The first completely nonsocialist cabinet, headed by the Center Party's young leader, Esko Aho, turned to Western Europe and applied for membership in the European Union later that year. In 1993, in a move that would have been unimaginable during the Cold War, Finnish Defense Minister Elizabeth Rehn successfully pressed for the purchase of 65 American Hornet jets for the Finnish Air Force. Meanwhile, the Finns became active investors in the Baltic states, especially in Estonia. Although events in Russia—particularly the victory of Vladimir Zhirinovsky's ultranationalist party in the December 1993 duma elections—caused jitters in Finland, the 1994 Finnish presidential election exemplified the almost complete repudiation of the foreign policies practiced during previous decades; all the major candidates, including the eventual winner, SDP's Martti Ahtisaari, supported Finland's membership in the EU. The Finns were, it seemed, ready for complete Europeanization.

While the Finns moved beyond Finlandization and toward Europe, however, it was obvious that the laws of geography would not allow them (nor the other Scandinavians) to simply ignore Russia and the Commonwealth of Independent States, the loose union established in December 1991 that included the successor states of the former Soviet Union. Given the discrepancy in living standards between Finland and Russia (the highest GNP gap between two neighboring countries in Europe) and the length of the border between the two countries, "a constant and probably increasing trickle of unregistered migrants from the erstwhile Soviet Union" became an increasingly acute concern for Finnish authorities during the 1990s. In addition, Finno-Soviet trade, which amounted to more than one-fifth of Finland's foreign trade during the Cold War, had crumbled already in the late 1980s (down from 27 percent of Finland's exports in 1982 to 11 percent in 1990) and contributed to high unemployment levels that approached 20 percent by the mid-1990s.[7] While Finland's Cold War–era security policy may have been "vindicated" in the early 1990s, while the negative image of Finlandization was abandoned by even its most vocal advocates, the foreign economic policies Finland had practiced left a devastating legacy.

BETWEEN BALTS AND BRUSSELS

In January 1992 Danish Foreign Minister Uffe Ellemann-Jensen spoke at the London Chamber of Commerce and Industry about the future of the Baltics in light of the end of the Cold War and the rapid progress toward European integration. His message was clear: "The Baltic Sea is no longer a blind alley on the outskirts of Europe, but will once more become a centre of activity and prosperity, become what some people refer to as the Baltic Growth Zone." Ellemann-Jensen added that the Baltic zone, to which Denmark, Sweden, and Finland were intimately linked, would be "one of four or five main areas of development in Europe."[8]

Ellemann-Jensen had captured the essence of what many hoped would soon be reality: an economically dynamic region around the Baltic Sea in which the more prosperous states—Germany and the Scandinavian countries—would invest in the new democracies with the end result being the creation of something akin to the medieval Hanseatic league, a free (or semi-free) trade zone where high growth rates would help the transition of the formerly communist states to democracy. Prosperity might also undermine the potential rise of nationalism and ethnic conflict, particularly in the Baltic states that have a large ethnic Russian population. If successful, the Baltic Growth Zone could also help in diffusing potentially intense security conflicts that might arise over, in particular, the landlocked Russian base of Kaliningrad. At the same time, the Baltic Growth Zone captures—because of its inevitable links to questions about EU enlargement, European security, and relations between the former "East" and "West"—much of the ongoing reconfiguration of the Nordic countries' position in the post–Cold War world and the confusion surrounding the cherished idea of a common Nordic identity.

To be sure, the idea of 'Norden' had lost part of its appeal already before the end of the Cold War. Having rejected the NORDEK plan in the early 1970s, the Scandinavians' regional cooperation had clearly suffered an almost mortal blow. Although the Nordic Council continued its meetings, although work on cultural interchanges and on practical matters (ranging from full social insurance coverage for Scandinavian citizens all over the region to the right to use their own languages in contacts with the authorities throughout Scandinavia, both agreed upon in 1981) continued, the Nordic countries were never destined to have effective integration in the "high" levels of economics, security, and politics. Even in the post–Cold War era, the Scandinavians appeared to be stuck with their specific model of cobweb integration.

The problem was that during this same time, the rest of Western Europe had stepped up the speed of integration. Thus, the Scandinavians, with the exception of the lone EEC member, Denmark, sooner or later had to face a choice between Europe and a growing degree of isolation, especially because the alternative to the EEC, EFTA, had lost most of its significance with the accession of its strongest member, Great Britain, to the EEC in 1972. Official debate in the late 1970s and early 1980s was muted, but new winds of change were on the horizon. In the 1980s the main constraint for Finland and Sweden was their neutrality, for Norway, the experience of 1972, for Iceland, the limited gains that accession could bring for a country reliant on the fishing industry. Then there was, of course, the fact that the Scandinavians were among the wealthiest people in the world. Their GNPs were near the top on every list, with Denmark, the lone EEC member, usually at the bottom of the Nordic group.

The reunification of Germany, the collapse of the Soviet Union, and the rapid progress toward European integration that was accelerated as a result of these events, thrust most Scandinavian governments into applying for membership in the European Union. As a temporary measure, the EC and EFTA countries established the European Economic Area (EEA) in 1992, but before the EEA began its operation in January 1994, Finland, Norway, and Sweden (along with Austria) had applied for EU membership (Sweden did so already in June 1991). At the same time the Icelanders, although part of the EEA, appeared to be in no hurry and did not even apply for membership in the EU.

The Scandinavians exhibited continued reluctance at the idea of being too closely associated with the continent. Already in June 1992, the Danish voters had delivered a major shock by rejecting the Maastricht Treaty, although a second referendum in May 1993 approved a modified pact. During the fall of 1994, referendums in Finland and Sweden eventually approved the treaty. In Norway, however, the referendum in late November 1994 resulted in a "no" vote (52.5 percent to 47.5 percent). The end result was that by 1995, Scandinavia had been split in two.

The complications for the idea and reality of Norden were clear. What would remain of Nordic cooperation now that some were in the EU while others were not? For example, would the border between Sweden and Norway become as tightly controlled as the other EU vs. non-EU borders such as the border between Germany and Poland? Or the one between Russia and Finland?

Although such an action was not about to happen, it was clear that the Icelandic and Norwegian decisions would leave them outside the mainstream of European development for the time being. Yet this turn of events was not necessarily negative. In the bridge building that had been such a large part of Nordic identity during the Cold War, the Icelanders and Norwegians occupied a minor, but potentially significant, niche between the EU and the United States. As NATO members, they have the opportunity to act as mediators in future conflicts between European and North American interests and could, once again, help solve some of the alliance's internal differences.

More importantly, however, Denmark, Finland, and Sweden could act as the gateway between the EU and the Baltic states. The Scandinavians have had an important role as midwives to a new European security structure, particularly in helping ease the privatization process underway in the former Soviet bloc; the long-term goal was to prevent the revival of old national animosities between, say, Germany and its eastern neighbors. More broadly speaking, the challenge was for the future of EU–East European relations and the potential further enlargement of the EU to the countries of the former

Soviet bloc, to which increased prosperity, democratization, and privatization were clear preconditions.

A June 1992 editorial in the *New York Times* after the first Danish referendum on the Maastricht Treaty explained the "no" vote against this background with a hint of optimism. The result was described as "the clearest sign yet that Europeans are uneasy about surrendering the attributes of sovereignty to a centralized authority." At the same time, however, the editorial stressed that concerns over potential German hegemony over the EU were an overreaction. From Washington's perspective, moreover, European integration meant more than just "a way to dampen old national conflicts and promote worldwide economic growth." The United States "[has] an interest in extending integration further east, where newly capitalist countries struggle to overcome a demoralizing legacy," the editorial continued. Thus, Denmark's rejection of the Maastricht treaty in 1992 "may force the E.C. to establish different levels of membership. That, in turn, would make it much easier to embrace the East." As a result, "Denmark's 'no' could yet contribute to wider European unity."[9] In short, the editorial implied that with their rejection, the Danish voters had opened a new era of post–Cold War bridge building.

Helping the newly independent Baltic states became, indeed, a vital challenge affecting the future security of post–Cold War Scandinavia. As John Fitzmaurice wrote, the Nordic countries "have vital economic, environmental and security interests in the region, which can best be safeguarded by strengthening regional ties across the Baltic and contributing to the viability of these new Baltic partners."[10] In practice this has meant that, although somewhat tempered by domestic economic difficulties, the Scandinavian countries, particularly Finland and Sweden, have invested heavily in the newly independent republics. By the mid-1990s the Baltics, particularly Estonia, had made great headway toward a market economy, a task made easier by their small populations (the combined total of approximately 8 million people is less than Sweden's population alone).

Scandinavian participation in promoting the Baltic Growth Zone is also a way of limiting the further rise of German influence in the region, as well as a way of allaying Russian security concerns. In a very clear sense, the Scandinavians are, therefore, still building bridges between East and West, albeit in a completely new international framework. In the post–Cold War world, the Scandinavians' vision of the future, although not necessarily a unified one, has clearly come to stress the idea of a "Europe" that, as Finnish Prime Minister Esko Aho said in the fall of 1994 in a speech at the opening of the Finnland-Institut in Berlin, "ranges from the Atlantic to the Urals."[11] Although his Gaullist statement would not have been welcomed in the United States during the Cold War, it certainly fits nicely with the idea that a broader (and looser) European Union is preferable to Washington than a narrow and more tightly knit, perhaps protectionist, one.

In the 1990s, the Scandinavians have not, therefore, been reduced to completely insignificant players in the reshaping of Europe. As Richard Latter put it in 1992, "Nordic participation in the European mainstream is essential; the 'Norden' option is indeed an echo from the past." Yet, Latter added with hope, what this fact also meant was that bridge building, the policy that appeared to have become a relic already in the 1980s, might well prove useful if refashioned to meet the challenges of a new era. Most importantly, the Nordic countries might provide a bridge between an economically prosperous European Union and the aspiring new democracies of Eastern Europe and the CIS. As he put it: "During the Cold War the Nordic countries developed a reputation for just this kind of effort which can now be directed to helping establish a stable European security environment."[12]

But it was not the structural bridge building between East and West that provided the most sensational headlines; that was, after all, a long and arduous process that would have to continue for years. Rather, it was the remarkable success of a Norwegian-engineered peace plan that produced one of the more spectacular results of modern conflict resolution and, momentarily at least, captured the attention of the world in 1993. The irony was that the Oslo Channel had little to do with American policy toward Scandinavia or East-West relations in Europe.

THE OSLO CHANNEL

On 13 September 1993, one of the most remarkable ceremonies of post-1945 world history unfolded on the White House lawn. U.S. President Bill Clinton, PLO Chairman Yasser Arafat, and Israeli Prime Minister Yitzhak Rabin took to the podium to announce the long-awaited reconciliation between the PLO and Israel. Almost everyone who had played a role in this or previous efforts to bring peace to the Middle East was there, including Jimmy Carter, Henry Kissinger, and George Bush. They all applauded as Shimon Peres, the foreign minister (and after Rabin's assassination in 1996, prime minister) of Israel, and Abu Mazen, one of Arafat's top aides, signed the documents that promised self-government for Gaza and the West Bank. Although the signing ceremony in the White House was an apparent tribute to American power in the post–Cold War world, the fact remained that for two years following the end of the Gulf War in the spring of 1991, the United States had not been able to muster the conflicting parties toward a successful peace agreement. The Israeli-Palestinian Accords had not been negotiated under American auspices, but in a series of secret talks that took place in secluded log cabins and country houses in Norway over a nine-month period starting in early 1993. In the end, it had not been American threats or promises but "the Oslo Channel"—symbolically recognized by the seating of Norwegian Foreign Minister Johan J. Holst alongside the former U.S. presidents—that had provided the last necessary push toward one of the potentially most significant achievements in twentieth-century conflict resolution.

The success of the Oslo Channel clearly suggests that small countries could have an important role in nurturing solutions to seemingly intractable local conflicts. Indeed, the accommodation between the Israelis and Palestinians in 1993 appeared to prove the point that was nicely captured in the title of Jan Egeland's (Norway's deputy foreign minister and one of the chief planners of the Oslo Channel) book, *Impotent Superpower: Potent Small State* (1989). Even in the wake of the victory in the Gulf War and the dissolution of the Soviet Union, the United States had found it frustratingly difficult to engineer a solution to the longstanding Israeli-Palestinian standoff. Instead, by extending bridge building into a new context, the Norwegians enabled President Clinton to claim the public relations benefits of an accord that he and his predecessor, George Bush, had been unable to deliver.

The success of the Oslo Channel was helped by the fact that in the 1990s, Norway was respected by both the Palestinians and the Israelis. Following World War II, Norway had been one of the strongest supporters of the creation of Israel, and the postwar Norwegian governments had created strong ties with the Israeli Labor Party. In the late 1980s, Norwegian Foreign Minister Thorvald Stoltenberg, along with his young deputy foreign minister Jan Egeland, forged a closer relationship with the PLO by, for example, introducing generous grants for humanitarian and medical aid in the Occupied Territories. With the aid of Terje Rod Larsen, a Norwegian academic who studied the living conditions in the Gaza Strip, and his wife, Mona Juul, a Middle East specialist in the Norwegian foreign ministry, Egeland was able to initiate the second track of negotiations that began in January 1993. The secret talks in Norway were filled with numerous practical problems. For example, at the beginning of the very first set of talks on 20 January 1993, the chief PLO negotiator, Abu Ala, was upset about the extensive searches he and his two partners were subjected to by the Norwegian immigration officials upon their entry. He threatened to go straight home without even meeting his Israeli counterparts. Terje Larsen, who bore the bulk of the strain involved in keeping the two sides at the negotiating table, was able to calm Abu Ala down by explaining that in order to stick to secrecy, the Norwegian authorities could not arrange any special treatment for the delegations, who came to Norway as "academic visitors." Despite this rocky start, the negotiations got under way and the two sides eventually met in secrecy numerous times over the subsequent months.

The climax came during Foreign Minister Shimon Peres's Scandinavian visit on the night of 17 August 1993. In a rather bizarre scene at Peres's guest house in Stockholm, Norwegian Foreign Minister Johan J. Holst placed a call to Yasser Arafat in Tunis at Peres's request. Peres wanted to finish the talks that night, he had told Holst, adding, however, that he did not want to speak to Arafat himself. At the other end, Arafat did not wish to carry on a conversation as important as this in his less-than-perfect English, and had Abu Ala do the interpreting while Arafat shouted instructions in Arabic in the background. Holst then acted as a "true" mediator during an overnight bargaining session that ironed out the final agreement on West Bank and Ghaza by 5:00 the next morning. On 20 August 1993, during Peres's brief stopover in Oslo, the two sides signed the Declaration of Principles on Interim Self-Government Arrangements. On 26 August, Holst and Peres made a secret trip to California to break the news and discuss the details of the agreement with Secretary of State Warren Christopher. A few days later, the deal was finally made public, although the final phase of negotiations, on mutual recognition, continued for several days.

The Oslo Channel was not, of course, solely responsible for the Israeli-PLO agreement signed at the White House in September 1993. The Norwegians had not offered anything substantive and had specifically refused to mediate; their role in the negotiations was purely that of facilitator. Nor was the agreement perfect; it soon came under attack from extremists on both sides. Nevertheless, it is hard to disagree with Jane Corbin's assessment that "[t]he quiet diplomacy of Norway was a new and significant part of the forging of the peace accord and may well become a model for mediation in other conflicts." It was further helped by the fact that Norway was "balanced between the sides [and] had the advantage that its own strategic resources of oil made it independent from the maelstrom of the Middle East."[13] The Oslo Channel was, without a doubt, one of the great success stories of the early post–Cold War years and indicated that bridge building could have a life beyond the East-West confrontation.

IS THE MIDDLE WAY DEAD?

Notwithstanding the brief period in the spotlight as peacemakers, Norwegians, and Scandinavians in general, could not escape the undeniable fact that they faced an ongoing identity crisis. Already in late 1990, for example, both neutrality and the welfare state were called into question. As the *New York Times* put it in December 1990:

> The end of the cold war and the beginning of a recession have plunged the neutral welfare states of Western Europe into an identity crisis. Most are nearly falling over themselves to join the European Community in the hope that membership will bring a return to prosperity and a new vision of the future to replace the "Swedish model" of political neutrality between East and West, extensive social-welfare programs and an economy combining capitalism with a sizable public sector.[14]

At the time this article appeared, the Swedes were, indeed, already taking serious steps to revamp the welfare state, reducing, for example, public expenditure by $3 billion in 1991; there were even proposals of privatizing the national health service and many other government-run operations (railroads, post office, electric utilities).

A few years later, Ole Waever described the Scandinavian identity crisis as follows:

> Nordic identity is in crisis. With the European revolution of 1989–91, the meaning of the term "Norden" has become unclear. In security terms, Nordic identity was defined by having lower military tension than Central Europe. In socio-economic terms, Nordic identity was dependent on the competition between capitalism and communism, offering a third way. At a deeper level, Norden represented a model of the enlightened, anti-militaristic society that was superior to the old Europe.

The end of the East-West confrontation, the dismemberment of the Soviet Union, and the accelerating speed of European integration seemed to have eaten away the very foundations of regional identity. With the USSR's collapse, there appeared to be no need for the Nordic Balance; with the discrediting of communism, the Middle Way and the welfare state seemed equally defunct; with the signing of the Maastricht Treaty, Europhoria had seized the day. The Scandinavians had lost their position as the great "modernizers," as the avant-garde society. It seemed, as Waever put it, that, "Suddenly the sources of the future are to be found not in Norden, but on the Continent. The less-European identity of 'Norden' is no longer a promise, but a threat—the threat of being [on the] periphery."[15]

Such notions were not simply utterances from a few select observers. The new nonsocialist cabinets elected in Sweden and Finland in the fall of 1991 had clearly signaled their intention to follow the Danish example and move further away from the Middle Way. Between 1991 and 1994, two of the youngest Scandinavian prime ministers led the charge. In Sweden, the 42-year-old conservative Carl Bildt declared that, "The time for the Nordic model has passed." In Helsinki, the Center Party's prime minister Esko Aho, five years younger than Bildt, similarly announced, "The Nordic model is dead." Bildt explained his enthusiasm for change by arguing that the Middle Way had "created societies that were too monopolized, too expensive and didn't give people the freedom of choice they wanted; societies that lacked flexibility and dynamism." To the new leaders, Scandinavia did not represent a superior form of society. Rather, the Middle Way ideology had nurtured national cultures that were "too grey and too conformist."[16]

It is remarkable that Bildt's words were reminiscent, almost identical, to the criticism of the Middle Way that had been expressed in the United States throughout the Cold War. In this sense, the new generation assuming leadership positions in Scandinavia was moving much closer to an "American" vision of a highly privatized economic system as the only credible foundation of a "good society." It was as if Bildt and Aho were acknowledging that President Eisenhower had been correct in his criticism of Swedish society back in 1960, a criticism that had caused an uproar from the Swedes and other Scandinavians (see chapter 4). At the same time, however, the popularity of anti-welfare politics in the 1990s was clearly linked to the immediate post–Cold War difficulties facing leftist parties throughout Europe—witness the political impotence of, for example, either the Labor Party in Britain or the German Social Democrats. The repudiation of communism had a clear spillover effect on the political fortunes of even the most moderate left-wing parties. As William E. Schmidt of the *New York Times* wrote: "the changes sweeping the Nordic countries are a direct result of what has happened elsewhere in Europe, where the influence of socialist politicians has waned and the political rhetoric has moved away from words like collectivity and solidarity, and toward notions such as privatization, deregulation and individual choice."[17] Moving clearly toward membership in the EU, the Scandinavians would be under even more pressure to standardize their programs with those of the other member countries, most of which did not come close to the Nordic countries in terms of overall spending on social welfare. By 1993 some observers, like the Danes Ib Jørgensen and Jens Tonboe, warned that with the apparent eclipse of the Middle Way, "We seem to be moving away from the Keynesian-Scandinavian welfare state and toward a Schumpterian workfare state of some kind."[18]

In the end, however, the shift did not result in a complete turnaround or in a clear-cut abandonment of the Middle Way. The "overreaching" of the welfare state had not destroyed Scandinavian societies or, for that matter, struck a mortal blow at the parties that were its foremost torchbearers. By 1994–1995, for example, the Social Democrats rebounded politically in Finland and Sweden as the more conservative parties were unable to solve post–Cold War economic difficulties. The Bildt and Aho governments may have made politically courageous, and perhaps fiscally responsible, decisions to slim down government spending, but doing so at a time of high unemployment (in Finland, close to 18 percent in 1994–1995) did little to improve their electoral success.

Therefore, a "privatization revolution" hardly took place in Scandinavia, or Western Europe in general, during the first half of the 1990s. In the end, all that seemed to occur was, as Nathaniel C. Nash of the *New York Times* wrote, "a modest belt-tightening by politicians. Major overhauls—passing through real economic pain to generate a renewed private sector that will create jobs— are not on the horizon."[19] The welfare state that was built after World War II was too deeply entrenched in the national psyche to be revamped overnight; it was simply not politically feasible. At the most, there was some tinkering at the edges. If anything, it was clearly acknowledged that the Middle Way—a mixed economy with large responsibilities given to the public sector—had actually always been closer to the mainstream of Western European economic thought and practice than could have been admitted during the Cold War.

TOWARD A NEW MILLENNIUM

Much has changed in the years following the collapse of the Berlin Wall and the dissolution of the Soviet empire. Nordic integration, the Middle Way, and

Scandinavian regional identity are being challenged by the forces unleashed in Europe during the early 1990s. But Scandinavian regionalism is not the only casualty. The internationalism of many Scandinavians—illustrated by, for example, the policy of bridge building—has been replaced by the need to associate more closely with European integration. Concurrently, the Americans appear to be in retreat. With the Soviet threat gone, Washington has less of a need to assume global responsibility. Nor does there appear to be much of an external market for the ideologically laden American rhetoric of the previous decades. The irony is that with the apparent victory of the United States in the Cold War, the "free world" has become, for the most part, an empty phrase.

At the same time, as we approach the end of this millennium, geography still looms large in defining the present and future of the Scandinavian countries and their relationship with the United States. Although the Soviet Union no longer exists, Russia and the CIS present another type of security threat to the Nordic countries. The specter of a nuclear holocaust may be gone, or at least diminished, but widespread economic dislocation in the Soviet successor states raises the question of large-scale immigration to Scandinavia. This concern is especially grave now in the mid-1990s when Russia suffers from severe internal problems, be they cracking down on various secessionist movements (as in Chechnya) or grappling with the social problems that have followed from the privatization revolution of the Yeltsin era.

There is, of course, no clear-cut solution. Nevertheless, with respect to Russia, the United States and the Nordic countries share a similar goal. For Washington, Helsinki, Stockholm, Oslo, Copenhagen, and, although to a lesser degree, Reykjavík, a democratic and gradually more prosperous Russia offers the best guarantee against the revival of old dangers and the exacerbation of new ones. Prosperity appears to be the key against massive outward migration from Russia and the best guard against the replacement of such relatively democratic rulers as Boris Yeltsin by right-wing nationalists (such as Vladimir Zhirinovsky) or the supposedly defunct communists, who experienced an astonishing revival in the December 1995 Russian parliamentary elections and whose leader, Gennady Zyuganov, emerged as Yeltsin's major, albeit ultimately unsuccessful, challenger in the 1996 presidential elections. In the second half of the 1990s, the Scandinavians continue to be in a position where they can attempt to build bridges to the East. This time, unlike during the Cold War, they can count on Washington's approval.

In retrospect, it seems clear that throughout the last half of the twentieth century, Americans and Scandinavians have helped reshape postwar Europe in fundamental, albeit clearly distinct, ways. As the major partner in NATO, the United States assumed a huge responsibility—however ulterior the motives may have been or whoever did the initial "pulling" or "pushing"— over the security of Western Europe, including Scandinavia. With the Marshall Plan and the support given to various European integration efforts,

Washington further encouraged the process that eventually led to the Maastricht Treaty, which, many hoped, would ultimately lead to the creation of the United States of Europe. At the same time, the Scandinavian model of a welfare state gradually became a part of the Western European consciousness. In this regard the Scandinavians, much like the Americans, were not enforcers but trendsetters, the ones who set an example. Whether they can continue to do so in the future is an open question.

CHRONOLOGY

1000	Leif Erikson in Vineland (Newfoundland)
1638	New Sweden established on the Delaware River
1809	Russia takes over Finland;
	Sweden acquires Norway
1905	Norway separates from Sweden
1914	World War I begins;
	Denmark (Iceland), Norway, and Sweden declare neutrality
1917	United States joins World War I;
	Finland becomes independent from Russia after the Bolshevik Revolution
1918	Civil War in Finland (Whites defeat the Reds);
	World War I ends
1939	Finno-Soviet Winter War begins (ends March 1940)

1940	Denmark and Norway occupied by the Germans, Iceland by the British
1941	Finland begins to act as cobelligerent with Germany against the USSR;
	United States takes over the occupation of Iceland
1944	Finno-Soviet Armistice;
	Iceland becomes independent from Denmark
1945	World War II ends
1946	Trygve Lie becomes the first secretary general of the United Nations;
	U.S.-Icelandic Keflavík Agreement allows only a contingency force necessary to operate the airport
1947	Paris Peace Treaty (Finland);
	Marshall Plan is announced;
	Denmark, Iceland, Norway, and Sweden participate in Paris talks, while Finland declines the invitation under Soviet pressure;
	First talks about a possible Scandinavian Common Market
1948	Finno-Soviet Treaty of Friendship, Cooperation and Mutual Assistance;
	Discussions begin for a Nordic Defense Union
1949	Denmark, Iceland, and Norway become founding members of NATO
1950	Norway and Denmark sign MDAP agreements;
	Korean War begins;
	Trygve Lie emphatically supports U.N. resolution to counter the North Korean attack, then fails to mediate an end to the conflict
1951	AFNORTH established;

U.S.-Icelandic Defense Agreement, American troops occupy the Keflavík base (Icelandic Defense Force);

Swedish government secretly agrees to comply with most Western export control regulations

1952 Finns deliver their last reparations to the USSR;

ERP ends;

Danish-American secret talks over base rights

1953 Eisenhower inaugurated and Stalin dies;

Nordic Council formed (Denmark, Iceland, Norway, and Sweden);

Dag Hammarskjöld becomes secretary general of the United Nations

1954 Scandinavian Labor Market established;

U.S.-Iceland defense agreement expanded

1955 Finland joins the United Nations;

Norway's Prime Minister Einar Gerhardsen visits the USSR

1956 Porkkala Naval Base returned to Finland;

Iceland's *Althing* calls for the United States to abandon the Keflavík base;

Finland joins the Nordic Council;

Urho Kekkonen elected president in Finland;

Hammarskjöld establishes a U.N. Emergency Force to deal with the Suez Crisis

1958 Sweden, Denmark, and Norway participate in the planning of EFTA;

Night frost crisis between Finland and the Soviet Union (resolved in early 1959);

Anglo-Icelandic cod war (continues until 1961)

1959   Nordic Common Market negotiations break down;

            Stockholm Convention, the founding protocol of EFTA, approved

1960   EFTA treaty becomes operative;

            Eisenhower's criticism of the Swedish welfare state sparks an uproar in Scandinavia;

            Gary Powers shot down over the USSR while heading toward a base in Norway

1961   COMBALTAP established, integrating Danish and West German forces under NATO's auspices;

            Kennedy-Khrushchev Vienna Summit;

            Finland becomes an associate of EFTA (FINEFTA);

            Following the British lead, Denmark applies for EEC membership;

            Note crisis between Finland and the Soviet Union erupts while Kekkonen is touring the United States;

            Sweden makes application for EEC associate membership;

            Dag Hammarskjöld dies in a plane crash in Congo;

            Swedish Foreign Minister Unden publicizes his "nuclear-free club" idea (Unden Plan) at the United Nations

1962   Norway applies for EEC membership;

            Cuban missile crisis;

            Sweden's Alva Myrdal becomes the head of the U.N. Eighteen Nations Disarmament Conference in Geneva

1963   Denmark and Norway withdraw their applications for EEC membership after de Gaulle rejects British entry;

            Kekkonen's Nordic nuclear-free zone proposal is rejected by other Scandinavians as a Soviet-sponsored move;

Lyndon Johnson tours Scandinavia in October, a month before Kennedy is assassinated

1964   TV-war in Iceland

1965   United States begins to deploy ground troops to Vietnam;

Olof Palme, Swedish minister of communications, openly criticizes the American policy and, despite U.S. pressure, the Swedish government refuses to apologize

1966   Swedish ambassador in Beijing opens talks with Hanoi and NLF (code-named ASPEN) in an effort to mediate an end to the Vietnam conflict (continued until February 1968);

Denmark proposes a security conference at NATO minister-ial meeting, eventually leads to the adoption of the Harmel Report in December;

Swedish diplomats help bring about the first set of meetings between Willy Brandt and Soviet ambassador to GDR and *Ostpolitik* begins to take shape

1968   Czechoslovakian crisis;

After a Danish proposal, negotiations begin for the establish-ment of a Nordic Economic Community (NORDEK)

1969   Finland offers to host CSCE talks;

SALT I talks begin in Helsinki, continue until 1972

1970   Iceland becomes a member of EFTA;

After two years of negotiations, Finland turns down NORDEK under Soviet pressure, the whole plan fades away

1972   Preparatory CSCE talks begin in Helsinki;

The Norwegians vote "no" to membership in the EEC

1973   Finland signs a free trade treaty with EC and a trade pact with COMECON;

Denmark becomes a member of the EEC;

Sweden and Norway sign free trade agreements with the EEC;

Swedish-American diplomatic relations frozen due to Olof Palme's criticism of the Christmas bombings (restored in 1974)

1975	Helsinki Accords signed

1978   Grey Zone agreement between Norway and the Soviet Union;

Kekkonen relaunches the Nuclear-Free Zone proposal

1981   American-Norwegian agreement on strengthening U.S. presence in the High North;

Soviet submarine shipwrecked near a Swedish naval base in Karlskrona (Whiskey on the Rocks), violations continue for several years

1984   Conference on Confidence and Security Building Measures and Disarmament in Europe holds its first meeting in Stockholm (continues until 1986);

1985   Mikhail Gorbachev comes to power in the USSR

1986   Olof Palme assassinated in Stockholm;

Reagan-Gorbachev Reykjavík Summit;

Finland becomes a full member of EFTA

1987   In Murmansk, Gorbachev calls for an Arctic Zone of Peace

1988   Sweden and the Soviet Union reach an agreement over the border line between Lithuania and Sweden in the Baltic Sea;

Danish *Folketing* stipulates that no vessels carrying nuclear weapons can enter Danish ports, Secretary of State Shultz warns about "extremely serious consequences"

1989   Gorbachev introduces Sinatra Doctrine, announces plans to destroy four Soviet nuclear submarines in the Baltic, and unconditionally recognizes Finland's neutrality;

At the Malta summit, Gorbachev tells Bush that he wants to move the Soviet Union toward "the Swedish model"

1990	Charter of Paris signed;
	Iraq invades Kuwait in August;
	Baltic states declare independence from the USSR
1991	Conservative-centrist governments take over in Finland (Esko Aho) and Sweden (Carl Bildt), declaring the "Nordic model" dead;
	Sweden applies for EC membership;
	United States and the Scandinavian countries recognize the Baltics' independence;
	Soviet Union ceases to exist;
	CIS formed
1992	In their first referendum, Danish voters reject the Maastricht Treaty; they accept a modified version later;
	Finno-Soviet FCMA Treaty canceled, replaced by a more general Russo-Finnish friendship treaty (without security clauses);
	Finland applies for EC membership
1993	PLO-Israeli talks in Oslo pave the way for a compromise;
	Norway opens negotiations for EC membership
1994	Clinton administration's Partnership for Peace (PfP) proposal meets with positive reaction in Scandinavia;
	In referendums over joining the European Union, the Finns and Swedes accept membership, while Norwegians reject it
1995	Finland and Sweden join the European Union

NOTES AND REFERENCES

CHAPTER 1

1. Franklin D. Scott, *The United States and Scandinavia* (Cambridge: Harvard University Press, 1950), 72–73.

2. Quoted in Henrik S. Nissen, "Adjusting to German Domination," in *Scandinavia during the Second World War*, ed. Henrik S. Nissen (Minneapolis: University of Minnesota Press, 1983), 106.

CHAPTER 2

1. Quoted in J. K. Paasikivi, *Paasikiven linja. Puheita vuosilta 1944–1956* (Porvoo: WSOY, 1966), 23.

2. Quoted in Karl Molin, "Winning the Peace: Vision and Disappointment in Nordic Security Policy, 1945–1949," in *Scandinavia and the Second World War*, ed. Henrik S. Nissen (Minneapolis: University of Minnesota Press, 1983), 331.

3. Marquis Childs, *Sweden: The Middle Way* (New Haven: Yale University Press, 1936).

4. Quoted in Nils Udgaard, *Great Power Politics and Norwegian Foreign Policy* (Oslo: Norwegian University Press, 1973), 125.

5. Quoted in Geir Lundestad, *America, Scandinavia, and the Cold War, 1945–49* (New York: Columbia University Press, 1980), 54.

6. James Barros, *Trygve Lie and the Cold War: The UN Secretary General Pursues Peace, 1946–1953* (Dekalb: Northern Illinois University Press, 1989), 19–26.

7. Quoted in Benedikt Gröndal, *Iceland: From Neutrality to NATO Membership* (Oslo: Universitetsforlaget, 1971), 37.

8. NSC 2/1: "Base Rights in Greenland, Iceland, and the Azores," 25 November 1947, *Documents of the NSC, 1947–77*, Reel I.

9. Ibid.

10. Quoted in Robert W. Matson, "The Helsinki Axioms: U.S.-Finnish Relations, 1941–1949," (Ph.D. diss., University of Oregon, 1981), 196.

11. Matthews quoted in Lundestad, *America, Scandinavia, and the Cold War*, 108.

12. Quoted in Jussi M. Hanhimäki, " 'Containment' in a Borderland: United States and Finland, 1948–1949," *Diplomatic History* 18:3 (Summer 1994), 357.

13. Ibid., 358.

14. George Maude, *The Finnish Dilemma: Neutrality in the Shadow of a Power* (Oxford: Oxford University Press, 1976), 15.

15. Kimmo Rentola, "Pessi ja illuusiot: Neuvostojohto ja suomalainen kommunismi 1944–1948," *Historiallinen Aikakauskirja* 92:3 (1994), 209.

16. Hanhimäki, " 'Containment' in a Borderland," 366.

17. Quoted in Gerard Aalders, "The Failure of the Scandinavian Union, 1948–1949," *Scandinavian Journal of History* 15: 2 (1990), 126.

18. Paul M. Cole, "Neutralite du jour: The Conduct of Swedish Security Policy Since 1945," (Ph.D. diss., Johns Hopkins University, 1990), 319.

19. Quoted in Hanhimäki, " 'Containment' in a Borderland," 367.

20. "Norway's Reply to Moscow," *Current History* 48 (March 1949), 171. The note is printed in its entirety on pp. 170–71.

21. "Program Designed to Decrease the Vulnerability of the Icelandic Government to Communist Seizure of Power," 25 November 1949, U.S. Department of State, *Foreign Relations of the United States, 1950* 3 (Washington, D.C.: U.S. Government Printing Office, 1981): 1457–58 (hereafter cited as *FRUS* followed by the appropriate year and volume).

22. State Department Policy Statement on Iceland, 15 May 1950, ibid., 1466.

23. Julius Moritzen, "Scandinavian Renaissance: Federation," *Current History* 44 (5 April 1945), 335.

24. Arne Olav Brundtland, "The Nordic Balance," *Cooperation and Conflict* 2:1 (1966), 30–63.

25. Bay to Secretary of State, 17 January 1949, *FRUS, 1949* 4: 36.

CHAPTER 3

1. Tage Erlander, *Tage Erlander 1949–1954* (Stockholm: Tidens Förlag, 1974), 131.

2. James Barros, *Trygve Lie and the Cold War: The UN Secretary Pursues Peace, 1946–1953,* (De Kalb: Northern Illinois University Press, 1989), 341.

3. Paasikivi's diary entries, 27, 30 June, 1, 6, 7 July, 1950, in *Paasikiven päiväkirjat*, II, ed. Matti Klinge and Yrjö Blomstedt (Helsinki: WSOY, 1986), 124–25, 128–29; Juhani Suomi, *Kuningastie. Urho Kekkonen 1950–1956* (Helsinki: Otava, 1990), 78–79; Risto E. J. Penttilä, *Finland's Search for Security through Defense, 1944–1989* (London: Macmillan, 1991), 48–55.

4. Cabot's diary entries, 26, 27, 29, 30 June, 1950, Cabot Papers, Fletcher School of Law and Diplomacy, Medford, Mass.

5. Memorandum by consultants of the National Security Council, 29 June 1950, *FRUS, 1950* 1: 329.

6. NSC 74: "A Plan for National Psychological Warfare," 10 July 1950; "Report on the Position and Activities of the United States with Respect to Possible Soviet Moves in Light of Korean Situation," 11 July 1950, both in *Records of the National Security Council*, 4th Supplement, UPA Microfilms, Reel 4 of 7.

7. Quoted in Donald E. Nuechterlein, *Iceland: Reluctant Ally* (Ithaca, N.Y.: Cornell University Press, 1961), 96–97.

8. Ibid., 106–7.

9. Quoted in Chris Prebensen, *Norway and NATO* (Oslo: Royal Ministry of Foreign Affairs, 1974), 15.

10. Poul Villaume, "Neither Appeasement nor Servility: Denmark and the Atlantic Alliance, 1949–55," *Scandinavian Journal of History* 14:2 (1989), 173.

11. ORE 26–50: "Current International Position of Sweden," 28 August 1950, HST Papers, PSF, Intelligence File, Box 257, HSTL.

12. NSC 121: "The Position of United States with Respect to Scandinavia and Finland," 8 January 1952, *FRUS, 1952–54* 6: 1758.

13. Paul M. Cole, "Neutralite du jour," 322–33.

14. Ibid., 352, 364–67.

15. Ibid., 352.

16. "Sweden—Closer to U.S. Now," *U.S. News and World Report* 33 (3 October 1952), 46.

17. NSC 121, *FRUS, 1952–54* 8: 755.

18. "Did Finland Outsmart Stalin?" *U.S. News and World Report* 33 (August 1952), 30–33. Kennan quoted in: "Minutes of the Chiefs of Mission Meeting," 25 September 1952, *FRUS, 1952–54* 6: 660.

19. Littgow Osborne, "Scandinavian Balance Sheet," *Foreign Policy Bulletin* (1 September 1952), 7.

20. "Paid in Full," *Time* (29 September 1952), 31. Emphasis added.

21. "We Helped Make Finland a Soviet Economic Serf," *Saturday Evening Post* (17 January 1953), 10.

22. Dulles to Helsinki, 7 July 1953, RG 84 (SD) Helsinki Classified General Records 1942–55, Box 33, WNRC. "Progress Report" on NSC 121, 25 August 1953, *FRUS, 1952–54* 8: 758–60.

23. Halvard Lange, "European Union: False Hopes and Realities," *Foreign Affairs* 28 (April 1950), 446.

24. "Changing Scandinavia," *Newsweek* 45 (21 March 1955), 59.

25. Memorandum of 153rd meeting of NSC, 9 July 1953, *FRUS, 1952–54* 8: 1463.

26. Ibid., 1465.

27. "European Attitudes Toward the United States," Memo by Assistant Secretary of State for Europe Livingston Merchant to Secretary of State, 24 August 1953, *FRUS, 1952–54* 1: 1469–80.

28. Bruce Olav Solheim, *Nordic Nexus: A Lesson in Peaceful Security* (New York: Praeger, 1994), 95.

29. Bay to State, 31 July 1953, *FRUS, 1952–54* 6: 1771.

30. Bell to State, 23 July 1953, ibid., 1763.

31. "McCarthyn kiritaival," *Suomalainen Suomi* 22 (March 1954), 185–87.

32. *Svensk Tidskrift* 40 (1953), 343, and 41 (1954), 186.

33. George Soloveytchik, "Europe's Quiet Corner: The Scandinavian Countries Today," *Harper's Magazine* 206 (February 1953), 57.

34. Henry A. Grunwald, "Sweden: The Well-Stocked Cellar," *Time* (31 December 1951), 21.

35. Soloveytchik, "Europe's Quiet Corner," 57.

36. William H. Sewell, Richard T. Morris, and Oluf M. Davidsen, "Scandinavian Students' Images of the United States: A Study in Cross-Cultural Education," *Annals of the American Academy of Political and Social Science* 295 (September 1954), 126–35.

37. All this in Franklin D. Scott, "The Swedish Students' Image of the United States," *Annals of the American Academy of Political and Social Science* ibid., 136–45.

38. NSC 5440: "Basic National Security Policy," 13 December 1954, *National Security Council's Documents*, 2nd Supplement, Reel 1 of 3 (UPA, MF).

39. Quoted in Tamnes, *The United States and the Cold War in the High North* (Aldershot: Dartmouth Publishing, 1991), 165.

40. NSC 5426: "Statement of Policy Proposed by the National Security Council on Iceland," 12 July 1954, *FRUS, 1952–54* 6: 1538.

41. "A Key Base Grows Shaky," *U.S. News and World Report* 30 (7 June 1954), 49.

42. Ibid., 52.

43. At the time Kekkonen was being treated in a Helsinki hospital and, from the pocket of his pajamas, gave the text of a speech he was supposed to have delivered to a *Maakansa* reporter who came to interview him. See Suomi, *Kuningastie*, 159–60.

44. Quoted in Suomi, *Kuningastie*, 161. For the whole text, see *Maakansa*, 23 January 1952. An English translation is in *Neutrality: The Finnish Position. Speeches by Urho Kekkonen*, ed. Tuomas Vilkuna (London: Heinemann, 1973), 53–56.

45. Jakobson to Helsinki, 11 May 1955, quoted in Jakobson, *Veteen piirretty viiva. Havaintoja ja merkintöjä vuosilta 1953–1965* (Helsinki: Otava, 1980), 63–64.

CHAPTER 4

1. Einar Gerhardsen, *I medgang og motgang: Erindringer 1955–65* (Oslo: Tiden Norsk Forlag, 1972), 69.

2. Robert S. Jordan, "The Legacy Which Dag Hammarskjöld Inherited and His Imprint on It," in *Dag Hammarskjöld Revisited: The UN Secretary-General as a Force in World Politics*, ed. Robert S. Jordan (Durham: Carolina Academic Press, 1983), 8.

3. *Die Welt*, 23 April 1955, quoted in Suomi, *Kuningastie*, 385–86.

4. NSC 5602: "Basic National Security Policy," 8 February 1956, *Documents of the National Security Council* (UPA Microfilms, Reel 4 of 5). Emphasis added

5. "Neutralism in Europe," NSC Staff Study, July 1955, WHO, NSC Staff, 1948–61, Planning Coordination Group Series, Box 2, Folder 9: Bandung (2), DDEL.

6. Ibid.

7. Ibid.

8. *Khrushchev Remembers. The Last Testament*, trans. and ed. Strobe Talbott (Boston: Little, Brown, 1974), 253–56.

9.   Jakobson to Helsinki, 27 September 1955, quoted in Jakobson, *Veteen piirretty viiva*, 75.

10.   Walmsberg to Secretary of State, 9 October 1955, RG 59 (SD), 660e.61/10–955, Box 2641, NA.

11.   Summary of Northern European Chiefs of Mission Meeting, London, 19–21 September 1955, *FRUS, 1955–57* 4: 571.

12.   Progress Report on NSC 5403: "U.S. Policy Toward Finland," 23 November 1955, WHO, NSC Staff, 1948–61, OCB Central File, Box 29: OCB 091.Finland (File #2)(1), DDEL.

13.   "Psychological Aspects of U.S. Strategy," 5 December 1955, WHO, NSC Staff, 1948–61, OCB Central Files, Box 83: OCB 091. Propaganda, DDEL.

14.   John Foster Dulles Papers, Box 96, "Neutrality," Seeley G. Mudd Library, Princeton University.

15.   "Action Program for Free World Strength," 5 December 1955, WHCF (Confidential File), 1953–61, Subject Subseries, Box 45: "National Security (2)," DDEL; "A Position Paper for NATO Ministerial Meeting," 8 December 1955, RG 84 (SD), Helsinki Classified General Records, 1942–1955, Box 31 (53–55), WNRC.

16.   Dulles's comment during a NSC meeting, 18 January 1956, quoted in Hanhimäki, "Containment, Coexistence, and Neutrality: the Return of the Porkkala Naval Base as an Issue in Soviet-American Relations," *Scandinavian Journal of History* 18:3 (1993), 226.

17.   Lyman B. Burbank, "Scandinavian Integration and Western Defense," *Foreign Affairs* 35:3 (October 1956), 149.

18.   Quoted in Jakobson, *Veteen piirretty viiva*, 78–79.

19.   Summary of meeting in Paris, 5 May 1956, *FRUS, 1955–57* 4: 58–60.

20.   The quotation from "Neutral is a Many-Sided Word," *Newsweek* (18 June 1956), 57. Eisenhower's press release is printed in *Department of State Bulletin* (18 June 1956), 1004–5.

21.   Dulles's speech in Iowa is printed in *Department of State Bulletin* (18 June 1956), 999–1004. For a transcript of the 12 June press conference, see *Department of State Bulletin* (25 June 1956), esp. 1064–65.

22.   Minutes of the 277th NSC Meeting, 27 February 1956, *FRUS, 1955–57* 19: 201–2.

23.   Figures taken from Gröndal, *Iceland: From Neutrality to NATO Membership*, 77.

24.   Ibid., 56.

25.   "Iceland: Where U.S. May Lose a Base," *U.S. News and World Report* 40 (13 April 1956), 46.

26.   "Icy Winds from Iceland," *Scholastic* 68 (April 1956), 14.

27.   "Iceland: Americans, Go Home," *Time* 67 (9 April 1956), 41.

28.   John Wuorinen, "Neutralism in Scandinavia," *Current History* 31 (November 1956), 280.

29.   Dulles quoted in Bennett Kovrig, *Of Walls and Bridges: The United States and Eastern Europe* (New York: New York University Press, 1991), 84.

30.   Eisenhower quoted in ibid., 99.

31.   Northern European Chiefs of Mission Conference, London, 19–21 September 1957, *FRUS, 1955–57* 4: 636–37.

32.   Ibid., 638.

33.   Robert Coe to State, 28 May 1957, *FRUS, 1955–57* 27: 522.

34. "Denmark: From Cradle to Grave," *Time* (10 November 1958), 35.

35. E.g., "Sex in School," *Time* 65 (6 June 1955), 37; "Sin and Sweden," *Time* 65 (25 April 1955), 29; "Controversy over Swedish Morals," *Coronet* 41 (December 1956), 126–32; "Sweden: the Welfare State," *Christian Century* (3 April 1957), 426; E. M. Korry, "Sex Education in Sweden," *Discussion* (15 October 1957), 34–36.

36. Peter Wyden, "Sweden: Paradise With Problems," *Saturday Evening Post* (19 December 1959), 23.

37. Quoted in Solheim, *Nordic Nexus*, 115.

38. Quoted in Allan Kastrup, *Med Sverige i Amerika: Opinioner, stömningar och upplysningsarbete* (Malmö: Corona, 1985), 288–89.

39. Ibid., 291.

40. NSC 6006/1: "U.S. Policy toward Scandinavia," 6 April 1960, *FRUS, 1958–60* 7: 678.

41. A. B. Horn (Helsinki) to Tom Brimelow FO/ND, 7 August 1957, FO 371/128584, PRO.

42. Väyrynen, "Finland's Role in Western Policy Since the Second World War," *Cooperation and Conflict* 12:1 (1977), 96.

43. NSC 5914/1: "U.S. Policy Toward Finland," 14 October 1959, NSC Files, RG 273, NA.

44. NSC 6024: "U.S. Policy Toward Finland," 30 December 1960, *FRUS, 1958–60* 10: 599.

45. Herter to Helsinki, 23 March 1960, *FRUS, 1958–1960* 10: 570.

46. NSC 6024, *FRUS, 1958–60* 10: 600.

47. 420th Meeting of the NSC, 1 October 1959, Whitman File, NSC Series, Box 11, DDEL.

48. NSC 5914/1: "U.S. Policy Toward Finland," 14 October 1959, NSC Files, RG 273, NA.

49. Zbigniew Brzezinski and William E. Griffith, "Peaceful Engagement in Eastern Europe," *Foreign Affairs* 39 (July 1961), quoted in Scott McElwain, "The United States and East Central Europe: Differentiation or Detente?" *East European Quarterly* 21:4 (January 1988), 454.

50. NSC 6025: "U.S. Policy Toward Iceland," 29 December 1960, *FRUS, 1958–60* 7: 666–67.

51. John Logue, "The Legacy of Swedish Neutrality," in *Committed Neutral: Sweden's Foreign Policy*, ed. Bengt Sundelius (Boulder, Colo.: Westview Press, 1989), 55.

52. Michael R. Beschloss, *The Crisis Years: Kennedy and Khrushchev 1960–1963* (New York: HarperCollins, 1991).

CHAPTER 5

1. Juhani Suomi, *Kriisien aika. Urho Kekkonen 1956–62* (Helsinki: Otava, 1992), 483.

2. Ibid., 475.

3. Comments on NSC Policy, March 1961, Kennedy Papers, NSC Files, Departments and Agencies, Box 283, John F. Kennedy Library (Boston, Mass.).

4. Kennedy's message quoted in Rusk's telegram to Gufler, 20 November 1961, *FRUS, 1961–63* 16: 420.

5. Väyrynen, "Finland's Role in Western Policy," 97.

6. Gufler to State Department, 2 January 1962, *FRUS, 1961–63* 16: 440.

7. Memorandum of Conversation, 28 November 1961, ibid., 431.

8. Quoted in Roy Allison, *Finland's Relations with the Soviet Union, 1944–1984* (New York: St. Martin's, 1985), 46.

9. Suomi, *Kriisien aika*, 497.

10. Rusk to Helsinki, 21 November 1961, *FRUS, 1961–63* 16: 421–22.

11. Rusk to Helsinki, 22 November 1961, ibid., 425.

12. Pascaline Winand, *Eisenhower, Kennedy, and the United States of Europe* (New York: St. Martin's, 1993), 282.

13. Frank Costigliola, "The Pursuit of the Atlantic Community: Nuclear Arms, Dollars, and Berlin," in *Kennedy's Quest for Victory: American Foreign Policy, 1961–1963*, ed. Thomas G. Patterson (New York: Oxford University Press, 1989), 48.

14. Quoted in Toivo Miljan, *The Reluctant Europeans: The Attitudes of the Nordic Countries towards European Integration* (London: C. Hurst, 1977), 176.

15. President's News Conference, 7 March 1962, *Public Papers of the Presidents: John F. Kennedy, 1962* (Washington, D.C.: U.S. Government Printing Office, 1963), 199.

16. Quoted in Juhani Suomi, *Presidentti. Urho Kekkonen 1962–1968* (Helsinki: Otava, 1994), 120.

17. Ibid., 128.

18. Quoted in Ingemar Lindahl, *The Soviet Union and the Nordic Nuclear-Weapons-Free-Zone Proposal* (New York: St. Martin's, 1988) , 82–83.

19. Quoted in Costigliola, "The Pursuit of Atlantic Community," 51.

20. Paul K. Conkin, *Big Daddy from the Pedernales: Lyndon Baines Johnson* (Boston: Twayne Publishers, 1986), 169.

21. Johnson's speech at the City Council of Göteborg, 4 September 1963, *Department of State Bulletin* (14 October 1963), 584–85.

22. Jakobson, *Veteen piirretty viiva*, 330; Suomi, *Presidentti*, 111.

23. Gufler to State, 7 September 1963, *FRUS, 1961–1963* 16: 502.

24. Johnson's address at a dinner given by Norwegian Prime Minister John Lyng in Oslo, 11 September 1963, *Department of State Bulletin* (14 October 1963), 589.

25. Johnson's speech at the Danish Student Association, 14 September 1963, ibid., 592.

26. Johnson's speech at the Joint Meeting of Vardberg Icelandic-American Society and Society for Western Cooperation, Reykjavík, 16 September 1963, *Department of State Bulletin*, (14 October 1963), 592.

27. Suomi, *Presidentti*, 116.

28. *U.S. News and World Report* (23 November 1964), 100–102.

29. *Med Sverige i Amerika*, 303; the titles in ibid., 300–302.

30. Quoted in Arne Ruth, "The Second New Nation: The Mythology of Modern Sweden," in *Norden—the Passion for Equality*, ed. Stephen R. Graubard (Oslo: Norwegian University Press, 1986), 250–51.

31. "A Nation Turning from Socialism," *U.S. News and World Report* (24 June 1968), 73.

32. A. Zanker, "Life in a Great Society, What One Country Finds," *U.S. News and World Report* (7 February 1966), 59.

33. D. W. Ferm, "Sex, Sin, and Salvation in Sweden," *Christian Century* 83 (September 1966), 1142–46.

34. Frederic Fleisher, *The New Sweden: The Challenge of a Disciplined Democracy* (New York: David McKay, 1967); David Jenkins, *Sweden and the Price of Progress* (New York: Coward-McCann, 1968); Roland Huntford, *The New Totalitarians* (New York: Stein and Day, 1971).

35. Gröndal, *Iceland: From Neutrality to NATO Membership,* 72.

36. Quoted in van Oudenaren, *Détente in Europe: The Soviet Union and the West since 1953* (Durham: North Carolina University Press, 1991), 209.

37. Quoted in Edward L. Killham, *The Nordic Way: A Path to Baltic Equilibrium* (Washington, D.C.: Compass Press, 1993), 183.

38. Willy Brandt, *My Life in Politics* (London: Hamish Hamilton, 1992), 251.

39. Willy Brandt, *People and Politics: The Years 1960–1975,* trans. J. Maxwell Brownjohn (Boston: Little, Brown, 1976), 109.

40. Quoted in Frederik Logevall, "The Swedish-American Conflict over Vietnam," *Diplomatic History* 17:3 (Summer 1993), 432.

41. *U.S. News and World Report* (18 March 1968), 78–79; (28 October 1968), 69.

42. Olof Ruin, *Tage Erlander: Serving the Welfare State* (Pittsburgh: University of Pittsburgh Press, 1990), 288.

43. Quoted in Allison, *Finland's Relations with the Soviet Union,* 111.

44. Quoted in Joan Hoff, *Nixon Reconsidered* (New York: HarperCollins, 1994), 236.

45. Henry Kissinger, *Years of Upheaval* (Boston: Little, Brown, 1982), 172.

46. Quoted in Logevall, "Swedish-American Conflict," 437.

47. Ibid., 440–41.

48. Quoted in Rico F. Carlos, "European Socialism, the Western Alliance, and Central America," in *Spain's Entry into NATO,* ed. Frederico G. Gil and Joseph S. Tulchin (Boulder: Lynne Rittner, 1988), 107.

49. Jukka Tarkka, *Suomen kylmä sota. Miten viattomuudesta tuli voima* (Helsinki: Otava, 1992), 146.

CHAPTER 6

1. This description is based on Chris Moseley, *Cruel Awakening: Sweden and the Killing of Olof Palme* (London and New York: St. Martin's, 1991), 6–8.

2. *Business Week* (23 July 1979), 95.

3. *Current History* 70 (April 1976), 184.

4. Ibid., 182.

5. Ibid., 181.

6. Ibid., 162.

7. Ibid., 178.

8. Henry Kissinger, *The White House Years* (Boston: Little Brown, 1978), 73.

9. G. Ginsburgs and A. Rubinstein, *Soviet Foreign Policy Toward Western Europe* (New York: Praeger, 1978), 5.

10. Walter Laqueur, *The Political Psychology of Appeasement: Finlandization and Other Unpopular Essays* (New Brunswick: Transaction Books, 1980), 14, 15–16.

11. In George F. Kennan, *Encounters with Kennan: the Great Debate* (London: Frank Cass, 1979), 20.

12. Viktor Vladimirov, *Näin se oli . . . Muistelmia ja havaintoja kulissientakaisesta diplomaattitoiminnasta Suomessa 1954–1984* (Helsinki: Otava, 1993), 336.

13. Quoted in Lindahl, *The Soviet Union and the NWFZN*, 113–14.

14. Ibid., 123.

15. Sol W. Sanders, " 'Finlandization' Threatens to Infect Norway," *Business Week* (24 April 1978), 53.

16. Quoted in Stanley R. Sloan, "NATO and Northern Europe: Perspectives on the Nordic Balance," *NATO Review* (June 1981), 12.

17. Tamnes, *The United States and the Cold War in the High North*, 239.

18. Quoted in Lindahl, *The Soviet Union and the NWFZN*, 28.

19. Quoted in Nils Andren, "Looking at the Superpowers," in *Neutral Democracies and the New Cold War*, ed. Bengt Sundelius (Boulder, Colo.: Westview, 1986), 168.

20. Olof Palme, *Sveriges Utrikespolitik* (Stockholm: Tiden, 1984), 72.

21. Quoted in Moseley, *Cruel Awakening*, 158.

22. T. M. Pasca, "Finlandization and the Finns," *The Nation* (21 May 1983), 634.

23. H. Peter Krosby, "Finland after Kekkonen," *Current History* 81 (November 1982), 383, 400.

24. Joyce L. Shub, "Finnish Line: Helsinki Grows a Little Bolder," *New Republic* (31 October 1983), 13.

25. Hecksher in *Center Magazine* (September/October 1979), 16; Ulf Himmelstrand, "Sweden: Paradise in Trouble," *Dissent* 26:1 (Winter 1979), 117–28.

26. Erik Willenz, "Why Europe Needs the Welfare State," *Foreign Policy* 63 (Summer 1986), 97.

27. Kurt Samuelsson, "The Swedish Model and Western Europe, 1945–1988," *Journal of International Affairs* 41:2 (Summer 1988), 384.

28. Arne Ruth, "The Second New Nation: the Mythology of Modern Sweden," in *Norden—The Passion for Equality*, 281.

29. Quoted in Roger D. Hansen, "The Reagan Doctrine and Global Containment: Revival or Recessional," *SAIS Review* 7:1 (Winter-Spring 1987), 42.

30. *Deterrence and Defense in the North*, ed. J. J. Holst, K. Hunt, and A. C. Sjoostad (Oslo: Norwegian University Press, 1985), 7.

31. Quoted in Martin Walker, *The Cold War* (London: Vintage, 1993), 292, 294.

32. Quoted in Kilham, *Nordic Way*, 212.

33. "Still Floating Oil," *The Economist* (10 January 1987), 46–47.

34. *The Economist* (14 April 1988), 56.

35. Kirsten Amundsen, *Soviet Strategic Interests in the North* (London: Pinter Publishers, 1990), 126.

36. Michael R. Beschloss and Strobe Talbott, *At the Highest Levels: The Inside History of the End of the Cold War* (Boston: Little, Brown, 1993), 110–11.

37. Ibid., 159.

38. *The Economist* (7 March 1987), 19.

39. *The Economist* (21 October 1989), 72.

CHAPTER 7

1. Quoted in Jan A. Trapans, "Averting Moscow's Baltic Coup," *Orbis* (Summer 1991), 437.

2. Ole Waever, "Between Balts and Brussels: The Nordic Countries after the Cold War," *Current History* 93 (November 1994), 390–94.

3. Margaretha af Ugglas, "Sweden's Security Policy in the Post–Cold War World," *NATO Review* (April 1994), 11–12.

4. *Yearbook of Finnish Foreign Policy* 18 (1991), 58.

5. Killham, *The Nordic Way*, 276.

6. John Lukacs, "Finland Vindicated," *Foreign Affairs* 71:4 (Fall 1992), 50.

7. Ibid., 62.

8. Quoted in Richard Latter, *Nordic and Baltic Security in the 1990s*, Wilton Working Paper (June 1992), 4.

9. "Denmark's No Needn't Derail Europe," *New York Times* (5 June 1992), A28.

10. John Fitzmaurice, *The Baltic. A Regional Future?* (New York: St. Martin's, 1992), 160.

11. *Yearbook of Finnish Foreign Policy* 21 (1994), 61.

12. Latter, *Nordic and Baltic Security*, 30.

13. Jane Corbin, *Gaza First: The Secret Norway Channel to Peace Between Israel and the PLO* (London: Bloomsbury, 1994), 210–11.

14. "Neutral Nations Looking to Europe," *New York Times* (7 December 1990), A13.

15. Ole Waever, "Nordic Nostalgia: Northern Europe after the Cold War," *International Affairs* 68:1 (1992), 77.

16. William E. Schmidt, "In a Post–Cold War Era, Scandinavia Rethinks Itself," *New York Times* (23 February 1992), A3.

17. Ibid.

18. Ib Jørgensen and Jens Tonboe, "Space and Welfare: The EC and the Eclipse of the Scandinavian Model," in *Scandinavia in a New Europe*, ed. Thomas P. Boje and Sven E. Olsson Hort (Oslo: Scandinavian University Press, 1993), 399.

19. Nathaniel C. Nash, "The Welfare State Is Alive and Welcome in Western Europe," *New York Times* (2 January 1996), C8.

BIBLIOGRAPHIC ESSAY

The history of Scandinavian-American relations, or the relationship between the United States and an individual Scandinavian country, has produced very few scholarly studies. Thus far only one book has taken a broad chronological approach on American-Scandinavian relations: Franklin D. Scott, *The United States and Scandinavia* (Cambridge: Harvard University Press, 1950). Because of the book's publication date, its discussion on the postwar period is limited. The same applies to Wayne S. Cole's *Norway and the United States, 1905–1955* (Ames: Iowa State University Press, 1989), although this book is an excellent introduction to the diplomacy between Oslo and Washington. On the other hand, such collected works as *Finland and the United States: Diplomatic Relations through Seventy Years*, ed. Robert Rinehart (Washington, D.C.: Institute for the Study of Diplomacy, 1993) offer only a sketchy account of the fascinating relationship between a Soviet borderland and the USSR's main rival in international affairs after World War II.

As a result, this work has been largely based on contemporary documents, journalistic accounts, and scholarly studies from various disciplines that, while not directly addressing the question of Scandinavian-American relations, illuminate various aspects of the issues discussed herein. With few exceptions (the background to 1945 and the immediate postwar period), this bibliographic essay is divided thematically rather than chronologically. Nor do I mention the "standard" works in the history of U.S. foreign relations since 1945. However, most of the works cited here have been used in writing many, if not all, the chapters of this book.

Some general introductions to Scandinavian history in English include: T. K. Kerry, *A History of Scandinavia* (Minneapolis: University of Minnesota Press, 1979); Edward L. Killham, *The Nordic Way: A Path to Baltic Equilibrium* (Washington, D.C.: Compass Press, 1993); David G. Kirby, *The Baltic World 1772–1993: Europe's Northern Periphery in an Age of Change* (London and New York: Longman, 1995); Franklin D. Scott, *Scandinavia* (Cambridge: Harvard University Press, 1975). For specific countries, see: Thomas K. Derry, *A History of Modern Norway* (Oxford: Clarendon Press, 1973); W. Glyn Jones, *Denmark* (London: Ernest Benn, 1970); David G. Kirby, *Finland in the Twentieth Century* (London: Hurst, 1979); Franklin D. Scott, *Sweden: The Nation's History* (Carbondale: Southern Illinois University Press, 1988); Richard F. Tomasson, *Iceland: The First New Society* (Minneapolis: University of Minnesota Press with Icelandic Review, 1980). Some non-English general histories include: Harry Haue et al., *Det moderne Danmark 1840–1992* (Copenhagen: Munksgaard, 1993); Osmo Jussila et al., *Suomen poliittinen historia 1809–1995* (Helsinki: WSOY, 1995); Stig Helenius et al., *Sverige efter 1900. En modern politisk historia* (Stockholm: Bonniers, 1991); Berge Furre, *Norsk historie 1905–1990. Vårt hundreår* (Oslo: Det Norske Samlaget, 1992).

General overviews of the Scandinavian countries' foreign policies include: *Foreign Policies of Northern Europe*, ed. Bengt Sundelius (Boulder: Westview Press, 1989); Max Jakobson, *Finnish Neutrality: A Study of Finnish Foreign Policy Since the Second World War* (New York: Praeger, 1968); Raimo Väyrynen, *Stability and Change in Finnish Foreign Policy* (Helsinki: Helsingin yliopisto, 1986); Barbara Haskell, *The Scandinavian Option: Opportunities and Opportunity Costs in Postwar Scandinavian Foreign Policies* (Oslo: Universitetsførslaget, 1974); *Norwegian Foreign Policy in the 1980s*, ed. J. J. Holst (Oslo: Universitetsførslaget, 1985); Thrainn Eggertson, "Determinants in Icelandic Foreign Relations," *Cooperation and Conflict* 10:1 (1975); Åke Sandler, "Sweden's Postwar Diplomacy: Some Problems, Views, and Issues," *Western Political Quarterly* 13:4 (1960); Krister Wahlbäck, *The Roots of Swedish Neutrality* (Stockholm: Swedish Institute, 1986).

The background to 1945 can be explored through numerous works. On the Vikings' exploration of North America, see: Erik Wahlgren, *The Vikings and America* (London: Thames and Hudson, 1986) and Else Roesdahl, *The Vikings* (New York: Penguin Press, 1987). A concise analysis of Nordic immigration to the United States can be found in Scott's *The United States and Scandinavia* cited earlier. On World War I, the impact of the Russian revolution, and the interwar period, see: Jussi Hanhimäki, "Before Friendship: The United States and the Finnish Revolution, 1917–1918," *The Maryland Historian* 20:1 (1989); Nils Ørvik, *The Decline of Neutrality, 1914–1941: With Special Reference to the United States and the Northern Neutrals* (London: Frank Cass, 1971); and Wayne Cole's *Norway and the United States*, cited earlier.

World War II, particularly Finland's struggles with the Soviet Union, has attracted a number of scholars. The 1939–1940 Winter War is covered in:

Allen F. Chew, *The White Death: The Epic of the Soviet-Finnish Winter War* (Lansing: Michigan State University Press, 1971); Eloise Engle and Lauri Paananen, *The Winter War* (Boulder, Colo.: Westview Press, 1986); Jukka Nevakivi, *The Appeal That Was Never Made: The Allies and the Finnish Winter War, 1939–1940* (London: C. Hurst, 1975); and Travis Jacobs, *America and the Winter War, 1939–1940* (New York: Garland, 1981). Andrew Schwartz's *America and the Russo-Finnish War* (Westport, Conn.: Greenwood Press, 1960) covers Finnish-American relations during the 1941–1944 "continuation war," but a more comprehensive study of that period is: Michael Berry, *American Foreign Policy and the Finnish Exception: Ideological Preferences and Wartime Realities, 1941–1945* (Helsinki: SHS, 1987). Finland is also touched on in Geir Lundestad, *American Non-Policy Towards Eastern Europe, 1943–47* (New York: Humanities Press, 1975). Other pertinent works include: Wilhelm Carlgren, *Swedish Foreign Policy during the Second World War* (London: Ernest Benn, 1977); Henrik S. Nissen, *Scandinavia during the Second World War* (Minneapolis: University of Minnesota Press, 1983); Peter Ludlow, "Britain and Northern Europe, 1940–1945," *Scandinavian Journal of History* 4:2 (1979); Annette B. Fox, *The Power of Small States: Diplomacy in World War II* (Chicago: University of Chicago Press, 1959).

The most extensively researched period is the beginning of the Cold War. For a general introduction to the literature, now somewhat outdated, see the essays in *Scandinavian Journal of History* 10:2 (1985). The most comprehensive account, although it does not discuss Finland or Iceland, is Geir Lundestad, *America, Scandinavia, and the Cold War, 1945–49* (New York: Columbia University Press, 1980). For other book-length studies in English that focus on single countries, see: Nils Upgaard, *Great Power Politics and Norwegian Foreign Policy* (Oslo: Norwegian University Press, 1973); and Tuomo Polvinen, *Finland in International Politics, 1944–47* (Minneapolis: University of Minnesota Press, 1986); and, most recently, Jussi M. Hanhimäki, *Containing Coexistence: America, Russia, and "The Finnish Solution," 1945–1956* (Kent, Ohio: Kent State University Press, 1997). An abbreviated version of the last work is also available in Finnish as *Rinnakkaiseloa patoamassa. Yhdysvallat ja Paasikiven linja 1948–1956* (Helsinki: SHS, 1996).

Of the many articles that address the various Scandinavian countries' policies in the late 1940s, the following are particularly noteworthy: Helge Ø. Pharo, "Scandinavia," in *The Origins of the Cold War in Europe: International Perspectives*, ed. David Reynolds (Yale, Conn.: Yale University Press, 1994); idem, "Bridgebuilding and Reconstruction: Norway Faces the Marshall Plan," *Scandinavian Journal of History* 1:2 (1976); Jussi M. Hanhimäki, " 'Containment' in a Borderland: The United States and Finland, 1948–49," *Diplomatic History* 18:3 (1994); idem, "Self-Restraint as Containment: United States' Economic Policy, Finland, and the Soviet Union, 1945–53," *The International History Review* 17:2 (1995); Mikko Majander, "The Limits of

Sovereignty: Finland and the Question of the Marshall Plan in 1947,"
Scandinavian Journal of History 19:3 (1994); Jukka Nevakivi, "Ratkaiseva väli-
rauha 1944–47: miksi Suomea ei neuvostolaistettu?" *Historiallinen
Aikakauskirja* 91:2 (1993); Gerard Aalders, "The Failure of the Scandinavian
Defence Union, 1948–1949," *Scandinavian Journal of History* 19:2 (1990);
Bernt Schiller, "At Gun Point: A Critical Perspective on the Attempts of the
Nordic Governments to Achieve Unity after the Second World War,"
Scandinavian Journal of History 9:3 (1984); Poul Villaume, "Neither
Appeasement nor Servility: Denmark and the Atlantic Alliance,"
Scandinavian Journal of History 14:2 (1989); Birgit Karlsson, "Neutrality and
Economy: The Redefining of Swedish Neutrality, 1946–52," *Journal of Peace
Research* 32:1 (1995). For an article that draws a clear distinction between the
preferences of the Copenhagen and Oslo governments, see Nikolaj Petersen,
"Danish and Norwegian Alliance Policies, 1948–49: A Comparative
Analysis," *Cooperation and Conflict* 14:2 (1979).

Security, particularly the notion of the Nordic Balance, is one of the most
heavily researched areas in postwar Nordic history. The term was coined by
the Norwegian political scientist Arne Olav Brundtland in "The Nordic
Balance," *Cooperation and Conflict* 2:1 (1966). In the same issue of that jour-
nal, one can find a broad overview regarding the possibilities of postwar
Scandinavian defense cooperation by Christian Lange and Kjell Goldmann,
"A Nordic Defense Alliance 1949–1965–197?" Many of the works that follow
address the U.S. (and NATO) role in sustaining the East-West balance in
Northern Europe after 1945: Wilhelm Alford, "Prospects for the Nordic
Security Pattern," *Cooperation and Conflict* 14:3 (1978); Nils Andren, *The
Future of the Nordic Balance* (Stockholm: National Defense Institute, 1984);
John C. Ausland, *Nordic Security and the Great Powers* (Boulder, Colo.:
Westview, 1986); Johan J. Holst, *Five Roads to Nordic Security* (Oslo:
Universitetsførslaget, 1973); idem et al., *Deterrence and Defense in the High
North* (Oslo: Norwegian University Press, 1985); Bo Huldt and Atis Llejins,
Security in the North—Nordic and Superpower Perspectives (Stockholm: Swedish
Institute of International Affairs, 1984); Bruce Olav Solheim, *The Nordic
Nexus: A Lesson in Peaceful Security* (Westport, Conn.: Praeger, 1994). On the
Finnish efforts to build a more credible defense, see Risto E. J. Penttilä,
Finland's Search for Security through Defense, 1944–1989 (London and New
York: St. Martin's, 1991).

NATO's role and the Scandinavian countries' relationship to the organi-
zation are discussed in: Nils Ørvik, *Semialignment and Western Security* (New
York: St. Martin's, 1986); *Western Security: The Formative Years*, ed. Olav
Riste (New York: Columbia University Press, 1985); Kirsten Amundsen,
Norway, NATO, and the Forgotten Soviet Challenge (Berkeley: Institute of
International Studies, 1981); Björn Bjarnason, "Iceland's Position in NATO,"
The Atlantic Community Quarterly 6:3 (1978); idem, "The Security of Iceland,"
Cooperation and Conflict 7:4 (1972); Rolf Tamnes, *The United States and the*

Cold War in the High North (Cambridge: Cambridge University Press, 1991); Clive Archer, "The United States Defense Areas in Greenland," *Cooperation and Conflict* 23:3 (1988); Nikolaj Petersen, "Abandonment vs. Entrapment: Denmark and Military Integration in Europe," *Cooperation and Conflict* 21:2 (1986); Benedikt Gröndal, *Iceland: From Neutrality to NATO Membership* (Oslo: Universitetsførslaget, 1971); Donald E. Nuechterlein, *Iceland: Reluctant Ally* (Ithaca, N.Y.: Cornell University Press, 1961); Elfar Loftsson, *Island i NATO: Partierna och försvarsfrågan* (Göteborg: Författarens Bokmaskin, 1981).

Soviet policy toward Scandinavia is treated in: Örjan Berner, *Sovjet & Norden: Samarbete, säkerhet och konflikter under femtio år* (Stockholm: Bonnier Fakta, 1985); idem, *Soviet Policies toward the Nordic Countries* (Lanham, Md.: University Press of America, 1986); Robert K. German, "Norway and the Bear: Soviet Coercive Diplomacy and Norwegian Security Policy," *International Security* 7:2 (1982); Ingemar Lindahl, *The Soviet Union and the Nordic Nuclear-Weapons-Free-Zone Proposal* (London: Macmillan, 1988); Bent Jensen, *Sovjetunionen og Danmark* (Copenhagen: Det Udenrigspolitiske Selskab, 1987); Milton Leitenberg, *Soviet Submarine Operations in Swedish Waters, 1980–1986* (Washington: CSIS, 1987); Roy Allison, *Finland's Relations with the Soviet Union, 1944–1984* (New York: St. Martin's, 1985); John Vloyantes, *Silk Glove Hegemony: Finnish-Soviet Relations, 1944–1974* (Kent, Ohio: Kent State University Press, 1975).

Finlandization has produced a virtual subfield of research. In addition to Allison and Vloyantes' works, one should note in particular: Harto Hakovirta, *Suomettuminen* (Jyväskylä: Gummerus, 1975); George Maude, *The Finnish Dilemma: Neutrality in the Shadow of a Power* (Oxford: Oxford University Press, 1976); idem, "Problems of Finnish Statecraft: The Aftermath of Legitimization," *Diplomacy and Statecraft* 1:1 (1990); idem, "The Further Shores of Finlandization," *Cooperation and Conflict* 17:1 (1982); Hans P. Krosby, "Scandinavia and Finlandization," *Scandinavian Review* 63:2 (1975). Two conflicting American views are offered in George Kennan, "Europe's Problems, Europe's Choices," *Foreign Policy* 14:1 (1974) and Walter Laqueur, *The Political Psychology of Appeasement: Finlandization and Other Unpopular Essays* (New Brunswick: Transaction Books, 1980). The most recent Finnish account that, unlike the official Finnish view during Kekkonen's presidency, argues that Finland did practice a form of appeasement that jeopardized its internal democracy is Timo Vihavainen, *Kansakunta rähmällään. Suomettumisen lyhyt historia* (Keuruu: Otava, 1991).

In addition to some of the works already mentioned, Finnish and Swedish neutrality and their efforts at various forms of bridge building are the subject of: Bengt Nilson, "Unden's tredje väg: Sverige i det kalla kriget, 1950–1952," *Scandia* 60:1 (1994); Bo Petersson, "From Avoiding the Subject to Outright Criticism: Soviet Commentators and the Vexing Case of Finnish Neutrality," *Nordic Journal of Soviet and East European Studies* 4:1 (1987); idem, "Essay and

Reflection: On the Soviet Union and Neutrals," *The International History Review* 11:2 (1989); Klaus Törnudd, " 'The Finnish Model': Neutral States and European Security," *International Journal* 24:2 (1969); Katarina Brodin, "The Policy of Neutrality: The Official Doctrines of Sweden and Finland," *Cooperation and Conflict* 3:1 (1968); idem, "The Unden Proposal," *Cooperation and Conflict* 2:2 (1966); Nils Andren, *Power Balance and Non-Alignment: A Perspective on Sweden's Foreign Policy* (Stockholm: Almqvist and Wiksell, 1967); Ulf Bjereld, "Critic or Mediator? Sweden in World Politics, 1945–90," *Journal of Peace Research* 32:1 (1995). Two noteworthy dissertations are Frederika Björklund, "Unity under Discord: The Swedish Debate on National Security during the Cold War" (Ph.D. diss., Uppsala Universitatet, 1992) and a coherently negative appraisal of Swedish neutrality, Paul M. Cole, "Neutralite du jour: The Conduct of Swedish Security Policy Since 1945" (Ph.D. diss., Johns Hopkins University, 1990). For a comparative look at neutrality, see *Neutrality in History*, ed. Jukka Nevakivi (Helsinki: SHS, 1993).

American views of neutrality since World War II are detailed in Jürg Martin Gabriel, *The American Conception of Neutrality Since 1941* (New York: St. Martin's, 1989), although the author's focus is mostly on Sweden and, in particular, Switzerland. Jussi M. Hanhimäki discusses Austria, Finland, Sweden, and Switzerland in "The First Line of Defense or a Springboard for Disintegration? European Neutrals in American Foreign and Security Policy, 1945–1961," *Diplomacy and Statecraft* 7:2 (1996). For a more quantitative assessment, see the Finnish political scientist Harto Hakovirta's *East-West Conflict and European Neutrality* (Oxford: Clarendon Press, 1988). For the 1980s, see also *Neutral Democracies and the New Cold War*, ed. Bengt Sundelius (Boulder, Colo.: Westview Press, 1987).

The most thorough works on the 1975 Helsinki Accords are John Maresca, *To Helsinki* (Durham, N.C.: Duke University Press, 1983) and Vojtech Mastny, *Helsinki, Human Rights, and European Security* (Durham, N.C.: Duke University Press, 1986). See also Thomas Krantz, "Moscow and the Negotiation of the Helsinki Accords, 1972–75" (Ph.D. diss., Oxford University, 1981). Of the more general accounts of détente, the following two were most useful for this study: Raymond Garthoff, *Détente and Confrontation*, 2d ed. (Washington, D.C.: Brookings, 1994) and John van Oudenaren, *Détente in Europe: The Soviet Union and the West since 1953* (Durham, N.C.: Duke University Press, 1991).

Marquis Childs's *Sweden: The Middle Way* (New Haven, Conn.: Yale University Press, 1936) has been followed by a plethora of books and articles, positive and negative, that assess the workings of social democracy. Childs himself provided a mildly positive reassessment more than four decades later entitled *The Middle Way on Trial* (New Haven, Conn.: Yale University Press, 1980). The most critical works appeared in the late 1960s and early 1970s. See in particular: Frederic Fleisher, *The New Sweden: The Challenge of a Disciplined Democracy* (New York: David McKay, 1967); David Jenkins, *Sweden and the*

Price of Progress (New York: Coward-McCann, 1968); Roland Huntford, *The New Totalitarians* (New York: Stein and Day, 1971). In addition, the following provide good overviews: Neil Elder et al., *The Consensual Democracies? The Government and Politics of the Scandinavian States* (New York: Blackwell, 1988); Leif Lewin, *Ideology and Strategy: A Century of Swedish Politics* (Cambridge: Cambridge University Press, 1988); Stephen Graubard, *Norden—The Passion for Equality* (Oslo: Norwegian University Press, 1986); Donald M. Hancock, *Sweden: The Politics of Postindustrial Change* (Hinsdale: Dryden Press, 1972). For an assessment of Sweden vis-à-vis the rest of Western Europe, see Kurt Samuelsson, "The Swedish Model and Western Europe 1945–1988," *Journal of International Affairs* 64:3 (1988). For an assessment on how the welfare state was revamped in Denmark and Sweden in the 1980s, see Herman Schwartz, "State Reorganization in Australia, Denmark, New Zealand, and Sweden in the 1980s," *World Politics* 46:5 (1994).

The problems and successes of Nordic integration and its relationship to broader European initiatives are covered in Wilhelm Agrell, "Nordic Integration and Cooperation—Illusion and Reality," *Cooperation and Conflict* 19:4 (1984); Preben Almdahl, *Aspects of European Integration: A View of the European Community and the Nordic Countries* (Odense, Denmark: Odense University Press, 1966); Stanley V. Anderson, *The Nordic Council* (Seattle: University of Washington Press, 1967); Toivo Miljan, *The Reluctant Europeans: The Attitudes of the Nordic Countries toward European Integration* (London: C. Hurst, 1977); Göran von Bornsdorf, "Regional Cooperation of the Nordic Countries," *Cooperation and Conflict* 1:1 (1965); Barry Turner, *The Other European Community—Integration and Cooperation in Nordic Europe* (New York: St. Martin's, 1982); Franz Wendt, *Cooperation in the Nordic Countries—Achievements and Obstacles* (Stockholm: Almquist and Wiksell, 1981). More specialized studies include: Klaus Törnudd, "Finland and Economic Integration in Europe," *Cooperation and Conflict* 4:3 (1969); Vibeke Sørensen, "The Politics of Closed Markets: Denmark, the Marshall Plan, and European Integration, 1945–1963," *The International History Review* 15:1 (1993); idem, "How to Become a Member of a Club Without Joining: Danish Policy with Respect to European Sector Integration Schemes, 1950–1957," *Scandinavian Journal of History* 16:2 (1991); Johan J. Holst, "Norway's Search for a Nordpolitik," *Foreign Affairs* 60:1 (1981).

On the end of the Cold War and its impact on Nordic security policy, see: Nils Petter Gleditsch et al., *Svaner på vildveje? Nordens sikkerhed mellem supermagtsflåder og europeisk opbrud* (Copenhagen: Vindrose, 1990) and Graethe Vaernø, *Lille Norden—hva nå? Splittelse og samling i EFs kraftfelt* (Stockholm: J.W. Cappelens, 1993). The impact of EU membership for Finland and Sweden as well as for Austria is discussed in Andreas Missiroli, "The New Kids on the EU Block: Austria, Finland, and Sweden," *International Spectator* 30:4 (1995). On the emergence of the Baltic region, see John Fitzmaurice, *The Baltic: A Regional Future?* (New York: St. Martin's, 1992). Scandinavian "identity problems" are nicely summed up in Ole Waever, "Nordic Nostalgia: Northern Europe after the Cold War," *International Affairs* 68:1 (1992), but see also Christer Jönsson, "International Politics: Scandinavian Identity Amidst American Hegemony?" *Scandinavian Political Studies* 16:2 (1993). The most comprehensive account of the Oslo Channel is Jane Corbin, *Gaza First: The Secret Norway Channel to Peace Between Israel and the PLO* (London: Bloomsbury, 1994). For a general account of the prospects of the EU, see the essays in *The Future of Europe*, Valerie Symes, Carl Levy, and Jane Littlewood (London: Macmillan, 1996).

On the two Scandinavian secretary generals of the United Nations, see James Barros, *Trygve Lie and the Cold War: The U.N. Secretary General Pursues Peace, 1946–1953* (Dekalb: Northern Illinois University Press, 1989); Robert S. Jordan, *Dag Hammarskjöld Revisited: The U.N. Secretary-General as a Force in World Politics* (Durham: Carolina Academic Press, 1983); Brian Urquhart, *Hammarskjöld* (New York: Harper and Row, 1972, 1984). On other major Scandinavian political figures, some of the more useful works include Olof Ruin, *Tage Erlander: Serving the Welfare State* (Pittsburgh: University of Pittsburgh Press, 1990); Juhani Suomi, *Urho Kekkonen*, 5 vols. (Helsinki: Otava, 1986–1994). On Olof Palme, see Chris Moseley, *The Cruel Awakening: Sweden and the Killing of Olof Palme* (London and New York: St. Martin's, 1991).

I have made some use of documentary sources, particularly in the first few chapters. The best printed source is the annual volumes in the *Foreign Relations of the United States*. Such annual series as the *Congressional Record*, the *Public Papers of the Presidents of the United States*, and the *Department of State Bulletin* provide some useful information about the public record of U.S. foreign policy. The decimal files at the National Archives provide a good source for day-to-day diplomacy. In the presidential libraries, the material available varies. The Truman, Kennedy, and Johnson libraries have surprisingly little of interest, while the Eisenhower Library is full of documents related to, in particular, the specter of neutralism in Scandinavia and Europe. An interesting private collection, located at the Fletcher School of Law and Diplomacy, is that of John Moors Cabot, who served as a diplomat in Finland and Sweden during the 1950s. Outside the United States, I made some use of the Public Records Office in London and the Finnish National Archives in Helsinki. In most Scandinavian countries, the rules for the use of national archives—and particularly materials related to foreign policy—are, however, quite strict (in general a 40-year rule is applied).

Memoirs proved less than satisfactory for this project. American leaders, whether presidents, secretaries of state, or others, have made scant mention of the Scandinavian countries. Only Henry Kissinger mentions them in any detail in *White House Years* and *Years of Upheaval* (Boston: Little, Brown, 1979, 1982), but even here the attention is limited to their relation to the pursuing of détente with the Soviet Union. Scattered references are found in

Harry S. Truman, *Years of Decision* and *Years of Trial and Hope* (Garden City: Doubleday, 1955–1956), and Richard Nixon, *RN: The Memoirs of Richard Nixon* (New York: Simon and Schuster, 1978). Eisenhower, Ford, Carter, and Reagan do not refer to the Scandinavian countries in any significant way. Of the many memoirs by Scandinavian leaders, the most useful are: Tage Erlander, *Tage Erlander*, 4 vols. (Stockholm: Tidens Förlag, 1970–1976); Jens Otto Krag, *Ung mand fra trediverne* (Copenhagen: Gyldendal, 1969); Hans Hansen, *Fra gamle dage* (Copenhagen: Rosenkilde og Bagger, 1961); Einar Gerhardsen, *Erindringer*, 3 vols. (Oslo: Tiden Norsk Forlag, 1970–1974); Urho Kekkonen, *Vuosisatani* (Keuruu: Otava, 1981); and Mauno Koivisto, *Kaksi kautta*, 2 vols. (Helsinki: WSOY, 1994–1995). Other memoirs of interest include those by two Finnish diplomats (and their country's ambassadors to the United Nations): Georg A. Gripenberg, *Finland and the Great Powers: Memoirs of a Diplomat* (Lincoln: University of Nebraska Press, 1965); Max Jakobson, *Veteen piirretty viiva. Havaintoja ja merkintöjä vuosilta 1953–1965* (Helsinki: Otava, 1980); and idem, *38. kerros* (Helsinki: Otava, 1984).

INDEX

See list of abbreviations on pp. xv–xvi for definitions of abbreviations and acronyms.

THE AUTHOR

A native of Finland, Jussi M. Hanhimäki studied at Tampere University (Finland) and at Boston University, where he received his Ph.D. in 1993. Prior to joining the International History Department at the London School of Economics in the fall of 1995, he taught in the United States and Canada. He has also been a guest lecturer at the School of Slavonic and East European Studies (University of London) and at Tampere University. He is a recipient of fellowships from the United States Institute of Peace, the Finnish Academy (*Suomen Akatemia*), the Social Sciences and Humanities Research Council of Canada, the Charles Warren Center for Studies in American History at Harvard University, the Contemporary History Institute at Ohio State University, and the Norwegian Nobel Institute. He has published numerous articles in such journals as *Diplomatic History*, *The International History Review*, *Scandinavian Journal of History*, and *Diplomacy and Statecraft*. He has also published *Containing Coexistence: America, Russia, and the "Finnish Solution," 1945–1956* (Kent, Ohio, 1997) and *Rinnakkaiseloa patoamassa: Yhdysvallat ja Paasikiven linja, 1948–1956* (Helsinki, 1996).

THE EDITOR

Akira Iriye is Charles Warren Professor of American History at Harvard University and visiting professor of history at the International University of Japan. His most recent publications include *China and Japan in the Global Setting* (1992), *The Globalizing of America: United States Foreign Relations, 1913–1945* (1993), and *Cultural Internationalism and World Order* (1997).